SPRING TURKEY HUNTING

SPRING TURKEY HUNTING

The Serious Hunter's Guide

John M. McDaniel

Photos by Nell and John McDaniel,
except as otherwise credited

Stackpole Books

Copyright © 1986 by Stackpole Books

Published by
STACKPOLE BOOKS
Cameron and Kelker Streets
P.O. Box 1831
Harrisburg, PA 17105

Printed in the U.S.A.

Library of Congress Cataloging-in-Publication Data

McDaniel, John M.
    Spring turkey hunting.

    Bibliography: p.
    Includes index.
    1. Turkey hunting.   I. Title.
SK325.T8M28   1986   799.2'48619   85-27723
ISBN 0-8117-1688-0

Contents

	Acknowledgments	7
1	Introduction	9
2	An Historical Perspective	19
3	The Challenge and Appeal	29
4	Biology and Spring Gobbler Hunting	37
5	The Spring Experience and the Hunter	61
6	Techniques and Strategies	71
7	The Tools	115
8	Camouflage	147
9	Calling, Calls, and Callers	155
10	The Physical Demands	183
11	Safety	189
12	Ethics	195
13	Working for the Wild Turkey's Future	199
	Selected Bibliography	211
	Index	213

Acknowledgments

Many people made this book possible. My thanks go first to my wife, Nell Reeves McDaniel, and my two daughters, Elizabeth Leyburn and Catherine Schielke. Each of them provided me with time, encouragement, help, and enduring patience. Nell not only proofed every draft but also provided valuable suggestions as to the content and organization of the manuscript. Most of the photographs were taken by us as a team.

Professional assistance was received from two Washington and Lee University secretaries, Anne Zeigler and Jeannette Jarvis. Jeannette typed the first draft of the book, and Anne did the second and third drafts. Anne's patience toward the end of her ordeal with the project deserves special mention. I am deeply indebted to both ladies.

W. Patrick Hinely Work/Play is responsible for many hours of darkroom work with my photographs. Also, he is to be credited for shooting the studio set-up shots.

Ted Goebel, a Washington and Lee undergraduate who developed map-making skills in our archaeology program, worked with me on all three maps. The final maps are a product of Ted's growing talents.

Hunter McCoy of the Washington and Lee print shop is responsible for putting the tables and maps in "camera ready" condition. His professionalism, good spirits, and patience, are deeply appreciated.

Kurt Russ, my colleague in archaeology at Washington and Lee, was invaluable in overseeing the effort of pulling the final product together in Lexington while I was here in Idaho. I will not cite the many problems that Kurt successfully addressed. His help made it possible for me to meet the deadline.

In the interest of not slighting someone, I will simply extend my sincere thanks to all those people—hunters, property owners, biologists, call makers, and others—who helped me learn about wild turkeys and their hunting. I owe a large debt for their generosity, unselfishness, patience, and encouragement. I trust some will come alive in this book. I additionally hope that the respect and admiration I have for each is obvious.

Finally, I acknowledge my debt to the wild turkey. This great bird has made my life richer. My hope is that the book will attract people, of both sexes, to the sport of wild turkey hunting. I am sure many of you who are attracted will become passionate hunters. The wild turkey's future rests with those of us who are hunters. We must lead the fight to protect habitat. Each of us should feel compelled to commit time and money to helping, on both the local and national level. The debt we have to the wild turkey demands nothing less.

John McDaniel
30 August 1985
Henry's Fork of the Snake River, Idaho

1

Introduction

The purpose of this book is to discuss in detail the strategy of spring wild turkey hunting. It is my goal to provide insights for serious hunters of all levels of experience. I trust the common denominator for readers is that they are determined to become more proficient spring gobbler hunters.

My preparation for this undertaking includes an intensive investigation of the literature concerning the hunting of the American wild turkey in the spring of the year. That exercise has been entertaining and informative. The bibliography includes the sources I have consulted that I believe are worthwhile. It is a selective list.

My literary research has been complemented by field data collection. My occupation, college teaching, has allowed me to invest hundreds of hours in research, photography, scouting, and hunting. Most of my hunting has been done in western Virginia; however, in the interest of achieving broader experiences, I made trips to Florida, Louisiana, and South Dakota.

The sport has provided me with many good friends who have shared their experiences with me. Their help has made this book possible.

It is my fervent hope that the book will serve the wild turkey. The bird deserves the respect of the American public. Those of us who enjoy turkey hunting must make a commitment to improving the status of this great gamebird.

I offer concrete suggestions as to what we can do to improve habitat and to increase public recognition for the wild turkey. It is intelligent to work together to further those goals; however, we should never forget that each of us is capable of

A wild turkey gobbler coming to the caller.

making his or her own contributions. We should demand it of ourselves. Most of us can find time for hunting, but few of us allocate equivalent time to the protection of habitat or to the education of others about this bird and the great sport he provides. It is fun to attend calling contests, but we should make the effort to attend the less entertaining sessions offered by biologists who can help us assure the wild turkey's future.

At the time I write, the picture is bright. Stable populations of wild turkeys exist in many parts of America. The sport enjoys rapidly increasing popularity; however, habitat destruction is a constant threat. The lessons of the late nineteenth and early twentieth centuries should not be forgotten. Increasing human population and the soaring demands for resources will impose more threats. We must not be satisfied with the abundance of wild turkeys today, but plan to protect them against the threats of tomorrow. Many conservationists believe hunters are selfish in motivation and shortsighted in plan. It is imperative that we prove their assessments wrong.

I trust this book will be fun to read. I enjoyed writing it. Reflections on the hunts, the friends who shared their experiences with me, and the great birds that tie it all together are among my most pleasant memories. I hope the book will take you back to those still-wild areas turkeys inhabit. I hope your pulse will quicken as you reflect on experiences that are similar to mine. For the beginner, I hope the stories will fill you with anticipation and a sense of challenge.

The hunting of this greatest of all gamebirds is available. You do not have to be of royal blood. That opportunity is a credit to this nation. In many countries of the world, the most prestigious game is pursued only by the very powerful or very rich. This American bird is available to hunters of all socio-economic backgrounds. We should not take this opportunity for granted.

We should be thankful for the opportunity to hunt, but also acknowledge the responsibility it imposes on each of us. We have an obligation not only to the future welfare of the wild turkey but also to the safety of our fellow hunters. It is becoming increasingly apparent that spring gobbler hunting can be dangerous. It is critical that we protect not only our fellow hunters but also our sport by developing a commitment to safety. We should encourage and support the development of educational programs oriented to safety. We should not tolerate hunters who act irresponsibly, and we must demand harsh punishment for those who jeopardize the lives of others.

Do not underestimate the challenge of becoming a capable spring gobbler hunter. The journey to competence is not easy. There are no shortcuts. There are no simple solutions in this book, no magic formulas, no foolproof tools. You will not buy success in spring gobbler hunting. You will have to work hard to become proficient. I am confident the advice the book provides will help you. I learned by trial and error. I shared my failures with other honest hunters, and they shared theirs with me. No advice is given simply because I read it somewhere. The strategies espoused as worthwhile are selected because they have been tested in the field.

If you are serious about this pursuit, I warn you that it can become addictive. It is important to have a family that understands. The demands you will impose on yourself and the investments you will feel compelled to make of time and money will be considerable. There will be times when you will be frustrated. I encourage you to persevere. The rewards that will accrue to you when you become proficient will be many. It is unlikely you will become arrogant about your skills, because wild turkey gobblers do not tolerate arrogance. As soon as you think you have figured out how to fool every spring gobbler, you will meet the bird that will demonstrate you are wrong.

IN PRAISE OF WILD GOBBLERS

The great bird is the source, the substance, and the symbol of the sport. He stimulates behavior in serious hunters that

A mature gobbler going into the "strut" or mating display.

is at once skillful, silly, competitive, reflective, arrogant, and humble. Addiction to the sport is a profound compliment to the wild turkey gobbler. Our respect for him is generated by myriad features of the bird's being.

The Endurance and Courage

The gobbler's endurance is challenged every winter by vicious storms. Late at night, I have stepped outside and wondered how he stayed on the wind-lashed limb. Somehow he does.

His courage is painfully obvious when you walk up after he has been immobilized by the shot. The largest bones in his body smashed, his muscles torn, he will hold his head high and his eyes will remain defiant.

One of the world's great hunting trophies.

The Physical Abilities

If you haven't seen a gobbler sprint across an open field, you have missed one of nature's great feats. The speed he generates contradicts his anatomy.

The first time I saw a gobbler make a long flight, it scared me. He flushed off the mountain, beat his wings twice, and glided over the valley. My stomach got light as I watched. The last time I'd had a similar feeling was when I'd watched the small dots fall easily from the slow plane. Each dot was a friend, and it was several long seconds before the chutes deployed. The gobbler didn't belong up there either. It was too high for something that large. Unlike the guys over the Fort Bragg drop zone, however, the gobbler was in command of his descent. I watched him glide over the dark woods, the light fields, the shining river, and lost him when he blended into the distant Blue Ridge. I don't know how far he went, but when I looked at the topographical map, I calculated he was 2,000 feet above the river. At that altitude, with his size, someone should have seen him on a radar screen.

His Grace and Beauty

Spring gobbler hunters have trouble understanding why people say our bird is ugly. One problem is that a turkey loses a great deal in death. John Audubon knew any bird's colors fade a short time after it dies, but it is more complex than that. A dead turkey has no structure. The head and neck become limp. Some animals, like a wild ram, look solid and still majestic after death. A turkey loses his strength and bearing. Poise and dignity are a part of every living gobbler. In death they are immediately gone. Look at the great paintings and photographs, and the quali-

ties are there. This is, physically, a grand creature. He exudes virility. To call him ugly is to prove that you have not observed the living bird.

His Presence

One evening a friend and I were perched on the roof of an old cabin overlooking several fields. It was just before the fall deer season, and we were hoping to see a good buck. Our patience was rewarded when two drifted into one of the fields. We watched with the detached interest characteristic of turkey hunters observing deer. We were trying to ascertain the number of points on the larger buck when a gobbler walked out of the trees. We both stood up and instantly lost our coolness.

"Look at him!"

"I can see the beard from here."

"Look at his head."

"Look at that stride—and check how tall he is."

"That boy owns Waynelee's field. I mean, he flat owns it."

I read a quote from Al Davis, owner of the Los Angeles Raiders professional football team, who said that years ago he had gone to a college football game to scout a fine player. His attention had been drawn to a different player, a freshman quarterback who walked with a slouch but had a presence. Davis said that Namath "tipped the field toward his sideline." A wild turkey gobbler tips any field. He, too, has a presence.

The impact of that presence can vary from one hunter to the next. Almost invariably, however, the effect is electric. Honest hunters admit to shaking hands, hyperventilation, a dry mouth, and a queasy stomach. For some, the effects are more severe. One experienced and competent hunter becomes violently ill after an encounter with a gobbler. Usually his illness is delayed until the affair is terminated. On at least one occasion, his nervous system did not accommodate the delay.

I was at home, working with my calls, when the doorbell rang and I heard my wife Nell say, "Bill, are you all right?" The tone of her voice made me sprint up the stairs. I turned to face my friend Bill, and before I could speak, he gushed, "It happened, John. X did it! He started groaning and panting like he always does, and when the bird came to within 50 yards, he leaned over to me and I thought he was going to whisper. Then he made this low, choking sort of sound, and before I knew what had happened, he vomited into my ear! It was horrible."

Nell moved to the stairs with the "I am now absolutely convinced these guys are insane" expression on her face. I looked at Nease's white face and anguished expression and began to laugh. The more I reflected, the funnier it seemed. No doubt the fatigue of the spring season contributed to my giddiness. Soon I was hysterical and fell to the floor, trying to ask Bill questions between convulsions of laughter. Bill soon began to laugh, and the situation deteriorated. In one gasp of reasonably coherent speech, I said, "Headline in Martinsville Bugle—X Vomits on Bill Nease as Gobbler Approaches Two Experienced Hunters." Bill said, "Just last week X said to me, 'Bill, it will happen. I just can't stand it when they come the last 20 yards. My stomach starts churning, and I begin praying for strength. I can't control it. I told Dr. Leach about it, and he just laughed at me, so I went to that young physician we took dove hunting. He was ready to send me to Charlottesville to

see a psychiatrist! He asked me what kind of relationship I had with my father. The boy thought I was crazy! I mean, none of those people know what a gobbler can do to you.'"

His Pride

I challenge you to find a creature that has more pride than a wild turkey gobbler in the spring of the year. His pride will get him in trouble, but you have to appreciate the way he feels about himself.

The best spring gobbler hunter I know was an 18-year-old G.I. in Paris when de Gaulle led the Free French down the Champs Elysees. In reflecting on his role as a witness to history, he said, "John, there were grown men and women around me, and they were all crying. The only other living thing I'd ever seen that had the arrogance and pride of that big Frenchman was a wild turkey gobbler. De Gaulle passed 20 feet from me, and I kept waiting for him to turn toward me and gobble."

His Role in Our World

For many of us, an impressive aspect of the wild turkey is that he will not tolerate destruction of his environment. He demands those precious still-wild places that exist in North America. He is not a bird of game preserves, "semi wild" hunting, or back yards. His attitude puts in perspective our obligations to our planet—and our children. If wild turkeys were relegated to zoos, our loss would be incalculable. A turkey in a pen is not a wild turkey. This great bird, and the other wild creatures that will not tolerate the crimes humans commit in the name of progress, or profit, help us maintain values con-

An example of the wild areas inhabited by spring gobblers.

cerning our world. He is a native American. We owe him a determined fight to protect his habitat. The human experience creates the opportunity and imposes the challenge. His survival is ours.

HUNTERS AND THE SUB-CULTURE

Turkey hunting will also introduce you to turkey hunters. You will encounter men and women—I hope the future will provide more opportunities for women—who will come from very different backgrounds.

Despite significant disparities in age, occupation, wealth, education, ethnic background, area of origin, political orientation, and religious belief, most turkey hunters share a sense of identification.

Those of us who have developed a passion for the sport acknowledge that our common interest can bring and hold us together. In many cases the only interest the participants have in common is spring gobbler hunting. It is enough.

So I invite you to join our ranks. For those who are already members — and may be senior to me in tenure — I hope some of the ideas in this book are provocative and a few of the stories are entertaining. I would enjoy hearing from any of you about your experiences and ideas.

2

An Historical Perspective

THE PREHISTORIC PERIOD

Archaeological evidence from a variety of areas proves that American Indians were hunting wild turkeys before Europeans entered the new world. Frequently turkey bones are the most common bird remains encountered on archaeological sites.

Analysis of skeletal material from two Virginia sites provides insights concerning the wild turkey in prehistoric times (Barber 1977, 1978). Barber's reports are particularly informative because they provide data from two environmental zones—the uplands and the coastal plain. At both sites the skeletal data indicated that the number of wild turkeys represented just over 5 percent of the total number of vertebrate creatures identified. At the upland site, located near the city of Blacksburg, only two species provided more individual skeletons—or parts of individual skeletons—than the wild turkey. The two species were the whitetail deer and the box turtle. Individual specimens of whitetail deer represented just over 45 percent of the total species count, and the box turtle accounted for 35 percent of the total.

The whitetail was again number one at the coastal site, near the city of Williamsburg, accounting for just over 21 percent of the total. The box turtle was again high at 18 percent. Additional species found in significant numbers in this tidewater environment were all species of fish at 11 percent (there were none at the upland site), muskrat at 18 percent, and raccoon at 11 percent. As stated above, the wild turkey represented just over 5 percent of the total.

These data support the concept that the turkey was important, but it was not the

An archaeological site being excavated.

primary focus of these prehistoric peoples. The greater reliance on the whitetail deer is correlated with the larger quantity of edible meat provided per creature. The box turtle's popularity is derived from the fact that its collection was relatively easy.

The Turkey as a Source of Tools

Various parts of the skeleton were used for tools—for example, awls and needles were made from the long bones of the legs and wings. One of the more intriguing applications involves the spurs of gobblers. Barber (1977) reports finding the leg of a gobbler from which the spur had been partially removed. This example is from the coastal site near Williamsburg. Barber says:

> . . . one (spur) of which was deliberately cut from the tarsometatarsal (large bone of lower leg). Although one might suggest that this male orientation is a result of unisexual flocking or gobbling lures, the sample is too small for speculation. [Barber 1977]

In conversation with me, Barber indicated that it was probable that the spurs were used as projectile points (Barber, personal communication, 1985).

Turkey feathers were used in a functional context to fletch arrows and for a myriad of decorative applications. There is also evidence to suggest that turkey skins, with feathers attached, were used as garments. The mantle, or cape, of wild turkey feathers maintained its importance until historic times. Mosby and Handley provide a picture of a wild turkey mantle of early twentieth century origin (Mosby and Handley, 1943:11).

A Spring Focus?

In my opinion, the turkey became a focus of prehistoric hunters when it was encountered during hunts for big game or at those times of the year when unusual opportunities for turkeys were combined with reduced chances for larger game. The spring would have constituted such a season as the mating behavior of the birds would have made them vulnerable. This seasonal emphasis on the turkey would have been intensified by the reduced vulnerability of large game as these animals adopted the more reclusive patterns of behavior associated with the time of the year during which their young were born.

Turkey-Hunting Methods of Prehistoric Peoples

It is difficult for the archaeologist to provide precise data on the hunting methods relied upon by prehistoric peoples. The basic problem is that our reconstruc-

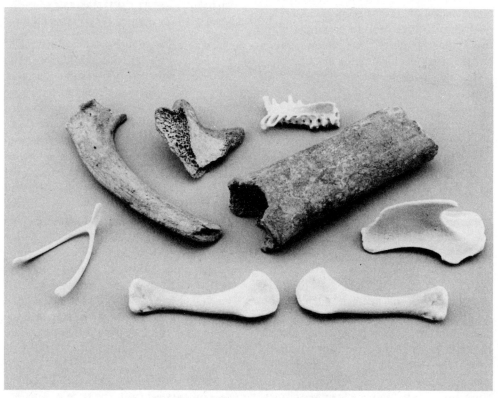

Faunal material from an archaeological site.

tions are based only on those material artifacts that survive in the ground. The tool inventory with which the prehistoric archaeologist has to work is hence made up primarily of the projectile points, knives, and other tools that were made from stone. This archaeological bias should not suggest that many other tool types, made of nondurable materials such as wood, were not important. Their absence in the archaeological record should be expected. In most cases the projectile points we excavate from sites that have associated collections of turkey bones were not designed for the hunting of turkeys. Even the smaller projectile points, commonly referred to as "bird points," were probably not used for hunting birds. It is likely that hunting techniques involved a combination of clever deception and relatively short-range capture or killing with tools such as snares, nets, bolas, traps, and a variety of nonstone projectiles propelled by hand, blow guns, slings, and bows.

There is little doubt that these prehistoric hunters would have developed skills in calling turkeys. It is fun to reflect on the possibility that certain bones excavated from prehistoric sites may have been used as calling devices. Occasionally the archaeologist will find a bone that is of the appropriate size and shape to have been used as a bone tube, or wingbone-type call. One such example is depicted in Griffin's *Archaeology of Eastern United States* (1952:Figure 24). Despite the provocative nature of artifacts such as the bone tube that could have been used as a calling device, it is my belief that most of the calling exercised by prehistoric peoples would have been done with their natural voices. When you consider the level of competence attained by contemporary

hunters with the natural voice, you can appreciate how subsistence hunters would have developed impressive skills.

In summary, the archaeological data conclusively demonstrates that prehistoric American populations harvested wild turkeys. Certainly, these hunters would have taken advantage of the vulnerability of the birds during their spring mating season. It is probable that deception involving the use of calls was exercised. Finally, it is also likely that a variety of entrapment or killing techniques was employed after the birds were attracted. Despite popular myths to the contrary, the tools used in killing the birds were efficient only at extremely close range.

SPRING GOBBLER HUNTING SINCE EUROPEAN EXPLORATION

Explorers were quick to carry stories of these incredible birds back to Europe. The American wild turkey was something new and grand. There were other impressive American animals and birds, but most of them were similar to creatures native to Europe. Our grouse were of different species, but they were at least comparable to the partridge of Spain. Our bears were also different, but there were bears in Europe. New waterfowl species were encountered, and their numbers were astounding, but all the explorers had seen ducks and geese before.

The wild turkey was unique — native only to the new world. The explorers devoted pages to the description of this creature. The reporters did not fail to make the point that the bird was delicious, a fact that significantly influenced its subsequent history.

Many records document the abundance of wild turkeys from the time of first exploration until the second half of the nineteenth century. Some of the records are no doubt exaggerated; however, it is clear that the American wilderness was well stocked with wild turkeys.

In most areas, a precipitous decline in wild turkey populations occurred during the middle of the nineteenth century. It is popular to assume that the primary reason for the decline was the aggressive hunting of the birds by settlers. In fact, it is probable that habitat loss was the critical factor. Unlike quail, deer, and ruffed grouse, the wild turkey will not tolerate significant alterations in habitat. Extensive timbering operations were extremely detrimental. The timbering was compounded by agricultural activities, which also reduced habitat.

The bird needs wild places. The very settlement of eastern America was an exercise in the reduction of wilderness. In the prevailing opinion of the time, the elimination of wilderness was a goal. The turkey, the black bear, the cougar, and the eagle were hostages to the mentality that saw wilderness as a barrier to progress. Robert Nash in his book, *Wilderness and the American Mind*, provides examples of the negative attitudes toward wilderness:

> Two components figured in the American pioneer's bias against wilderness. On the direct, physical level, it constituted a formidable threat to his very survival. The transatlantic journey and subsequent western advances stripped away centuries. Successive waves of frontiersmen had to contend with wilderness as uncontrolled and terrifying as that which primitive man confronted. Safety and comfort, even necessities like food and shelter, depended on overcoming the wild environment. For the first Americans, as for medieval Europeans, the forest's darkness hid savage men, wild beasts, and still stranger creatures of the imagination. In addition civilized man faced the danger of succumbing to the wilderness of his surroundings and reverting to savagery himself. The pioneer, in short, lived too close to wilderness for appreciation. Understandably, his attitude was hostile and his dominant criteria utilitarian. The conquest of wilderness was his major concern [Nash 1982:24].

The attitudes addressed in the quote from Nash were not effectively challenged until the beginning of the twentieth century at the earliest. Mosby and Handley (1943) pay eloquent tribute to the damages caused by timber cutting in the late nineteenth and early twentieth centuries in Virginia. The primary reason they cite for the decline of wild turkey populations during the first quarter of the twentieth century was the loss of habitat to lumbering and agriculture.

There is no question that the acceleration in aggressive lumbering activities in the latter part of the nineteenth century was a critical factor. The advent of the small portable sawmill at the turn of the nineteenth century allowed timber cutters to gain access to the most isolated tracts of timber. As these small portable mills began to take trees from even the highest slopes and the most isolated hollows, the wild turkey began to lose critical "refuge" areas. The effect thus was not simply the destruction of habitat but loss of the last buffer zones the birds had enjoyed. The mobility and aggressiveness of the lumberers was such that no ridge was too distant for their saws. In my home state of Virginia, the situation reached its height between 1905 and 1915 when over 2,000,000 board-feet of timber were cut by over 3,500 different lumber mills (Mosby and Handley, 1943). The devastation of the forest was compounded by the fires that ravaged the wood waste from the cutting.

From the bountiful perspective of 1985—with the great explosion in the popularity of spring gobbler hunting in so many areas—it is hard to appreciate the fact that many intelligent people felt the bird was on the verge of extinction in 1915.

It is true, of course, that in areas that were not subjected to significant human population increases or lumbering, the birds maintained healthy populations during those lean years. In the traditional spring gobbler states of Alabama, Florida, Louisiana, and Mississippi, fewer inroads were made on habitat. In this small core of states the tradition of spring hunting was carried forward while hunters in North Carolina, Virginia, Pennsylvania, and other states lamented the drastic decline in turkey populations.

It is instructive to reflect on the attitude directed to the plight of the wild turkey during this period—from 1890 to 1950—when most populations were at an all-time low. In his classic book, *The Wild Turkey and Its Hunting*, published in 1914, Edward McIlhenny stated:

> Since the days of Audubon it has been prophesized that the wild turkey would soon become extinct . . . In the states of Florida, Alabama, Mississippi, North Carolina, Georgia, Louisiana, Texas, Arkansas, and Missouri, and the Indian Territory (Oklahoma) the wild turkey is still to be found in reasonable abundance, and if these states will protect them by the right sorts of laws, I am of the opinion that the birds will increase rapidly, despite the encroachment of civilization and the war waged upon them by sportsmen. [McIlhenny 1914]

This quote not only is prophetic in the context of what the future would hold,

but it also stresses the importance of the Deep South as a core area during those difficult years of the early twentieth century.

This southern area became the birthplace of modern spring wild turkey hunting techniques. It was here that spring seasons flourished decades before they were developed in northern areas. Many states that now maintain impressive populations have a short history of spring hunting. The spring season has enjoyed a remarkable resurgence in the relatively recent past.

RESURGENCE— THE VIRGINIA EXAMPLE

In many states, the wild turkey has made an astounding recovery from the grim days of the first part of the twentieth century. A review by Mosby and Handley (1943) that attempted to ascertain when wild turkeys were last seen in 31 Virginia counties provides a range of "last seen" dates from "prior to 1890" to 1937. It is clear that the status of the turkey as late as 1952 was poor in many parts of Virginia (Coggin and Perry, 1975). The first step in an attempt to re-establish the wild turkey in areas in which it had formerly enjoyed success was initiated in 1916 with the establishment of the Virginia Game Department (Mosby and Handley, 1943). This step not only provided the first effective game laws oriented to the protection of the bird but also mandated the formation of a corps of game wardens to enforce the laws. From 1916 forward the bird enjoyed state protection (Mosby and Handley, 1943). Obviously, more was needed than simply protection. In the 31 counties mentioned above, there would be no popula-

The hardwood mountains of Virginia provide superb habitat for spring gobblers.

tion growth unless some method was developed to reintroduce the bird.

The first attempts at reintroduction in Virginia provide important lessons to those involved in wildlife management. In 1929, the recently formed Commission of Game and Inland Fisheries began a restocking program, using turkeys reared at game farms. This effort was implemented for almost 10 years, but the results were extremely disappointing. The game-farm birds did not establish themselves in even the best habitats into which they were introduced. This failure was undertaken at the expense associated with the release of 1,400 game-farm turkeys (Mosby and Handley, 1943).

Faced with the failure of the game-farm birds, researchers at the Virginia Cooperative Wildlife Research Unit at Virginia

Polytechnic Institute at Blacksburg, Virginia, tried a new approach. W. W. Bailey and H. S. Mosby are credited with developing the concept that successful restocking would be realized only if pure wild-stock turkeys were established.

Mosby describes critical details in this success story:

> Twenty-four captivity-reared wild turkey hens were assigned for the project by the State Game Commission, and several settings of eggs from native wild stock obtained from the Santee River Swamp of South Carolina were supplied by W. E. Wise of Parker, Virginia. Mature wild gobblers on the Camp Lee Military Reservation, Prince George County (an area that had not seen the eradication of the original wild stock), where the propagation field work was conducted, were introduced to mate with the captivity-reared hens. [Mosby and Handley 1943:20]

The stocking program involving these pure-strain turkeys was not begun until about 1940 in most of those sections of Virginia from which the birds had been eradicated.

THE POPULATION EXPLOSION FROM 1960 ON

Table 1 provides a comparison of the data for annual kills for the state of Virginia for 1952 (Coggin and Perry), 1967 (Coggin and Perry), and 1982 (Virginia Commission of Game and Inland Fisheries Big Game Harvest Summary Printout 03-1-85). These years were selected because they are 15 years apart and because the final year (1982) brings us to contemporary data. As the data indicate, we have seen a phenomenal increase in the harvest of wild turkeys in the last 30 years. The major factors in this resurgence include the following:

1. The gradual expansion of areas suitable for exploitation by wild turkeys.

a. Critical to this process has been the natural reseeding, and subsequent growth to mast-producing age, of hardwood trees in those areas that were timbered during the logging extravagances of the first quarter of the twentieth century.

b. The reduction in intensive agriculture and the accompanying depopulation of

TABLE ONE
TOTAL LEGAL KILL OF WILD TURKEYS FOR
STATE OF VIRGINIA

1952	1967	1982
1,608	3,218 Percent increase from 1952 figure = 100%	18,417 Percent increase from 1952 figure = 1,045%

Virginia hunters have enjoyed great success in recent years.

some areas made them suitable for maintaining turkey populations. As fields reverted to second-growth timber, they provided additional cover and food.

c. The tremendous increase in state and federal programs oriented to the management of wildlife on public lands. As more private property was placed under federal and state control, programs were initiated to improve the areas for wildlife. Perhaps more importantly, the public tracts provided large areas that would not be sold or exploited without public concern for the implications of those actions.

2. The development of an intelligent stocking program assured that the birds would be introduced into those areas deemed capable of sustaining them. Critical to this stocking program was:

a. Stocking birds of pure wild strain.

b. Introducing an adequate number of birds to assure survival of a viable group.

3. Implementing intelligent laws that would control the human harvest of the wild turkey.

4. Increasing interest in the sport of wild turkey hunting. This growth in interest paid dividends by both:

a. Encouraging hunters and landowners to implement intelligent management practices on private land, and

b. Stimulating hunters to bring political pressure to bear to see that dollars were invested in improving wild turkey hunting.

In the context of our specific interest, the data from Table 1 not only demonstrate the wild turkey's ability to flourish under intelligent management practices but also indicate that the implementation of a spring season did not deplete wild turkey numbers.

The recent initiation of the spring season in Virginia (in most counties the first one was held in 1962) should be considered by anyone interested in the history of spring gobbler hunting. In many sections of the nation the activity is not yet 25 years in age. With rare exception, only in the Deep South core states have spring seasons extended back for generations. In most areas, it is a relatively new sport.

3

The Challenge and Appeal

ATTITUDES

For most Americans, the word "hunting" suggests the fall or winter seasons. The concept of October's "Hunter's Moon" suggests that hunting occurs after the advent of cool weather. Almost any painting of contemporary hunters depicts the men dressed in warm clothes.

The spring gobbler season demands a reassessment of these perceptions. As the popularity of the spring season has grown, more and more hunters have adjusted their seasonal patterns of outdoor activity. For most of us it demanded a reduction in time previously allocated to fishing. In the spring, you fished. Suddenly an exciting new opportunity was presented, and a choice had to be made. Some people claim to be avid spring fishermen as well as spring gobbler hunters. Few can do both. Consistently successful

spring gobbler hunters must allocate considerable time to their sport. As I said in my first book:

> It is nice to talk of how in May one can hunt turkeys in the morning and fish for trout in the afternoon; however, if you expect to kill your gobbler regularly in the spring you will fish very little. You must invest full days for consistent success with spring gobblers. The season may end at 11 A.M., but you have to scout in the afternoons and practice calling in the evenings. In addition, the 2:30 A.M. alarm will dampen the enthusiasm with which one awaits the 3:30 P.M. hatch of mayflies. The turkey asks a lot. The successful turkey hunter pays his dues. [McDaniel 1980:8]

Some hunters have difficulty in accepting the philosophical basis of spring hunting. The ideas they express are either: it is unfair to take advantage of a bird engaged in sexual pursuit; or, the spring is a time for rebirth and creatures should not be killed. I know avid fall and winter turkey hunters who articulate such ideas, and I am convinced they are sincere. I will add that out of a group of 100 hunters presented with the challenges and thrills of the spring, I doubt if more than two or three will develop negative attitudes.

The argument that it is unfair to take advantage of the bird's breeding season is not persuasive. In our traditional fall seasons many creatures are engaged in breeding activity. Hunting deer scrapes, bugling elk, or calling moose are all exercises in taking advantage of the breeding seasons — albeit in the fall.

One friend who claims to have felt the spring season was "too strange" a hunting experience said that one of the elements he missed most was returning to a warm and cheerful fire after the hunt. He said, "One of the most enjoyable aspects of the hunt is to look forward to the warmth of a fire after a cold day in the field. When I came in from the spring hunts I was sweating and uncomfortable — to me it just isn't hunting."

It is different. To those of us who have been captivated by it, the uniqueness is one of the appeals. Often I will photograph wildflowers or pick a small bunch to take home. If I am particularly lucky, I may find morel mushrooms. Often I think my wife is more excited about a good collection of the delicious morels than she is about a beautiful gobbler — although she loves both.

I enjoy seeing the creatures that are absent in the fall and winter seasons. Small birds are more plentiful in spring, and it is rare when I don't encounter a few that I have to use a book to identify.

I also relish the richness and warmth of the spring woods. At times the winter woods are so grey and quiet that a hunter feels like an intruder. In the spring the woods are alive, warm, and friendly. The rich smell of the soil and the new growth are stimulating. It is relaxing to lean up against a tree in the warmth of the sun. Sit up against the same tree in the fall, and you will be shivering to maintain warmth in response to a coldness that is measured in color, texture, and sound as well as temperature.

From my perspective, the spring allows us to exercise intimate contact with a different type of environment — even if we are in the same area we hunt in the fall. The intimacy is achieved only by spending time in the area, not just walking through it. After several spring seasons I realized that prior to my spring hunting I really knew the woods only in the fall and winter. The spring season makes a hunter a naturalist for all seasons.

THE CHALLENGE

The challenges imposed by spring hunting are unique. They are particularly attractive to many spring hunters simply because you are less likely to kill a mature gobbler by sheer good luck than any other highly respected and yet widely available game trophy. There are very few authentic stories of novices blundering into a mature gobbler in the spring. In contrast, every rural area has the "young boy kills huge buck on first hunt" tale. This point is not made to be disrespectful to deer or deer hunters. Any deer hunter will agree that if you sit at a good crossing, your chances of having a deer pushed to you are very good. All you need do is stay relatively alert and shoot with a modest degree of speed and skill to kill the deer when it appears.

What success will the inexperienced spring hunter have if you tell him to sit in one place and wait for a gobbler? Only someone interested in trying to argue a difficult position would make a case for such a strategy. In spring hunting there is no simplistic method. To enjoy any measure of success you must be able to call and, perhaps more importantly, you must know when to call and from where. Finally, the mature gobbler will not afford any easy chances even after you have him within range. You must develop a high level of skill in hiding yourself and making a shot without allowing the bird to detect you.

The first deer I ever killed provides an illustration of this point. The cold, December, Pennsylvania woods had so chilled my pre-adolescent 105-pound body that I was shaking violently. I sat in front of the huge old oak where, four weeks before, a buck had walked up to me as I hunted squirrels. I told the men I wanted to sit there until they began their first drive. The drive started at nine, and after two hours on the stand I was more interested in their arrival than I was the deer that had been the focus of my dreams the night before.

When I heard the barrage of shots up on the mountain, my attention shifted from the cold to my purpose for enduring it. I heard him bounding down the ridge long before I saw him. When he appeared, my eyes riveted on the bright ivory antlers. The thrill of seeing the buck sent increased shivers through my body. The deer ran right toward me, and I watched as an observer rather than as a participant in the drama. At a scant 30 yards he stopped, no doubt wondering about this short figure

in bright, Woolrich red — this was before the advent of blaze orange. With the buck looking right at me, I raised the rifle and watched in horror as the front bead danced above and below him with the shaking of my body. Desperately, I moved a foot forward and braced the rifle against a small sapling. The buck perceived this strange movement and reacted by jerking his head up and stamping one front foot against the ground. I can still see — almost 30 years later — the sharp movement of his head. With the rifle jammed against the tree, the sight now wobbled within his chest cavity, and I jerked the trigger to end my ordeal. The buck crashed to the ground.

The head of the little buck hangs above me as I write. Below it are a collection of mature gobbler feet. As I reflect on the intense moments that culminated in the killing of the turkeys, the comparisons with the unfortunate little buck are impressive. No mature spring gobbler would tolerate the display I made in front of the buck. Young, shaking boys are not going to harvest many mature spring gobblers. In contrast, you could fill the Los Angeles Coliseum with mature bucks killed by shaking boys like the one on Jericho Mountain in Pennsylvania in December 1957.

Young, cold boys are not the only hunters who will find mature spring gobblers too tough. Many hunters who have established reputations for killing a deer every year suddenly decide that some aspect of spring gobbler hunting is not to their liking. Some say, "They are just too easy to call." Others find the challenges of catching hatchery trout too thrilling to allow turkeys to interrupt. To each his own. But let me offer a comment on the challenge. Spring gobbler hunting is tough. If you are going to be good, it will demand dedication, hard work, and a period of learning before you, on your own, begin to realize a measure of consistent success. There are a lot of stories about hunters calling mature gobblers up the day after they first picked up a call. A few of those stories — including one involving a young friend of mine — are true. But most men kill their first gobbler only after an investment of considerable time and effort. One I know, a fine athlete and a good all-around hunter, worked 93 days before he killed a gobbler by himself. If someone takes you out, tells you where to sit and you kill a bird, that's a different accomplishment.

The difficulty of the spring hunt becomes the attraction and ultimately the explanation for the consuming addiction. We do not, as spring gobbler hunters, have an exclusive lock on a difficult sport. The deer hunter who hunts only for trophy bucks and takes them *consistently* has imposed a tremendous challenge on himself. Remember now, I'm not referring to one big deer in a lifetime — that can be achieved by anybody with a measure of good fortune.

ATTITUDES TOWARD THE BIRD

Accolades directed to the wild turkey vary tremendously in the manner in which they are articulated. Two committed hunters can sound as if they are speaking two different languages. One superb turkey hunter I know is a lawyer in the state of Florida. His occupation, dress, and use of language are testimony to the economic and educational opportunities he was given. He would be the first to admit to those advantages. When he talks of wild turkeys, the intensity of his admiration is

there. His language use may be atypical, but his love for the bird fits. In his words: "The American wild turkey gobbler is the ultimate game creature. No other creature imposes greater challenges or provides greater thrills for those of us blessed with the opportunity to hunt him." My friend from Florida works in well-fitting suits, but when he changes into his old camouflage hunting clothes, an observer sees another side of him. He may not look it as he dines in the finest restaurants of America, but he is one of the physically toughest hunters I have ever tried to stay up with. He is a credit to the subculture.

Another good friend quit school to cut timber when he was 12. His parents were poor, and he had few opportunities. Few of the sentences he utters are grammatically correct. He writes and reads with difficulty. He is very bright and a superb turkey hunter. When he expresses his admiration for the great creature, the intensity of his feeling is evident: "He is the king of our mountains. There is no creature that is close." I relish the company and give thanks for the friendship of both these men. I've learned from both of them. I respect them both.

ARROGANCE AND THE
SPRING GOBBLER HUNTER

I once wrote that "arrogance is an occupational hazard of wild turkey hunters." I still enjoy the sentence. Arrogance is dangerous. Pride can quickly become arrogance, and we should try to maintain a pride in our bird without being arrogant. It is not easy. Many uninformed individuals have been critical of the turkey. That may be a stimulus to our arrogance. As a result, some of us may become pugnacious.

We were sitting around a small campfire in a deep West Virginia hollow. The young state game biologist was making an argument about the relative difficulty of hunting trophy deer and mature gobblers. He was, in a spirit of good companionship, arguing the merits of the deer. I sat looking down into the hypnotic embers and had an idea what was about to transpire. James, a good friend and one of West Virginia's great gobbler hunters, sat on his haunches across from the game biologist, and he too stared into the fire. As he stared he poked a small stick into the fire. The more the game biologist talked, the more active James' manipulation of the stick became. I listened to the game biologist:

"Now, James, you have to admit that some of those gobblers will do stupid things. Why, old man Conley said some kid bought one of those $4 calls and killed a 20-pounder the next day! Come on, you have to admit they are capable of stupid behavior."

James just kept poking the stick into the fire as the game biologist continued: "Why, your friend Raymond told me he has already called up four good ones this spring. Now, how many trophy bucks is a good hunter going to have a crack at in the fall?"

James didn't say a word, and I wished I were elsewhere.

"I've got you on that one," said the game biologist, sensing he had made a good point. "James, you have to admit I'm right."

James looked back to the fire and then, with the most decisive of motions, he drove the small stick into the coals. The sparks flew up, and I involuntarily recoiled backward. I looked up to see James staring intently at the young biologist.

James said very slowly, as if explaining something to a child: "The wild turkey gobbler is the king of these mountains. He always has been, and he always will be. Anybody who suggests otherwise is a damned fool."

Now I stared into what was left of the fire to avoid looking at either man. The young biologist laughed and said, "Well, I guess there is no sense in discussing it with you. You know I respect the turkey. He is a great bird, but you refuse to listen to common sense. Even John will admit a trophy buck is a great creature, right, John?" Wishing I could disappear, I just stared into the fire. James terminated my ordeal by standing up, looking off at a distant ridge, and saying, "Six years in college, and he argues that a whitetail buck is more of a game creature than a gobbler. Education is wonderful." Then, without another word, James walked down to his truck.

I've been exposed to similar situations in various social circumstances. As a professor, I frequently encounter academicians who perceive turkey hunting to be childish or a waste of time. For those who tease about it and push that teasing past what I consider common courtesy, I have developed a stock answer: "I will ask you to do one thing before you continue to make fun of turkey hunters. Come on a hunt with me, just once. But before you agree to do that, I'll add that I doubt you are tough enough to stay with me for the first hour of the hunt—let alone the whole morning. If you do stay with me for the first hour, your wife will probably have to send the rescue squad in to get you after I walk out." No one has accepted the challenge yet.

The game is tough. The very schedule is too much for many people. We are talking about a season that in most states extends for at least a calendar month. To achieve consistent success, you cannot afford to miss many mornings. Don't forget for a second how early those mornings are and how enervating the hunt can be. Unless you are camping in the woods, you must invest a measure of the early morning (late night?) to traveling to the area the turkey inhabits. Even when you live within wild turkey range, as I do, a hunt is usually at least a 30-minute drive and a 30-minute walk away. In my time zone that means the alarm is often set for 3:30 a.m. or earlier. The very strain of the early mornings makes many people what we call "twice-a-spring hunters." Twice-a-spring hunters are enthusiastic before the season and on the first morning. It is usually on the second morning that the recognition of the degree of difficulty comes through. Most decide two mornings are enough. Every once in a while one of these guys will kill a gobbler. They never kill turkeys with consistency, and it is incredible how many of them hunt for years at the two-morning pace and never kill one.

All of us can go for a couple of days and feel fine. It is toward the end of the first week that the fatigue begins to take its toll. Unless you are camping without your family, the dream of going to bed at 8 p.m. remains just that for most of us. We learn to function on five hours or less of sleep. It is not easy. The sport does not cater to those who need comfort and rest. Many of us admit to headaches and pain after a week. For me, salvation in the morning is not just a hot cup of good coffee but also a washbowl full of cold water into which I immerse my face for several seconds. A good friend, upon seeing that bizarre act, calls it the "death bucket," suggesting that it brings me back from the verge of death.

Fatigue is imposed by the nature of the hunt as well as the schedule. Even if you are careful to keep your equipment to a minimum, you probably will carry 25 pounds of gear and clothes into the woods. Add a few steep hills or dense swamps, and the day will leave your legs tired. At times you will feel as if you cannot move, and yet the desire for the bird will somehow allow you to muster strength.

It is my conviction that the single most important trait all successful turkey hunters bring to the spring season is a degree of physical and mental toughness. The season makes such demands that the toughness is a prerequisite to consistent performance. It is an interesting lesson to see this same toughness in hunters from varying socio-economic situations. It becomes the common denominator of the group. You simply must be able to face painful fatigue and have the will to continue. Many newcomers to this sport simply can't tolerate the demands on a regular basis.

THE APPEAL

In talking with dedicated wild turkey hunters, I have developed a conceptualization of what it is that attracts and holds most of us to this demanding sport. First, and of critical importance, I believe we hunt because we respect and enjoy the intimate interaction with our prey and the setting in which that interaction takes place. We derive enjoyment from that experience whether it culminates in the death of a turkey or not; however, the killing of the gobbler must be the goal. If we are simply looking for turkeys, or photographing them, the intensity that characterizes the hunting experience is lost. Those who are addicted to spring gobbler hunting immensely enjoy the natural setting in which the quest takes place. We derive satisfaction from the beauty of the woods, and the other animals and birds that are on the stage but are not the focus of our hunting attention.

Second, the difficulty of taking a mature gobbler contributes directly to the appeal of the sport. We feel a sense of accomplishment when we succeed, and that success gives us pride.

Finally, I believe we enjoy the freedom the sport provides. This freedom may be particularly important. As hunters we are masters of our fate. We plan and implement the hunt ourselves. In spring gobbler hunting we take no orders, we have no superiors. I often thought that if I were told when, where, and how to hunt, much of the essence of the activity would be lost. We relish the freedom of the pursuit.

No one has to be there to tell us if we did well. That comes from within as it has for thousands of years. We know we are not just lucky. A phony can make mileage in many career areas. He will never make a first-class spring gobbler hunter.

We must admit that the appeal may differ from one person to the next. I know one good hunter who has learned very little about the flora and fauna of the woods in which he hunts. He is not a particularly good naturalist. That is unusual. Another man who is also very good is essentially a competitive hunter. To him, the satisfaction lies in outperforming others. He is not abusive, but the direction of his effort is obvious. However, for most of the great spring hunters I know, the key attractions are respect for the turkey, satisfaction in meeting the challenges the hunt imposes, enjoyment of the natural surroundings, the freedom that hunting confers, and the intense thrill generated by the act of killing a gobbler in an ethical manner.

4

Biology and Spring Gobbler Hunting

The existence of a spring wild turkey season is a recognition of biological facts. The sport is predicated on the implications of the sexual behavior of the birds.

The wild turkey is essentially a gregarious creature. The survival of the young birds depends on their staying within the protection afforded by their brood. Separation from other young turkeys is in itself reason for panic. The preoccupation of the mother turkey is to hold her brood together. During the non-spring months most of the turkey's vocalizations are oriented to establishing, or maintaining, contact with other members of their groups.

The influence of the sex urge disrupts this behavioral pattern. We are told that it is the exposure to increased daylight that triggers a hormonal response causing turkeys to begin sexual activity. When the gobbler recognizes this impulse to breed, he responds to it by isolating himself from other mature gobblers and by beginning to gobble.

It is important that the aspiring spring hunter realize that the gobbler is not accustomed to going to the hen. It will not take many mornings of observation to demonstrate that the hens usually move to the gobbler. He is not hard to find—thanks to his gobble.

THE GOBBLE

The gobble is certainly one of the most thrilling of wild calls. Its biological role is to indicate to the female turkeys that a male is available and eager to mate. The frequency of the gobble is influenced by a variety of factors. At times, a gobbler will gobble incessantly. In other situations, he will rarely gobble. Some birds have a pro-

The thrill of the gobble is an important part of the spring experience.

clivity to gobbling; others are unlikely to gobble more than a time or two on any given morning.

There is a general relationship between the quality of gobbling and age. You can with some measure of accuracy gauge the age of a bird by the tone of its gobble. A young bird typically has a short and discordant gobble. The more mature gobbler will produce a longer, clearer gobble.

There will be differences even within the same age class, and you may be able to identify a specific bird by the tone of its gobble.

Gobbling can be both goal oriented and reflective. A turkey that gobbles is usually trying to attract a hen; however, a loud noise such as thunder can stimulate gobbling. When the gobbler is attempting to attract a hen, he often will increase his gobbling if a reluctant hen does not come. He does adjust his gobbles to the hen's response. When the hen is in his company, he will typically reduce his gobbling. The arrival of the hens will occasionally bring about a total cessation of gobbling. He will continue to strut and display, but not gobble. Occasionally the call of a distant hen will elicit a gobble, but in many cases he will remain silent.

The Range of the Gobble

The gobble can sound so loud that you might think it could be heard for miles. In fact, under many conditions the gobble does not carry well at all. Under the worst conditions of weather, terrain, and heavy vegetation, the sound will not be audible to average human hearing at 200 yards. It always impresses me how much farther some other sounds, such as the crowing of a rooster, will be heard. One factor that impedes the range of the gobble is the location from which it is made. Vegetation and contours absorb the sound and limit its range. One of the errors most frequently made by spring hunters is overestimating the distance to a gobbling bird. Every experienced hunter has encountered situations in which he was unable to hear a gobbler that a nearby companion heard distinctly.

The gobble that sounds so loud when the bird is on the roost will sound very different when he is on the ground. The difference is a function of the acoustic advantages of elevation. A call made from the ground immediately begins to encounter sound barriers—ranging from light brush to ground contours. The turkey on the roost is above many of these barriers, and his call will carry farther. This is the reason the call of a flying crow, hawk, or other bird will carry such distances. There

is nothing to impede the sound waves.

The hunter must learn that under many conditions the gobble cannot be heard at extreme distances.

THE GOBBLER'S DISPLAY

The gobble may be the most important aspect of the gobbler's mating ritual from the hunter's perspective, but it is only part of the process. The display of the turkey is referred to as the strut. It is more impressive than most avian sexual displays because of the size of the wild turkey. To strut, the bird jerks his body into a compact position by lowering his wings, fanning his tail, and tucking his head down tight against his chest. As he changes his position, he attains the characteristic puffed-out appearance by stretching his skin. Once he has attained the bulbous shape, he moves in a very slow and graceful manner, taking very short steps and dragging his primary feathers.

When observing the display, I am always impressed by the apparent hypnotic state of the bird. There is no question that during the strut itself the bird is more vulnerable to predation. On several occasions I have watched a gobbler strutting with several hens and been impressed with the far greater wariness of the hens than of the gobbler. After first observing this phenomenon, I tested the selective wariness of the birds by attempting to stalk them while the gobbler was in strut. In every instance the hens identified the threat before the gobbler did and fled while he continued his display. The reason the gobbler is not too vulnerable—obviously gobblers survive to breed, so the activity cannot be too disadvantageous—is that the display is frequently interrupted. The gobbler goes in and out of strut with some regular-

A gobbler in sexual display.

ity. When he goes out of strut he immediately achieves his full range of wariness.

One of the most fascinating aspects of the strut is the pulmonary puff—the sound made when the gobbler places his tail in the display position. Many hunters have tried to describe the sound, and it is not easy to do. To my ears it is best imitated by filling your cheeks with air until they are fully expanded, and then quickly opening your mouth to allow the air to escape. Some pressure has to be applied to your cheeks for this to sound realistic. Once I was on the coast and heard the wind catch the sail of a very small boat, and the sound—though louder—was very similar to the puff of the gobbler. The sound does not carry far at all. Some hunters claim they can hear it at a range of 100 yards; however, that seems too far to me. I would say that for most hunters the maximum audible range is about 75 yards. When you hear him strut, he is close! Many turkey hunters have been placed in a state of abject panic by suddenly hearing this noise. I wish I had camera footage of myself and a friend several years ago when, after two hours of apparently futile calling, we were sitting together against a large oak and enjoying the warmth of the late morning. I had been calling periodically, but neither of us had the alertness you must try to maintain. When the gobbler went into strut behind us, he couldn't have been 20 yards away. Our reactions would have been no less violent if a hand grenade had been thrown at our feet. The gobbler registered our frantic responses and quickly disappeared. It was almost impossible to believe his shock treatment had not been planned.

Whenever I have had an opportunity to observe the display of birds for an extended period of time, I am always impressed with the smooth, graceful, controlled nature of the activity. There is little rapid or aggressive movement. When several gobblers are in attendance — which is not uncommon — it is rare to witness antagonistic behavior among them. The words serene and controlled best describe the scenes I have been privileged to see. Unlike the rutting bucks I have watched, there is no loss of coordination on the part of the gobblers. Twice while fall turkey hunting I have seen bucks so intoxicated with lust that they literally were uncoordinated and wobbling erratically on the trail of a doe. In contrast, I have never seen a gobbler lose the dignity that characterizes his display.

It also is rare to observe much interaction with hens. This sounds contradictory to the biological purpose of the event, but my observations typically show the hens behaving in a manner that is best described as oblivious. After arriving at the gobbler's breeding location they will pick at the ground, scratch at the leaf cover, fluff their feathers, scratch themselves with their feet, raise their heads to alertly observe, and generally seem totally uninterested or impressed by the gobbler's beautiful display. Often the mating ritual will end suddenly as the hens drift away and the gobbler, after a few more lovely displays, walks off.

CONFLICTS BETWEEN MALES

During my years of spring hunting I have only twice been close to gobblers fighting. On both occasions the conflict was violent but short-lived. On numerous occasions late in the season I have simultaneously called more than one gobbler a long distance. When these gobblers met after their long trek, they never engaged in any hostile or aggressive behavior. In every case they strutted together — often in a manner so synchronized that it appeared to have been choreographed — and came to me together. The conflicts that I anticipated did not materialize. It is my suspicion that the frequency of conflict as a result of competition for mates, or as a function of territorial disputes, is exaggerated. The violent conflicts are a last resort. I am not suggesting the turkey decides against violence. It is rather a selection for behavior that avoids conflict. This behavior extends to other animals. For those fortunate enough to be in the woods during the rutting season of deer, it is instructive to observe how drastically altered the behavior of the normally reclusive bucks becomes. As I mentioned, I have watched them wobble after a doe,

A pair of gobblers displaying the lack of conflict that is characteristic of their interaction during the spring.

grunting loudly and seemingly oblivious to the threats they normally would identify. For all the deer I have seen in rut, I have yet to observe a fight. Clearly they take place, but it is easy to exaggerate their frequency.

THE BIOLOGY OF THE BIRD FROM THE PERSPECTIVE OF A PREDATOR

If you were to design a creature that would be difficult for a human to kill, it could turn out to be a wild turkey gobbler. Various biological attributes make this bird incredibly wary.

Of primary importance are his acute senses of hearing and vision. The only way to appreciate these qualities is to hunt him. I have never been comfortable with the comments that compare a turkey's vision or hearing to man's. To say "he sees 10 times as well" is at best a guess and at worst a vague estimate. A valid comparative test simply isn't possible. The true measure of the bird's senses has to be

An alert wild turkey gobbler.

gained under field conditions. Experienced hunters learn that the slightest movement or softest sound will be detected by a gobbler. You must develop a new sense of what is unacceptable sound or movement when hunting. The whitetail deer has established in many of us guidelines for acceptable behavior. You learned that if you made slow movements as you adjusted to the approach of a deer, you would not be detected. Even detection did not necessarily result in instant flight of the deer. Many hunters would stop a deer with a quick whistle and have time to make a deliberate shot. If we were particularly skilled at standing still, we would often have deer walk directly to us.

Spring gobblers make different demands. A wild turkey will identify the slightest movement by a hunter—a source of amazement to experienced deer hunters. I still find it incredible that a moving bird is capable of identifying my slight movement at ranges up to 100 yards. The visual acuity of the bird when moving has not received adequate attention. A good hunter recognizes that his scrutiny of the woods is much more effective when he is stationary—this incredible bird seems to lose little of his powers of observation even while moving.

Every hunter has his own favorite story about the gobbler's hearing. All of us have made calls that sounded as if they would not be audible to a human at 20 yards, only to have a gobbler respond at 250 yards. Most of us have tested the hearing of the birds by making small sounds as they passed at 75 or 100 yards' distance. The results of these crude experiments have always increased our respect for their hearing. Many of us have watched a turkey suddenly become alert upon hearing a sound made by a distant hunter or vehicle.

These situations are particularly instructive when we measure how long it is before the approaching hunter or vehicle is audible to us.

Suffice it to say that we are highly unlikely to encounter any creature with a superior combination of auditory and visual capabilities.

THE TURKEY'S RESPONSE TO THE THREAT OF PREDATION

Superb hearing and vision are helpful in avoiding predation only if they stimulate effective evasive tactics. The deer that stamps his foot at a hunter has identified a possible threat. The critical point is that the foot stamping is not conducive to successful escape. Unlike the deer, the wild turkey is blessed with tremendously quick reactions to perceived threats. A gobbler that sees movement does not engage in assessment—he takes flight. He may flee in the air or on the ground—that is dictated by a variety of factors. But he always attempts escape instantly. The most impressive and instructive pictures that come to my mind when I reflect on mature gobblers are of their rapid escape procedures. A gobbler sneaking along a hillside can instantly throw himself down the slope in a violent and seemingly uncontrolled flush. Another picture is the speed with which a bird can run into heavy cover. The speed doesn't seem possible.

Wariness

The word wariness, applied to a game creature, can indicate many types of behavior. Those qualities that confer "wariness" are diverse. The senses are certainly relevant. The unusually acute hearing and vision of a wild turkey contribute to his

The bobcat, one of many predators that pursue the wild turkey.

wariness. The analysis becomes more complex if you reflect on why the turkey responds so quickly after identifying a threat. Is it because he is so wary? This explanation initiates an exercise in circular reasoning. It is also very easy to make the error of attributing human-like reasoning to the turkey. We use adjectives such as clever, intelligent, and cunning. If we are to understand this marvelous creature it is important that we avoid the error of attributing to him human qualities. Human intelligence is qualitatively different from that of turkeys. We all have spoken of the "old gobbler that outsmarted me," but such a tribute distorts what we mean. What we are acknowledging, in these awkward attempts at articulating respect, is the inherent wariness of the great bird.

The Turkey's Persistent Suspicion

Their wariness is compounded because they unconsciously recognize their vulnerability. If it were not for their persistent suspicion, they would be vulnerable. A turkey is big enough to be obvious to most predators and yet small enough to be a likely target. A comparison with deer is instructive. Deer have no threats that come from above. Great horned owls do not prey upon deer. The turkey has enjoyed no such immunity. Turkeys have evolved as targets for a great many predators—hawks, owls, eagles, snakes, wolves, foxes, bobcats, raccoons, skunks! At some stage in the bird's life cycle, virtually every predator in an area will be happy to add a turkey to his menu.

It seems reasonable that a creature that has faced so many types of predators would evolve effective evasive behavior. The wild turkey gobbler has evolved under the harshest selective pressures and, from

an evolutionary perspective, developed the ability to cope with those threats.

The only turkeys that survived to pass their genes onto subsequent generations were those that could both identify threats and—this is the critical point—respond quickly to those threats. Only the perceptive *and* the quick survived. Until the advent of the human predator—which occurred relatively late in the evolutionary history of deer—there was no predator that selected against a deer that would stamp its feet at a suspicious object 40 yards away. If that object happened to be one of the few non-human predators that was a threat—say a mountain lion—the deer had time to sprint away before the lion made its rush. For the turkey, in contrast, only those birds that instantly threw themselves out of the ambush would have a chance of avoiding the agile fox or bobcat. Also, a turkey stamping his foot at a swooping owl or goshawk would gain nothing but exercise before a quick death. The shadow of the avian predator demands instant response.

One might argue logically that other small birds and animals that are vulnerable to predation should have developed increased wariness. A rabbit seems to be on every predator's list of game to be eaten, so why did he not become the ultimate North American game creature? I believe there is a reasonable explanation. Rabbits and other small game animals and birds enjoy two critical advantages that made it unnecessary for them to develop particularly efficient predator-evasion techniques. First, they are small, and if they remain immobile they can avoid detection. A wild turkey is a master at hiding, but his relatively large size will not allow him to depend primarily on hiding for protection. His size increases his vulnerability. He is obvious. Many small game animals instinctively developed the technique of remaining motionless to avoid predators. The second point is that the wild turkey never enjoys huge numbers, even in the best environments. Unlike quail, the reproductive biology of the turkey does not allow frequent re-nesting following nest destruction by predators. A cold late spring storm in wild turkey range can raise havoc with the entire hatch. This creature never is abundant in the sense that quail or grouse can be abundant, and his very scarcity has demanded a selection for wariness.

"A TURKEY IS REALLY DUMB"

The above statement has been encountered in the monthly outdoor magazines. The readers are subjected to the following theme: "Don't be in awe of turkeys. In essence they are stupid birds, and if you apply the techniques I will provide, you will learn they are easy to fool."

Again, the problem is that stupid, silly, and foolish are words that effectively describe only human behavior. "Stupid turkeys" is an inane phrase. A turkey does not exercise rational thought. There is no evidence to indicate that he can think in the abstract or reason in any manner approaching that of humans.

Most of these "turkeys are dumb" articles provide a few stories illustrating the mistakes a gobbler can make and the ease with which they can occasionally be killed. Any game animal is vulnerable when pitted against an intelligent and dedicated human hunter—that is axiomatic. The articles are deceptive in that they confuse wariness with "intelligence" and imply that the wariness of the wild turkey has been exaggerated. They are wrong.

You will have hunts in which the vulnerability of the bird is demonstrated. But to use an easy hunt to make a case for the "stupidity" of the bird is a gross distortion.

THE TURKEY'S ABILITY TO LEARN

Though it is inappropriate and in fact futile to talk of a "smart" turkey, there is no question that, like other non-human animals, this creature can learn from experience.

Wild turkeys will adjust to hunting pressures in the spring. They will learn from experiences. If you doubt this last comment, I suggest you exercise the following test. Find a mature gobbler a week before your spring season, and try to call him to you for a photograph. If you succeed, spend at least four or five more mornings in the area making similar calls in attempts to attract him again. After he has been fooled, it will be very difficult to call him from the same place with the same type of call. He will "learn" that the particular call from a specific area is something to be avoided.

One factor which makes spring gobbler hunting tough is excessive calling by hunters—not just poor calling, but the amount of calling. An excellent call that is made too frequently or too loudly can repel rather than attract. Gobblers subjected to excessive calling will develop a reluctance to respond to any call. This is not to say it is impossible to call such birds but rather that the task will be more difficult.

Increased human activity in the turkey woods can itself make it difficult to call the birds. Again, it is important to be precise. It is not that "those turkeys know the season is in." Such essentially childish statements are often encountered. A local farmer provides a story of the huge gobbler that used his fields for the month before the fall hunting season, only to disappear as soon as the season commenced because "he knew when the season began!" The only animal that can calculate calendar dates is *Homo sapiens* — period. It is true that wary creatures will quickly adjust to the increased pressure that is often imposed during a season. In most cases the adjustment is not to move from an area but rather to become more wary and less susceptible to even good calling.

It is my conviction that a mature gobbler not only will become more wary in general but also will "learn" to recognize a specific tone or rhythm of calling. It is difficult to assess how long the memory of this call may remain with him. Evidence I have collected suggests it can prevail for an entire month.

Many hunters have made statements attributing high intelligence to specific gobblers that refuse to enter certain types of areas. A common story is: "That bird on Atlas Mountain is so smart he refuses to walk down a logging road." Again, we have to be careful about attributing problem-solving ability to the bird. There is no doubt that gobblers will avoid areas. The question is what underlies the avoidance. No gobbler ever "decided" that he "would avoid all logging roads." The gobbler cannot conceptualize a logging road. What has occurred is that a bird has learned that a section of open ground — which happens to be a logging road — is dangerous. That explanation is very different from suggesting the bird first conceptualized the physical entity we call a logging road and second, decided to avoid all such roads.

IDIOSYNCRATIC BEHAVIOR OF GOBBLERS

Some gobblers develop unusual patterns of behavior. In many cases this behavior makes them more difficult to hunt. The non-gobbling gobbler is a classic example. Again, we should refrain from explanations that have the bird "deciding" to curtail his gobbling so as to reduce the threat of being killed by spring hunters. That explanation has the same biological validity as a Bambi story. What occurred is that a gobbler was born with genes that influenced his gobbling behavior. The effect was to reduce his frequency of gobbling. That behavioral trait is fortuitous in the context of avoiding human predation. If the bird is able to mate successfully, it is likely that the trait will be passed on to some of his male offspring. If the advantage is maintained in subsequent generations, it is probable that more "non-gobbling gobblers" will be encountered in the future. This scenario is biologically viable. It does not demand that any turkey or group of turkeys decide on a policy of non-gobbling.

It is my belief that the selection for reduced gobbling is taking place in areas that have been subjected to intense hunting pressure. I know from my records that there has been a statistically significant reduction in the average number of gobbles made by gobblers over the last 10 years. The key years in this alteration were 1975 and 1976. My records show significantly increased gobbling activity in the years prior to these dates. It is interesting to note that a tremendous increase in the popularity of spring gobbler hunting began at approximately the same time in

Many gobblers develop unique patterns of behavior.

Virginia. It is probable that birds with a proclivity to gobble frequently were selected against during these early years. Hence the suggestion that we may be creating populations of birds that are less likely to gobble frequently is reasonable. Please do not misunderstand what I am saying. I am not saying that in the future you will not encounter a bird that gobbles

a lot. My point is that the frequency of such encounters may decline in areas that are subjected to heavy hunting pressure.

THE GOBBLER'S WEAK SPOT

It has often been said that we would never kill a turkey if they had the sense of smell of whitetail deer. It is sobering to

Even a young gobbler displays a bearing and posture that demonstrate his pride.

reflect on the increased difficulty that would face turkey hunters if we had to contend with gobblers with yet another acute sense.

Despite the popularity of the statement about the sense of smell, I believe we would face a greater challenge if mature spring gobblers would lose their pride and arrogance. Most gobblers make the fatal

mistake because they can't accept the concept that the coy hen doesn't recognize that he, the gobbler, is worth walking to. The gobbler is so arrogant that he just has to show the hen what a mistake she has made by not coming to him. The mind of the turkey does not conceptualize the situation as I have articulated it, nor does he operate with human pride; however, that does not obviate the fact that he simply cannot tolerate a hen that will not come to his call.

Any spring hunter who has not attempted to call *mature* gobblers in the fall and winter has missed a great lesson. In those seasons, the absence of this sexual pride and arrogance greatly changes the behavior of the gobbler. When the sexual ardor is not there, it is *much, much* more difficult to call a mature gobbler.

THE ROLE OF THE HEN

Hunters often overlook the significant role of the hen in influencing the behavior of the gobbler in the spring. Of critical importance is the fact that the hen typically is attracted to the gobbler. All conventional strategies of spring gobbler hunting are predicated on the assumption that you can convince the gobbler to come to you. However, we should never overlook the fact that by enticing the gobbler we are altering the normal course of events. If this is not normal, you may ask, why are gobblers at times so eager to go to the hen? The explanation of this apparent contradiction lies in biological data. After the hen has laid her total complement of eggs, she will stay with her nest most of the time. Up until this critical decision is made, she visits the gobbler each morning. When instinct triggers her to begin constant incubation of the clutch, she loses the desire to visit the gobbler. From the hunter's perspective, this initiates a period when the still-eager gobbler is deprived of the focus of his attention. When he gobbles in the morning, the occupied hen does not respond. The gobbler's reaction to this humiliating situation is to begin to gobble more actively. If you are clever or lucky enough to be within calling distance

of the gobbler at this time, you may see just how aggressive a gobbler can be. The behavior of the hen alters his behavior—he becomes frustrated and confused by the sudden decline in his popularity. On the first morning he encounters this situation, he may refuse to go to the recalcitrant hen. On each morning that follows, the chances of his succumbing to the temptation to seek her out become greater.

Initiation of Incubation

The date when the hens begin to stay with their nests is fairly consistent from year to year. Obviously, this date will vary from one area to the next in the same manner that the gobbling season varies with latitude. In my first book, I called this period the "hot time." In most states, the earliest phases of the legal season will be prior to this period.

Data I have collected for western Virginia indicate that five consecutive calendar dates during our 25-day season have provided for 62 percent of the mature gobbler kills recorded. These five key dates normally fall at the end of the first week of the season. In contrast, the first five days of the season have provided only 15 percent of the kills and the last five days only 10 percent. It is my belief that the primary factor influencing the productivity of the five "hot" days is that hens begin to stay with their nests during this period. It is true that several other factors may have some influence. For example, our worst weather normally is during the first week, and the lower figures for the last week may in part be a result of reduced hunting activity, as some hunters will have killed their legal limit of birds by then. But the fact that over 60 percent of the mature kills have been recorded during 20 percent of the calendar dates substantiates the high productivity of this period. It is hard for some hunters, accustomed to the advantages conferred by the first day of a pheasant or deer season, to believe that the best hunting for spring gobblers is often not on the first day of the season.

It is true that barren hens, those that have lost nests, or those that are not sitting for other reasons will be available to gobblers long after the majority of hens have begun to stay with the nests. It is simply bad luck to encounter a gobbler with these non-nesting hens. In general, the more hens there are in an area, the higher the chance that some will still be with the gobblers. The statement that hens are still with the gobblers is often offered in disgust by hunters early in a season. It is used to explain why the gobblers have not been vulnerable to the call. It is a valid excuse. It is hard to convince a gobbler to leave hens in his home area to gain the company of a hen in a foreign area. It is not impossible, but as we shall discuss later, accomplishing it involves special techniques and a measure of good fortune.

SPRING ALTERATIONS IN RANGE AND POPULATION STRUCTURE

Mature gobblers will stay together during the fall and winter seasons. I observed a band of six mature and two immature gobblers on four different occasions during November 1984. During eight full days of observation I found the group four times. On two of the occasions, both immature gobblers were present; on the other, just one of the jakes was in the company of the mature birds. I believe the area used by the gang of gobblers was approximately 800 acres in size. Their movement indicated a regular pattern of travel

that gave them access to areas that maintained food sources.

Observation in the spring of 1985 indicated a dispersion of the group and much reduced mobility for all the gobblers. I never saw the entire group after mid-April 1985. The largest group of gobblers observed in the area consisted of two birds. Observation, both visual and by listening to gobbling, indicated that the gobblers had dispersed well beyond their 800-acre fall range.

SPRING TERRITORY

My observations indicate that the territorial behavior of gobblers needs careful analysis. A dominant gobbler maintains a primary range as depicted on Map 1; however, he does not restrict himself to this area. I have frequently observed as many as three mature gobblers displaying together in the same area. Antagonistic behavior is the exception rather than the rule when two gobblers meet.

Under certain circumstances a gobbler will travel a long distance—certainly beyond any primary range—to gain access to a hen. Toward the later stages of the spring, when most of the hens are on their nests, I have had gobblers travel over 700 yards to a hen call. In several instances, they came while another mature bird gobbled incessantly within 100 yards of my call. These experiences have convinced me that gobblers do not respect rigid definitions of spring range.

Another behavioral characteristic of gobblers in spring is the enduring relationship often established between an immature and a mature bird. I have observed these odd bachelor couples on many occasions. The two birds travel and stay together for extended periods of time in the

MAP 1
Spring Range For Three
Dominant Gobblers

KEY

Listening Post: ⬤

Stream: ⚫ ⚫⚫ ⚫⚫ ⚫

Scale: 1" = 1000'

Contour Interval: 100'

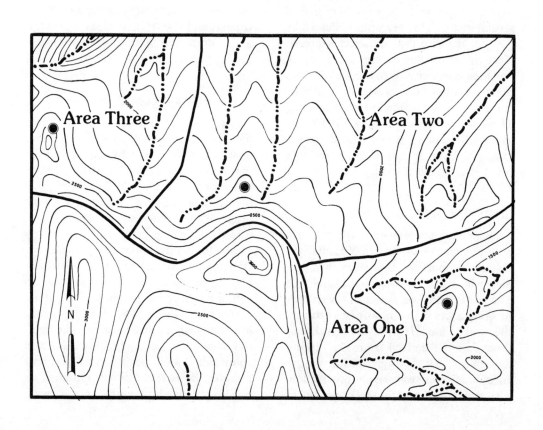

spring. Frequently I have had them both come to my call, and invariably the young gobbler will come in front of the mature bird.

STRUTTING AREAS

Secluded areas that are relatively free of dense cover will often be selected as displaying areas by gobblers. The birds seem to recognize their vulnerability to predation during the display and select areas that make it less likely that a stealthy predator will be able to sneak to within close range.

It is my belief that a mature gobbler will have several mating or strutting areas within his spring range. On one property I hunt, different edges of a huge, open field were used by one gobbler over a period of several years. This example indicated to me that the bird did not select a precise place but was rather looking for an open, flat area conducive to his display. In another situation in deep woods, a gobbler made use of two different strutting areas. These areas were approximately 500 air-yards apart but separated by a deep hollow, which made the walking distance between them much greater.

ROOSTING AREAS

Despite popular stories to the contrary, my observations in western Virginia provide no support for the belief that gobblers will frequently roost in the same tree. The most impressive aspect of my data on roosting areas is just how many different sites will be used. (I stress the fact that *all* these data are derived from the Virginia mountains. My spring hunting experiences in other states have not provided me with enough information to comment on

possible variations in this behavior in other types of terrain.)

I have found that the most attractive type of roosting location for a mature gobbler is at the head, or top, of a mountain hollow, where the two ridges that form the sides of the hollow will curve together as they join the mountain. The small bowl just below where these ridges meet is an ideal roosting spot. The bird will usually be in a tree just off the contour of one of the ridges. Such an area provides significant protection from wind and weather. Map 2 shows several of these prime roosting areas.

NESTING AREAS

Hens select nesting places that are characterized by nearness to water and dense vegetation. Most of these areas will be low in elevation. Typical nesting locations are depicted on Map 2.

IS HE FOOLED OR NOT?

A gobbler that comes to a call will often provide biological evidence of the degree to which he has been fooled. A gobbler that has only sex on his mind will allow his excitement to literally change the color of his head and face. The bird with the bright blue and white face and head is fooled. The blue color of the head is caused by an infusion of blood that is precipitated by involvement in the sexual display. In contrast, a gobbler that comes in with a bright red head is not totally committed to the sex act. The bird with the red head can be gone in an instant. The strutting bird with the bright blue head/face coloration can quickly gain alertness; however, he is less likely to attain it as quickly as the bird with the red head.

MAP 2
Roosting & Nesting Areas
KEY

Listening Post: ⬤

Old Logging Road:

Roosting Area:

Nesting Area:

Stream:

Parking: A

Line of Travel: ➡

Scale: 1" = 500'   **Contour Interval: 100'**

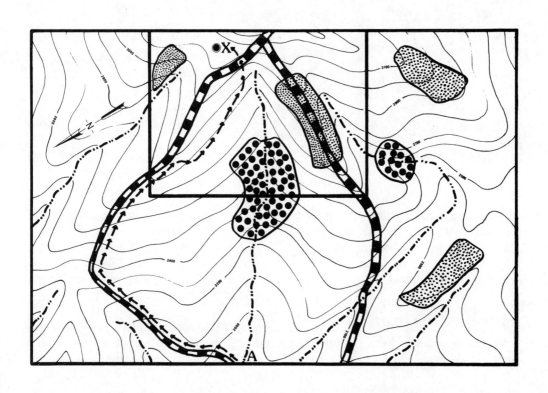

A mature gobbler.

Most young, sexually immature gobblers will come with the characteristically red head. The experienced spring hunter always wants to see the blue and white rather than the red head.

IS HE YOUNG OR OLD?

All spring gobbler hunters enjoy the long, thick beards and curved spurs of mature gobblers. Despite popular opinions to the contrary, in some cases it is difficult to determine if a gobbler you are working is mature. The following criteria are helpful in making age assessments under field conditions:

1. The general size of the bird. It has been my experience that mature spring gobblers will be approximately 40 percent

larger than immature ones. In our area the smallest of immature birds will weigh from 12 to 12½ pounds and the largest from 15 to 15½. A 40 percent increase establishes the characteristic size range of our mature gobblers — from 17 pounds to 21 pounds with an occasional bird outside that range. The size of gobblers, and turkeys in general, varies significantly from one area to the next, but this 40 percent

greater size of the mature birds should remain consistent.

The substantially greater size of the mature gobbler makes him easy to identify when birds of both age categories are together. Unfortunately, this criterion is more difficult to rely upon if you are observing only one large bird.

2. The size of the beard. The beard of most immature birds protrudes only a few

An immature gobbler.

Three beards showing age variations. *Top:* **the young gobbler;** *middle:* **the two-year-old gobbler;** *bottom:* **the mature three-year or older gobbler.**

inches from the chest feathers. The maximum protrusion I have seen is about four inches. In contrast, the mature bird's beard will normally measure eight inches or longer. As soon as the beard reaches eight inches, it begins to hang down rather than protrude. At shotgun range this key is often easy to pick up.

3. The tone of the gobble. In most cases the gobble of an immature bird will be discordant and shorter than that of a mature bird; however, some young birds develop mature-sounding gobbles. They will never have the ringing, bold gobble of the three-year-old or older dominant gobbler, but the gobbles are easy to confuse with those of some two-year-old birds. Some men claim they never fail to identify the

gobble of a mature bird. I will not challenge those assertions, but after hundreds of hours of field observation, I know I can be fooled.

4. Behavior. Most young gobblers will not engage in the strut. Often an immature bird will be seen in the company of a mature bird, and he will gobble but not engage in strutting.

There are exceptions to this rule. I have encountered immature birds that engaged in a characteristically mature sexual display. They would not only strut but also demonstrate the mature bird's physiological changes stimulated by the sexual excitement — such as the changing of the colors of the head and face.

5. One of the best ways to determine the age of a gobbler in the spring is the contour of the outer edge of his tail feathers.

Tail feathers of the mature gobbler on the left and the immature gobbler on the right. Notice the uneven outer edge of the immature bird.

Three spurs demonstrating age variations. *Left:* **the young gobbler;** *middle:* **the two-year-old gobbler;** *right:* **the mature three-year or older gobbler.**

The immature bird will have an irregular outer tail contour, a function of the molting process of the year-old bird. This key is very important in the field in those situations in which the bird approaches the hunter in heavy cover and never gives him a look at his beard. Occasionally, this uneven tail contour—which is obvious when the bird is in strut with the tail fanned—will be the only visible key the hunter has to the age of the bird.

These traits I have just addressed are selected because they can be useful under field conditions. Obviously, spur length of a mature bird will be different from that of the immature gobbler. Unfortunately, the spur length is not usually visible in hunting situations.

5

The Spring Experience and the Hunter

THE SPRING EXPERIENCE

You look at the watch yet another time. (A hunter could argue that there is no time in one's life when hours, minutes, and seconds—those arbitrary divisions of time that man imposed upon himself in his relatively recent past—seem so important.) It is almost 8:30 p.m., and you wonder where the time has gone. You pick up the phone, dial the familiar number hoping Gary will answer—it embarrasses you to get Linda because you call so often during the spring season. No luck. Linda is, as always, pleasant and you wait for Gary's familiar voice—anticipating the question: "Did you get him?" The answer is, "No. How about you?" Again a negative. It is well into the second week of the season, and Gary's voice transmits the fatigue you feel. The conversation is typical. Each man listens with interest to the story

of the other's hunt. A few questions are asked: "You mean where the two streams come together under Piney?" "Was he with hens?" Finally the conversation turns to the next day. You tell Gary where you plan to go, and you conclude with a quick "Good luck." You glance back at the watch and realize you are behind schedule.

The excitement that carried into the evenings of the first few days is no longer sustained. You check your equipment rapidly and move upstairs, desperate for rest.

Nell is putting the two girls to bed as you enter the room. She says, "Well, I think Daddy might beat my girls to sleep tonight." You smile as the girls laugh. You say goodnight, feeling a bit guilty, and head for the bedroom.

It is a "good tired." You know you'll quickly relax into a deep sleep. If every

American adult were a spring gobbler hunter, there would be no market for sleep aids. You check both alarm clocks and glance one last time at the watch — 9:30 is not bad. In the instant before sleep you think about the spot you have chosen for tomorrow's hunt. You see the ridges, the hollow, the small stream, and you review the access route you will use. The final picture, as always, is of the great bird.

You move quickly to the alarm in the vain hope you will not disturb Nell. She says "Good luck" as you move toward the door. You move down the stairs slowly, trying in vain to limit the creaking sounds of the old oak. Each landmark on the short trip to the kitchen is familiar. You speak softly to the retriever you know is under the breakfast table. The solid thumping of his tail is welcome. The bright light in the kitchen is a bit of a shock, and you realize there is some pain. You move to the sink and fill it with cool water and immerse your head. The cold takes your breath away, but when you dry your face you feel better. A flick of a switch and the coffee pot begins to make noises that are not heard during the loud breakfasts with the family. You take the retriever out for a quick walk, and the April morning is cool. The stars are bright, and there doesn't seem to be any wind. You get impatient with the dog and pull him back toward the kitchen's bright light.

Sitting alone at the table, you drink the strong coffee slowly. You think about Jesse, who goes every morning without any kind of hot drink, and you wonder how he does it. You realize you are smiling as you stare at the wall thinking of your friend. You quickly glance at the watch, and as always there is little time left. You go downstairs to get the pack and the gun

and to put the camouflage paint on your face. The exercise with the camouflage has become a ritual. You are careful to cover all the visible areas. The final step is putting on the boots. It is surprising how many precious minutes you consume by this simple task, but finally you are ready. You check the coffee maker carefully to make sure it is off because you don't want to ruin another one. Finally you gather up the pack, gun, and hat and move awkwardly outside. You open the door of the Wagoneer slowly, anticipating the sound of the latch. You start the engine and back out into the street. You use the parking lights as you don't want to flash the headlights on the neighbors' homes. As you head down the familiar street, you glance at your watch — five minutes behind schedule.

The town is as still as it is dark. At the one major intersection you pause; a pickup truck crosses in front of you, and a man you do not know smiles from behind his camouflage. You smile back, acknowledging your relationship.

The road is familiar, and the trip provides a pleasant rest before the hard climb. You park the vehicle and make sure you have all the tools before you lock the car and turn to the familiar trail.

The first 100 yards are tough. You feel the tightness in your legs as you pull up the slope. When you reach the old logging road, your heart is responding to the strain. The road is relatively flat, and you begin to feel strong. The route is familiar, and you anticipate the curves the long-departed loggers etched on the landscape. You are higher now, and there are no lights. You move at the familiar pace and enjoy the seclusion and the modest adventure of being alone on the dark mountain. At the long-deserted farm site you stop to rest, opening your shirt and taking off your cap to cool down.

From this vantage point the distant Interstate is visible, and you watch the lights of the few vehicles that move slowly along it. Another set of lights on a distant mountain calls attention to a hunter or hunters who are gaining access. Concerned by possible competition, you look at the closer ridges, hoping not to see the flashlight of a nearby hunter. There is none. You glance at the watch—late. You readjust the pack and gun and move off again.

The last 400 yards are tough. Your legs ache, and your breath comes in gasps. Finally you reach the spot from which you always listen, and take off the pack and sit down. Despite the cool morning, you are soaked with sweat.

High on a narrow ridge, the location lets you hear gobbling from four different roosting areas. You check the wind, and though there is some breeze, it isn't bad. If it doesn't start to blow, it could be a great morning. You rearrange your gear and button your shirt. It doesn't take long to cool off after the climb.

After making sure everything is in the pack in the event there is a need to move quickly, you stand up and prepare to make an owl call. As you prepare to call, you feel yourself alter the way you hold your mouth. The first note of the call sounds loud and a bit strained. The subsequent notes sound better, and you wait with anticipation. There is no response.

Light begins to enter the woods, and you strain to hear a gobble. Prime gobbling time is about 10 minutes away. The 10 minutes pass slowly. Prime time arrives, but apparently no one told the gobblers of Big House Mountain.

He is 10 minutes late and a long way off. When he gobbles, you try frantically to determine his position. He helps by gobbling twice in succession. He is on one of the ridges they have been on before. It is not the best place, but you can get to him. You put on the pack, grab the gun, and are off down the ridge at a fast trot.

You feel the excitement as you run. He continues to gobble, and each call sends a thrill through you. After 200 yards on the old road, you turn off it to get to the ridge the bird is on. In the thicker cover you walk at a fast pace, your mind racing as you consider strategy. Finally, you reach the point from which you need to get a more precise fix on his location. You stop, your breath coming in gasps. He does not make you wait long. It is a great call—a booming, mature gobble that suggests a three-year-old bird. He is 400 yards away and on a small spur ridge.

It is a favorable situation. You stay well back from the edge of the ridge as you move toward him. A hen calls from below him. He cuts off her raspy yelps with his great gobble. Another hen calls, and he double gobbles. The chorus is a thrill, but the competition is a serious threat to your chances for success. When you reach the spur ridge, he is going crazy and he doesn't sound as if he is much over 200 yards away. Should you call from here? Because of the presence of the hens, you take the chance on getting a bit closer. You head down the ridge, not at all sure your decision is correct. Each time he gobbles you want to stop, but the calls of the hens convince you to move closer. Finally, at an estimated 150 yards, you stop, locate a nice large oak atop the ridge, and carefully move to it as he and the hens scream at each other. In position, you take out the calls with trembling hands and glance at the watch. It is 6:45 a.m. You make the decision to use the raspy slate call. With the big shotgun across your knees, you prepare to make the first call.

The long hours of practice and the past successes give you confidence as you stroke a series of quick, loud yelps. His quick response is the thrill it always is. You touch the big shotgun and make sure you are ready, well aware that a shot might be hours away. You hear one of the hens call and enjoy her quick yelps. It is great to hear them. There is a good chance you will hear him come off the roost, and you strain for the sound. He is gobbling a lot now, and you hope that no other hunter will hear him. Another hen calls from a different direction. The gobbler is playing no favorites. He responds to every call. He sounds ready to accommodate any hen — even the immobile one on the ridge 150 yards above him.

You glance at the watch and decide to wait a full five minutes before calling again. You begin to count his gobbles and lose track at 31. After four minutes you can't wait any longer, and hit him with another fast series with the raspy slate. He gobbles back. He likes the slate. You relish the tension. You hear his body hit the leaves an instant before hearing the more muffled gobble. He is on the ground. You pull the gun up in the hope that he might try the raspy hen first. Your vain hope for quick victory is shattered by the loud cutting of one of the hens. The gobbler goes crazy. It sounds as if the two birds are together. There are more loud hen calls, a string of gobbles, and then silence. You try another loud call on the slate, and the gobbler interrupts whatever he is involved in to let you know you should come down to join the fun.

You debate your next action. There is a chance he will move up the ridge with his hens. Also, if you are patient, he might come to you after spending some time with the hens. You decide the best course of action is to try to sound like several hens in the hope of attracting the hens and their friend. To implement this strategy, you place all your calls in positions of readiness. You first use the mouth diaphragm, making some soft yelps and a few purrs. This time there is no response. You pick up the small, flat, slate call. The rough texture of the corn cob on the striker feels familiar. The yelps from the slate sound good, and you enjoy the very act of calling. The gobbler's response excites you — it is clearly closer. You make several low clucks and purrs on the call, and a hen yelps back. You estimate the distance to the bird to be 100 yards, and you reassess the quality of your chosen position. The ridge is fairly open and wide, and it appears to be the kind of location the gobbler will enter.

There is a temptation to let the birds move naturally up the ridge, but that is balanced by the greater temptation to play a role in encouraging them. As is customarily the case, you succumb to the desire to play an active role and make several more calls on the slate. Each time, you receive what you perceive to be searching responses from the hens with the gobbler. The gobbler's calls now sound as if they are coming from a stationary position. You can picture the scene. The great gobbler will be going in and out of strut near the middle of the ridge. His movements are measured and dignified. There will be nothing rushed or aggressive about the display; rather it will be graceful and controlled. The hens, probably three or four of them, will be close to him but behaving in a way that suggests they are oblivious to his display. You have watched the performance on a number of occasions and have yet to see a hen seem eager to mate with the hard-working gobbler. The hens do make the effort to travel to the gobbler, and then they will stay with him for hours, but during these extended periods they seem to lose interest in the biological purpose of the meeting. The actual mating is the briefest part of the entire interaction.

Imagining the activity just down the ridge, you glance at the watch and realize that the bird has been on the ground a half hour. You must be patient. Your best tactic is to continue to respond to the hens and try to convince them to come up the ridge with their preoccupied friend. You decide to try the tube call despite the fact it is most effective at longer distances. The calls sound good, and you enjoy the rhythm. The gobbler is apparently not impressed.

You consider imitating another gobbler, to make the bird jealous; however, you resist the temptation because your success with the jealousy strategy has been modest. The idea of changing locations does not seem reasonable, because you are so close. You look at your calls and realize you have not yet tried the old box. As you prepare to call, you realize how stiff your body has become since first sitting. Your legs are cramped, and you shift your body in a vain attempt to gain comfort. The box feels awkward in your stiff hands, and you rehearse the stroking motion before letting the lid touch the sides. The call sounds too loud. You question the intelligence of the choice. A hunter does not get within 100 yards of a mature gobbler every morning, and it is depressing to think you have wasted the precious opportunity. Concerned about the way the first call sounded, you quickly stroke another and the great bird gobbles back instantly.

He gobbles from the same spot and with the same volume with which he has been gobbling intermittently for the last half hour, but you *know* this is not a random gobble but communication. The quickness of the reply is not the sole convincing factor. There is a quality of urgency in the call that experienced callers can identify. You begin to tremble. You place the box down quickly and move your hands to the dead weight of the cold shotgun. The gobbler aggravates your palsy with two more aggressive gobbles. You know his head is pointed toward you and his small brain is focused upon you. You bring the gun up and place it on your raised knees and stare down the rib. Your pulse rate doubles. A glance at the watch indicates it is 7:15 a.m. The woods are silent, and you strain for sounds of the birds. Five minutes pass, and the big gun begins to tire your hands. You move slightly, trying to adjust the weight. The sound of a squirrel bouncing through the leaves hits you like an electric shock.

He gobbles again, but it does not seem appreciably closer. Again it is time for a decision. He is interested in this hen up the hill, but is he interested enough? Should you call again? Despite the many mornings of experience, you are not sure. You just wait. Now he begins to gobble actively again, and you perceive he wants encouragement. He is just arrogant enough to expect this new hen to do what all the others have done and come to him. Your failure to move does not make him suspicious, just angry. You can sense the impatience in his gobble. There is a chance he will come; however, you know there is a chance he will stay with his hens and insist you come to him. It is a standoff.

Looking down the barrels of the shotgun now, you feel the tightness, anticipation, thrill, and fear. "The challenge is to be cool," you tell yourself, as you always do. The effect of the counseling is no better than it ever is. If anything, you grow tighter. He gobbles again, sounding as if he is in the same location—a good 75 to 100 yards down the ridge. The next call is that of a hen, and her coarse yelps are closer. She calls again, and you estimate she is 50 yards away. Despite the intensity of the moment, you register the tone and coarseness of the hen's yelp.

At this juncture you debate making another call. The tiny diaphragm call is pressed against the roof of your mouth. The hen yelps again, and you perceive a spirit of urgency in her call. You return the call with the diaphragm, without thinking. You feel your head bob as you make the yelps. The gobbler's double gobble sends a fresh wave of excitement through you. Involved, you make several clucks and purrs on the call and a series of low-volume yelps. The hen responds, and she is still closer. You look down the ridge, adjusting the position of your body as you strain to hear the sound of the bird, or birds, walking. Seconds race by, and your left leg begins to cramp. The hen makes another call. Your heart is racing now, and while your head is locked in position, your eyes race from one edge of the ridge to the other.

When the rhythmic sound of the walking comes, it is steady and bold. You bring your face down to the stock of the gun. Where is the bird? You begin to wonder if your fix on the sound is accurate, and you lift your face to look just to the right and left of the spot from which it seems to be coming. You begin to panic with the realization that a failure to obtain an accurate fix on the bird's position will result in your being caught unprepared. Your new con-

cern intensifies the tension, and you feel your head move slightly. "Don't move your head," you say to yourself as you try to remain composed.

The first clue to the hen's arrival is a flash of black directly above the gun barrels. She sounds much closer. She walks steadily and calmly through the light cover of the open ridge. You cannot resist the temptation to watch her for an instant before looking behind her for the gobbler you know is coming. Despite the camouflage, you feel conspicuous. You try to pull together and wish you could breathe with less movement. The hen scratches at the forest floor and then lifts her head and surveys the ridge with those impressive eyes. Satisfied with the security, she lifts her wings in a stretching motion and fluffs up her feathers before taking two more quick steps.

The gobble hits you like a physical force. As soon as you hear the sound you know what has happened. The gobble comes not from the ridge—in the direction of the hen—but at a right angle and just off the contour. He has paralleled the approach of the hen just off the ridge top. He is probably within 30 yards. If the hen were not in front of you, you could rotate 90 degrees and wait for him to pop up; however, you know the slightest movement will alert the hen, and her quick cluck will be the end of the affair. You move your eyes to the edge of the ridge and feel desperate. The hen comes closer. Now she is 25 yards away. She looks back down the ridge and makes a soft yelp. The gobble that greets her call is even closer. He has moved along the edge and is almost directly opposite you and, despite being off the contour, is probably closer to you than the hen. You swing your eyes to the left to focus on the spot from which the gobble came. Because it is a full 90 degrees to the left of the direction in which you are facing, your vision is blurred and you consider trying to slowly turn your head. Fifteen years of experience with the birds convinces you to reject the idea of any movement.

The next sound you hear is the puff of the strut. The gobbler is in display just off the contour. You can see the hen moving in front of you as you strain to focus on the dropoff of the ridge. Your eyes water with the strain, and your vision blurs. You move your eyes back toward the hen and try to relax. She is 15 yards away now. There is nothing you can do.

You see the dark blur at the edge of the dropoff and know instantly it is the top of his great tail as it fans in his strut. He is climbing up on the ridge. You feel your breath come quicker, and you alter your grip on the shotgun, which points 90 degrees away from the gobbler. The bird is 15 yards away, and you are incapable of decisive action. *(If you think it is time to swing the gun quickly to the left and jump up to surprise the bird, this book will be a help to you. Such a move would be an exercise in sure failure. The first rapid move, and your next view would be of the gobbler climbing over mature hardwoods 80 yards down the hollow.)* You know your only chance is to hope he will walk in front of you.

As you try to focus on the dark blur, the hen comes still closer. You glance back at her, and she is not 10 yards away. You will not go undetected much longer. A sudden flash of white tells you his head is now above the contour. You strain to see him clearly, but the rotation of your eyes continues to blur the image. You see more of the dark blur rise above the ridge. His progress is slow but steady. The blurred

shape grows, your pulse rate increases, and beads of sweat trickle down your immobile face. The blur diminishes in size, and you know he has gone out of strut. The sudden, incredibly loud gobble hits you, but your physiology has no higher plane to attain. The pulse can race no faster. The bird fluffs back into strut and moves slightly more into your line of vision. He is moving toward the hen and toward the aiming plane of your barrels. After several interminable seconds he comes into better focus at an angle of 45 degrees from the direction in which the gun is pointed. He looks, and no doubt is, twice the size of the mature hen. His head is as big as a baseball. The massive beard hangs down, and despite the intensity of the moment, you notice that it is curved and bounces slightly with each step he takes. Just 10 more yards and you can bring the gun on him.

Suddenly the hen putts and you see her eyes are on you. The gobbler freezes. The hen begins a series of clucks and raises her head. The game is up. You have to act. You swing the gun. He does not flush. He does not run. He does the one thing that leaves you without a chance. He throws himself over the contour of the ridge in one violent motion. You jump up and stagger on cramped legs to the edge of the contour. Reaching the edge of the ridge, you watch as he beats his way up above the trees 80 yards in front of you. The escape is perfect. He had been 15 yards away, and you were unable to get a shot.

You stand on the ridge and shake with the thrill of the moment. It is over. A spring turkey hunter does not get a second chance. You debate your actions and realize you are smiling. It has happened again. He had been in the most precarious of positions and somehow had extricated himself. You are proud of what he accomplished. No one could convince you any other game creature could have exercised such a perfect escape.

PORTRAIT OF A
SPRING GOBBLER HUNTER

Something about the man attracts your attention. I'm not sure what it is. He is of only average size. It may be the eyes. They are clear and light blue, and most of the time they twinkle—at times they burn. It may be the way he moves. He is no longer in his 40s, but he moves as if he were 25. He bounces up stairs. He walks at a rapid pace all the time. It is a relentless, constant motion.

He is a very gentle person. My children were at ease with him the first time they met him. Both my girls are shy, but they enjoy his company. All dogs seem to recognize he understands their place and predicament.

In the woods the quality that sets him apart from most good turkey hunters is his intelligence. As they say on Madison Avenue, he is a very bright guy. The uninformed do not give hunters credit for making use of intelligence. The primary reason James is so good is that he is so bright.

He also has the requisite toughness. The toughness is both physical and mental. At 53 he can walk 25-year-old men into the ground. He also has the tenacity to hunt when he is hurt. Two years ago he pulled a muscle in his leg, and a physician, who is a turkey hunter, told him he would miss the season. He wrapped his leg, hobbled up the ridges, killed two birds in two states, and never missed a day. I could see the pain in his face. When I asked him why he pushed himself so hard, he simply said,

"That's part of it, John—you have to be able to get it done when it isn't easy." The toughness endures. A lot of local hunters are successful early in the season, and then the strain gets to them and they just go through the motions. James is deadly the last day.

He has developed and refined all the necessary skills. Some friends rave about his calling. He works at it and is never satisfied. I once watched him try to master a new type of call. He was already a master of at least four types and yet was trying to learn another. I teased him and said, "Sandy Koufax didn't bother to throw a knuckleball—why do you need that strange call?" He looked up and asked who Koufax was. There is a clue there. He doesn't waste his time with the distractions that make it hard for most of us to spend enough time mastering the skills.

He shoots very well. How good is he? Who knows. I've watched him break clay pigeons with boring regularity, but I'm sure he would be no threat to the best European pigeon shooters. One thing I can assure you—if a gobbler makes the fatal error of showing James his head and neck at less than 40 yards, the chances the bird will survive the encounter are slight.

One thing that has always impressed me about James is that he listens. He always is attentive to my stories about both my successes and failures. I believe he still learns from them. It may just be a function of his intelligence, but he clearly is a good listener.

He is also proud. There may even be a trace of arrogance. Once we went to listen to some turkey-hunting experts at a seminar held at a local high-school gym. The program was adequate, and the calling was excellent. One of the men must have weighed 350 pounds. I asked James what he thought of the show. He said, "They really are first-rate callers, John, no question about that, but I don't care how strong that fat boy is, there is no way he can hunt with us in our hills. Our gobblers won't accommodate fat boys." I laughed, and as he turned toward me I could see the fire in his eyes.

The reputation that James has established has nothing to do with his occupation, his family, or his wealth. He has never won a calling contest, written a book, received a degree in wildlife biology, or been the Master of Ceremonies at a turkey seminar. He wouldn't be caught dead in cowboy boots, or wear a turkey beard as a tie. No one taught him to hunt. He learned the hard way. He knows what to do because he learned by trial and error. He has befriended a few of us who asked him questions about turkey hunting. If we were really lucky, he took us along and showed us how it should be done. He never tried to impress us with his skills; in fact, he told more stories about his failures than his successes. He did talk a lot about the birds. The lesson was that they deserved, in fact demanded, respect. His eyes took on a different look when he talked about the abuses the birds had suffered.

I was with him once when we encountered another hunter at a check-in station. The man was with three friends, and they were in the process of checking in a small gobbler. The hunter who had killed the bird threw it out of the bed of a pickup truck and looked at us and said, "See, I told you boys that gobbler could still fly." The beautiful young gobbler fell in a heap next to the Exxon pumps. One of the man's friends followed his lead and picked the bird up and tossed it in the air. Several more raucous remarks were made for the

benefit of James, me, and two teenage girls, who smiled coyly at the drama. The man in the back of the pickup, in an effort to solicit a response from James and me, said, "Hey, fellows, feel free to shoot that bird if he flies again." James turned to go inside the store, and I followed, feeling very uncomfortable.

The proprietor said hello to me and greeted James in the deferential manner accorded to men who are great turkey hunters in small towns in the American South. James asked if he could check in a gobbler, and I noticed that his voice sounded strained and unnatural. The proprietor was quick to say he would check the bird, and we went back out to get it. The four men were still involved in the skit with the young gobbler. The audience had been augmented by a husband and wife who laughed loudly at every line. James walked directly to our vehicle and took the gobbler from the back seat. When I saw his face, I knew we would be lucky to leave the little store without incident. The man in the back of the pickup saw our bird, and he half yelled, "Lord have mercy, now there is a gobbler!" James didn't look his way. The man added, "Well, boys, there is a man with a real gobbler." I sensed from the tone of his voice he would be willing to let James take center stage. James stopped and looked at the man in the truck. I could not see James' face or eyes, but the man by the pumps stopped tossing the turkey and the man in the truck stopped talking. James turned quickly and walked into the store. I followed, wondering if the four strong, young men might attack the old man and his small friend.

James checked in the bird and answered the routine questions. He thanked the proprietor and provided a few polite but short answers to the inevitable questions about the status of the local turkey population. He then bought a Dr. Pepper, asked me if I wanted one, turned, and carried the bird out of the building. The four men were standing by the entrance to the store. As we met them the man said, "That is a beautiful gobbler you killed, sir." James turned and looked up at the huge young man, who towered over him. He said, "Your bird is also a beautiful creature, and you should be ashamed of the way you treated it. If you ever want to be considered a turkey hunter, the first thing you will have to do is learn to respect these great creatures." The young man muttered, "Yes, sir, we were just acting silly. We didn't mean any disrespect."

It wasn't over. The gentlest man I've ever met—the only person outside the family that my eldest daughter relaxed with when she was going through her first rough encounter in school—jerked his body up until his eyes were close to the man's face and shouted, "You God-damned idiot! You didn't mean any disrespect when you threw the bird in the dirt? Are you *that* stupid and common? And

you boys," he said, spinning with athletic quickness toward the three accomplices, "you didn't mean any disrespect when you tossed the gobbler up in the air? I'd like to see you tossed in the air and dragged through the dirt."

All three men just looked down at their feet. James stood there as the four tough-looking young men muttered apologies. They did not turn as we walked to our vehicle and drove off. I didn't say a word and felt very uncomfortable as we made the trip back into town. Finally, two blocks from my home, he said, "I'm sorry for that display, John, but don't ever let the bastards get away with desecrating a gobbler." I smiled and said something about the fact I hoped he hadn't expected me to pull a revolver if they attacked us. "Not a chance, John—the big mouths have hearts of jelly." As he said it, the blue eyes were twinkling again, and I knew better than ever why those of us who hunt with him just laugh when someone suggests that "the big fat man who won the calling contest must be the best turkey hunter in the world."

6

Techniques and Strategies

STRATEGIES FOR PRE-SEASON SCOUTING

If one is to realize consistent success, he must have a source of information concerning the specific areas frequented by gobblers. The key word here is consistent. Obviously, anyone can blunder into a gobbler; consistently successful hunters locate a number of gobblers before the season begins.

A Strategy for the Home Area

The great majority of hunters, this one included, have a general area that they hunt more frequently than others. For most of us, the choice is made because the area is near our home. For scouting the home area, the following strategies have proven efficient:

Maintain detailed records of your pre-

vious hunts. A review of these data is extremely valuable when you are trying to determine which specific hunting properties will be most likely to produce. The first step I engage in each spring is to review the notes I have maintained over the years.

If an area is not subjected to environmental alterations such as logging, or to significantly increased hunting pressure, it will generally sustain its attractiveness to gobblers for many seasons. Obviously, there will be shifts in population density, but after several years you will begin to see patterns emerge in the productivity of various properties. Reviewing these historical data should be your first step as you plan the allocation of your precious time each spring. Obviously, if you are contemplating your first spring season, you will have no data to analyze. Then you should immediately begin this process of collecting information. If you have data from previous years, you will need to go into the field to seek clues about the present situation.

Morning Scouting

Traditionally, hunters have been encouraged to use the preseason to go out at dawn and listen for gobbling. Obviously this pays dividends, but I submit that there are more productive and efficient ways of collecting information on the location of gobblers.

There are two practical problems with morning scouting. First, there are mornings when gobblers are vocal and others when they are not. On one morning during prime gobbling time, you can go to a property you know has gobblers and not hear a sound. The answer to why the birds decided to be silent won't be found in barometric pressure, wind velocity, or phases of the moon. Obviously, multiple visits will decrease the likelihood of an atypical morning; however, this demands a tremendous investment of time. The second problem is the time demand of early-morning listening. Let me provide a word of caution to the first-year hunter who plans to listen for birds each morning for a six-week period before the season. Rising at 3:30 or 4 a.m. is debilitating. Unless you are on vacation for the entire spring and completely removed from the responsibilities of a family, the hours will wear you down. It is not a problem if you hunt only on the weekends, but if you try to hunt most mornings of the season, the decision to scout for six weeks prior to the season becomes a game plan for exhaustion. You must have strength to hunt effectively, and while it may not be macho to admit it, a long string of early morn-

ings without the opportunity to nap in the afternoon will make you a less efficient hunter. So if you want to hunt as many mornings as possible, be realistic about your scouting schedule.

A friend of mine and I, when we first caught the disease, tried to scout every morning and hunt every day, and at the end of the season we were ill and doing things our wives and friends still laugh about. One of the stories my family enjoys most concerns a confrontation my friend and I had with a farm gate. We were driving into a superb hunting property when Gary brought the jeep to a stop, and I dutifully climbed out of the passenger's seat, in a state of semi-conscious exhaustion, to open the gate. Gary drove through, and I closed the gate and then walked around *to the driver's side* of the car, opened the door, and climbed in on top of Gary. The point that most effectively demonstrates our level of exhaustion was that neither of us was very quick to address the rather profound error I had made. For several long seconds we just sat there on top of each other, trying to figure out what had gone wrong. Such fatigue clearly could cause dangerous behavior, and it is important that we recognize the serious implications of exhaustion.

Afternoon Scouting— The Intelligent Alternative

One good way to reduce the level of fatigue and still collect important data is to scout in the afternoons. True, birds will not gobble as frequently then, but in my home range the six weeks before the season is a period during which turkeys leave ample sign—consisting of the scratching they make while searching for food. I have found heavy scratching in April. Even if warm weather has resulted in a decline in

An example of turkey scratching.

scratching, dustings and tracks will provide data on populations.

Though most of the tracks and scratching will be made by young turkeys and hens, I have *never* found an area with extensive sign that did not provide good hunting later in the spring. Obviously, large populations of hens will attract gobblers, and as long as the sign is found within six weeks of the spring season — *not* during the fall or winter — gobblers will be in the area.

These afternoon scouting sessions are also a wonderful time to learn the terrain of the areas and find good places from which to call.

Sharing Information

Most hunters are selfish. That statement is harsh, yet accurate. One reason most of us develop a rather selfish attitude is that often our generosity is exploited. If you are an experienced hunter with a measure of reputation, many inexperienced hunters will seek out your counsel. Only a fool invites everyone to his prime areas. If you know someone who will tell you about a bird he has found, you have a friend who is unusual indeed. In such a case it should be your obligation to respond with generosity and consideration. Such partnerships are one of the enjoyable aspects of spring gobbler hunting. But believe me, there are not many people who will demonstrate such generosity. Many of the inexperienced hunters you befriend will quickly forget any debt and begin to compete for local reputations and become secretive and competitive.

If you find a hunter who will share information, you should both work to maintain the relationship. Two hunters can provide a wealth of data for one another.

The Critical Pre-Season Error

For several years I enjoyed carrying a camera into the woods during my pre-season scouting sessions. My belief was that as long as I didn't spook the birds, the photography would not jeopardize my chances of calling birds during the season. Though I tried not to alarm gobblers after they came to me, I began to see a pattern develop as I returned to work these birds during the season. In general, in any area in which I called to birds before the season, it was more difficult to get them to respond later in the year. In some instances my return to the area during the season would be a full two weeks after my scouting visit.

My concern about the effects of pre-season calling does not apply to calls made to *locate* birds. I do not think that calls designed to locate birds, such as gobbling, will result in the turkeys being suspicious of calling during the season. The key element is not calling the bird *to you.*

PLANNING THE INTELLIGENT HUNT

The scouting procedures I have outlined

are critical in providing the foundation for consistently successful hunting. Even after defining several good areas, the hunter faces the challenge of selecting the one that is most likely to be productive on any given day. This choice should not be left to some spur-of-the-moment whim. On the contrary, a number of factors should be considered. Included are the following:

1. *The anticipated hunting pressure on the day you plan to hunt:* I define properties I call "Saturday areas." These properties are secluded, making it unlikely that other hunters will hunt them. For example, hunting pressure is more likely to be controlled on private property than on public land. Also, there is tremendous variation in access to private properties, depending on the owner's attitude and the physical accessibility of the tract. My Saturday properties are generally those on which my hunting partners and I are able to exercise the greatest control. In most cases that means leased or very isolated properties.

Don't exclude from your precious list of hunting areas properties that experience heavy pressure. I try to plan my hunts of these more accessible areas for those times when there will be reduced hunting pressure. Some I hunt only on weekdays; others I visit only late in the season or during inclement weather. Some properties get such intense pressure that I remove them from my list.

2. *The productivity of a property during a given year:* I rely not only on the notes I have taken during the year but also on reports from my hunting partners and friends. As I said while discussing scouting techniques, prime spring hunting areas generally remain productive; however, some properties will show significant

variations from year to year. In most cases, unfortunately, the change will be for the worse, and it will usually be correlated with altered land-use practices such as extensive timbering. It is important to maintain an unbiased perspective when assessing the value of any property. Do not commit yourself to a property because you had a great spring season there three years ago. You must continually reevaluate properties.

3. *Weather:* On some properties the hearing and hence the hunting will be much better on a windy day. I maintain a list of properties that offer advantages on days of high winds. It is more difficult to find properties that offer advantages in the context of rain, but there are some that become particularly difficult to hunt because of deep mud in logging roads or because steep, rocky ridges become dangerous when wet.

4. *The amount of pressure you and your partners have imposed on the area:* Even if the area is leased and you are confident no one has illegally gained access to it, two or three hunters can overhunt a property. I have learned that the chances of calling a gobbler—not just hearing one—will increase if the property has been "rested" for at least a day, or better yet two days, after each hunt. One of the factors contributing to the difficulty of calling a gobbler is intense hunting pressure. Check your calendar, and rest your areas. Obviously, if you are going to rest an area, you must have a number of options. The more good properties you have lined up, the greater your chances of success will be.

So, on the eve of a hunt you should carefully assess weather conditions, anticipated hunting pressure, the current status of the gobbler population, and the number of times the area is known to have been hunted.

EVENING LOCATION OR ROOSTING

Despite popular opinion to the contrary, many highly successful hunters operate with occupational schedules that deprive them of the opportunity to "roost" birds—that is, discover the place where they will spend the night. Using the plans outlined elsewhere in this book, you can be very successful even if you are not able to roost a gobbler; however, roosting a bird or birds gives you a tremendous advantage. The key to roosting is to listen in a good area. Effective pre-season scouting should put you in such an area. When you walk to a good location from which to roost birds—that is, one that affords effective listening—you should concentrate on not being detected. Unlike early morning when darkness is a great asset in allowing undetected access, in the afternoon entry into the woods demands stealth and the use of personal camouflage. Many hunters are unsuccessful at locating gobblers in the evening because they have alerted the birds as they entered the woods. The first critical step is silent, unobtrusive travel to a good area.

Obviously, a critical consideration is to listen from places close to roosting areas; however, some areas are not good choices, because they do not allow you to hear well. A stream, for example, often creates so much noise that any location near it will be a poor place from which to listen.

Any location that is good to listen from in the morning will usually be fine in the afternoon. It has been my experience that the closer I am to the roosting areas in the evening, the better. I have located birds in the evening by the sounds they made as they flew up onto the roost. These sounds are audible over a surprising distance, but they do not carry like the gobble. Hence, I attempt to get closer to roosting areas in the evening than I do in the morning.

Stimulating a Response

It is highly advantageous to hear the gobble of a bird, since it's impossible to determine a turkey's sex or age by the sound it makes flying up to its roost. At times gobblers will cooperate and gobble at least once after establishing themselves on their perch for the night. Often the gobble at this time will be a responsive reaction to some loud sound. Another gobble, the hoot of an owl, or a clap of thunder will often stimulate the call. It is very difficult to predict what might elicit the response. Most experienced hunters try several sounds to get a response. The owl call is probably the most popular. It is important to perfect your owl call since a realistic imitation will result in more responses than a poor one.

Often the gobble itself can be an extremely effective call at roosting time, and some experienced hunters rely on it alone.

Hen calls, particularly the loud, sharp ones such as the cackle or cutting calls, are often highly effective stimulators. These calls will be discussed at length in the section on calls.

I enjoy roosting birds on an evening when there is a thunderstorm because gobblers that will not respond to any of the locating calls will frequently gobble at thunder. My success in these situations has tempted me to try a small signal cannon, like those used to celebrate scores at college football games. So far, my wife and daughters and my own sense of decorum have persuaded me not to drag one of the cannons into the woods. It would probably work.

One of the most important lessons of roosting is that failing to hear a gobble in a good area does not mean a bird is not there. I have often tried unsuccessfully to roost a bird, gone back to the same area the next day, and encountered one or more gobblers in the area in which I had heard nothing the evening before. The advantages conferred by getting a fix on a gobbler's location the evening before a hunt are considerable; however, do not rule out areas because of a failure to hear gobbling in the evening.

Gaining Access to the Roosted Bird

If a gobbler gives away his location in the evening, the strategy for the hunt becomes straightforward. You will plan to locate yourself in a position the gobbler will readily come to. The route to the spot is as critical a consideration as the selection of a good calling location. If the gobbler detects you en route, the rest of your efforts, regardless of the skill with which they are exercised, will be futile. Hence, enter his domain carefully. Techniques that will help you enter the woods without being detected include the following:

1. Walk rather than drive at least the last 1,000 yards to the selected location.

2. Use a flashlight only during the dark of the moon or on overcast nights. In most cases—if you give your eyes a chance to adjust to the low light—you will be able to walk without artificial light. I carry a tiny flashlight but only use it to work my way around obstacles such as a log across the trail or a fence. The light is also ready to flash an instant warning to another

hunter or to allow me to avoid a skunk. On most mornings I never use it. I watch many men walk into the woods with the powerful beam of a large flashlight bouncing off trees for their entire journey. I am confident gobblers are spooked by such activity.

3. When possible I follow old logging roads and open trails. I try to avoid walking through hardwoods or thick areas because of the noise I inevitably make. I believe that one of the great advantages of certain properties I hunt is their extensive network of logging roads. These roads are invaluable for quiet access to roosting areas; they also let me move toward birds I am working without being detected.

4. Often a hunter must move through woods during the last phase of his trip to the calling location. During the last several hundred yards of the route, I go very slowly and try to move at the pace and cadence of a walking deer. This is time-consuming and unnecessary during the early stages of the route.

5. During the last stages of access I try to take advantage of any contour that will protect me from detection by the gobbler. Map 2 demonstrates my point. If my destination is listening post X and my route is along the dotted line from A to X, I will leave the logging road to take the more difficult path that puts the contour of the ridge between me and the area in which I think the gobbler is located. This reduces my chances of being silhouetted on the ridge, but more importantly, the ground mass that is placed between me and the bird effectively muffles the sound of my progress. Since the hearing of the bird is so acute, any technique that reduces noise is advantageous.

Do not assume that your duel with the gobbler begins after you lean back against the tree you have selected as an appropriate location. The way you have gained access to that tree will be critical to the success you subsequently enjoy.

THE LISTENING POST

On some mornings you will not have the advantage of knowing where a gobbler is located. In these situations you will want to be in a place that gives you the best possible chance of hearing a gobbler—or better yet, gobblers—at dawn. My hunting partners and I call these locations "listening posts."

A good listening post should place the hunter close to a number of known roosting areas. The key to establishing a valuable listening post is that it be within hearing range of at least several probable roosting spots. Maps 1 and 2 show appropriate locations for listening posts. One location I use provides access to nine proven roosting areas.

One common error the inexperienced hunter can make in selecting a listening post is to misjudge the distance at which a gobble is audible. I have had aggressive young hunters come to me with a topographical map to show me an area they planned to hunt. As they defined the spot from which they would listen, it was clear that they expected to locate gobblers several air miles away from the location. If you are over 750 yards from a gobbler in most areas, he will be impossible to hear. If topographic or climatic features intervene or if weather conditions are poor, the range at which you can hear the gobble is much reduced.

This alteration in the ability to hear is an impressive factor to those of us who have an opportunity to hunt in various parts of the country. Sound carries well in some places, quite poorly in others. The most impressive lesson I learned from a Florida hunt was that gobbles did not carry as well in the flat swamp as they did in our mountains.

Access to the listening post should allow quiet travel. If you alert a bird on your way into the woods, the chances of calling him are reduced tremendously. I try to use logging roads or open ridges to travel to listening posts. There should also be a network of easily traveled trails that lead from listening posts to likely roosting areas. This factor explains why it is difficult to select a listening post from maps alone. A location may look perfect on a map, but if it is covered with dense vegetation, it will be impossible to travel quickly.

Listening posts should comprise appropriate places from which to call a gobbler since occasionally a bird may be roosted close to your location.

THE APPROPRIATE CALLING PLACE

Nothing is more important than the intelligent selection of an appropriate place from which to call. A great location will give the hunter a critical advantage; conversely, a poor one will all but guarantee failure for even the most proficient of callers.

Location is critical because there are many areas that turkeys will not enter. Gobblers sense the insecurity imposed by certain types of terrain. An inexperienced hunter recognizes that few turkeys will march out to the middle of a plowed field in response to a call, but the same hunter often does not understand that there are also areas within woods and swamps that turkeys will avoid. For example, it is very difficult to convince a gobbler to enter dense cover.

Topographic features are important. Gobblers are more inclined to travel up than down when being called. The old advice—"get to the same contour or slightly above the gobbler"—is in general reliable; however, it should be used with intelligence. For example, turkeys enjoy traveling in clear corridors when possible. It is no coincidence that the best place to look for turkey tracks is in old logging roads. You should always consider these roads as probable routes by which a turkey will approach, even if the route does not place you above the turkey. I would much prefer to be below a turkey on an old logging road than above him in thick cover. The ease of travel is the critical consideration. Despite popular opinion to the contrary, gobblers will come downhill to a call. The accompanying photographs depict two coming downhill to my call.

A ridge top is a natural avenue of approach. In hardwood forests a ridge will afford easier travel than the slopes ascending to it. A ridge that supports large hardwoods and relatively little ground cover is often an ideal location from which to call. One of the poorest locations is in the bottom of a deep gully or ravine—particularly one that supports dense vegetation. In flat country too, there will be areas that are more frequently used by turkeys. Most such zones will be characterized by mature trees and relatively open ground cover. Areas of dense brush and briars will be used much less frequently.

Appropriate Distance

One of the most overworked and poor-

Two gobblers begin to come down a hill to the caller.

est pieces of advice provided to spring hunters is: locate yourself 200 yards from the bird. This advice distorts the importance of distance. The appropriate distance will vary with the time of day, time of the season, topography, vegetation, and the type of access you have to the gobbler. At times 200 yards will be approximately correct, but at other times it will be incorrect. The guiding principle should not be attaining a specific distance from the gobbler but rather getting close enough for him to hear you call and yet staying far enough away so he does not detect you.

Do not underestimate the willingness of an unspooked bird to travel long distances to a good call. Clearly there is an advantage if you can get close to a bird, but you can call them from over 500 yards away.

The two gobblers progressing down the hill.

After he has been alerted, he will not travel any distance to any call.

So if you find an ideal spot — say a nice flat, open ridge top at the end of a logging road that angles gently down toward the gobbler — use it. If I am confident I can reach the spot without alerting the bird, and if it is close enough for him to respond, I will call with confidence there

whether the location is 400 yards from the bird or 125. It is stupid to get in a poor situation — say in a dense clump of laurel on a steep hillside across a stream from a gobbler — just because it happens to be "200 yards from the bird." In general, the earlier in the season it is, the closer I will try to get to a gobbler. During the early season it is more likely that a bird will be

The two gobblers after making the descent.

with hens, and their presence makes it less likely he will travel a long distance to another call.

The Ideal Location

If you can find a place where two or three ridges join, you have a good start. If the area supports mature hardwoods, even better. If old logging roads run up all three ridges to meet where they join, you enjoy an additional advantage. Finally, if the spot where the ridges meet is relatively flat, the situation is ideal.

Map 3 depicts such a location. While looking at this map, consider some of the advantages of the location:

1. It is in an area where birds are likely

MAP 3
Strutting Areas And Best Places From Which To Call

KEY

Listening Post: ⬤

Old Logging Road:

Strutting Area:

Nesting Area:

Stream:

Line of Travel: ➡

Best Place from Which to Call: ■

Scale: 1" = 250'

Contour Interval: 50'

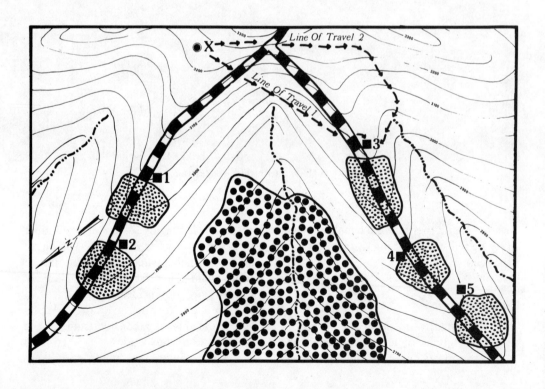

to be roosting—the heads of three hollows are within calling distance.

2. You can travel from listening post X to calling location 1, 2, 3, 4, or 5 along either of the two logging roads.

3. The logging roads and open timber make the gobbler feel comfortable moving there.

4. The grade up the ridges is not so steep as to discourage the birds but is steep enough to help protect the hunter from visual detection.

5. The location is sufficiently far from hunter access via public roads so that your chances of being able to work a bird without being disturbed are good.

6. The logging roads allow the caller the opportunity for quick and quiet movement on a bird that refuses to come.

7. The proximity to nesting and strutting areas makes it a likely place from which to hear gobblers.

There is no question in my mind that the mistake most frequently made by hunters is failing to choose an appropriate place from which to call. The hunter will often not recognize the error because he will attribute his failure to the quality of his calling. Remember that if you are in an appropriate place, you can call a gobbler with a variety of calls. A poor location won't produce regardless of the quality of your call.

SITTING STRATEGY

Very few inexperienced hunters know how to sit while calling. I can watch a hunter sit in a blind for 10 minutes and guess with accuracy his level of experience and his chances for success. An experienced hunter knows he cannot afford to move until he is ready to shoot, and even

then any movement must be made with skill.

Inexperienced hunters think that the mandate, "You can't afford to move!" really means you cannot make exaggerated movements. It does not. It means you should strive to avoid *all* movement. It is not easy, and even experienced hunters often are forced to make modest movements; however, the challenge is to avoid all movement.

A key to making that possible is to use a sitting position that will be comfortable over an extended period of time. Also you should take the time to silently clear debris from the sitting area. Make sure you are as comfortable as possible when you do sit down.

I sit as pictured in the accompanying photo. My calls are between my legs. The need to pull items from pockets assures significant movement. Obviously you must move to pick up a call, but its location between your legs screens the movements as much as possible. I fold my small daypack up and sit on it. The pack provides a pillow and also keeps dampness from making me uncomfortable. I don't carry a cushion, because it is bulky and I think unnecessary.

The best description I have ever read about the importance and the challenges of sitting still was written not by a turkey hunter but by a big-game hunter, Ted Trueblood:

> Holding still, which should be the easiest of all hunting skills, is actually one of the most difficult. It requires no effort. It is restful. It gives you a chance to think. Yet it is desperately hard to sit still, really still, even for a few minutes. I would rather walk steadily all day than sit perfectly motionless for an hour.
>
> There is a world of difference between sitting on a stump and sitting *still* on a

The right-handed hunter (not camouflaged in this demonstration sequence) is seated in an appropriate position for the arrival of a gobbler from the direction the arrow points.

stump. You can sit and visit with your companions, or eat your lunch, or simply rest, and an hour will fly by before you know it. But when you sit down with the deliberate intention of remaining absolutely motionless, the seconds become minutes, the minutes hours, and the hours days [Trueblood 1978:169].

There was a man who knew the chal-lenge of sitting still. He would have been a great turkey hunter.

Another important tactic is to place yourself in a manner that allows the most efficient coverage of the area from which the turkey is likely to approach. One dis-advantage of sitting is that it restricts body mobility. You cannot pivot effectively, so the arc to your front that you can cover with your shotgun is restricted to approximately 170 degrees. To best take advantage of this restricted arc, rotate yourself so that the zone from which the bird is most likely to come will fall in the middle of the arc. If you are a right-handed shooter, that means you should be seated with your body facing to the right of the anticipated angle of approach. In the accompanying photograph, the arrow depicts the anticipated angle of the turkey's approach. By facing 45 degrees to the right, the hunter has placed the anticipated angle of arrival precisely in the middle of the 170-degree span he can cover with his gun held at his right shoulder. The next photograph shows the maximum coverage to the left, and the photo after that shows the range of motion to the

The maximum range of motion to the left for the hunter seated as in previous photograph.

right. The error many hunters make is to face directly at the spot from which the bird is expected. This position makes it impossible to adjust to a bird that comes from slightly more to the right than antici-pated.

One way to expand the area you can cover — at the cost of some movement and awkwardness — is by shooting your gun from your "off" shoulder as depicted in the final photo of this series — that is, shooting the gun from your left shoulder if you are right handed. As the photo-graph demonstrates, the arc is increased to approximately 250 degrees. This is not easy, but it is possible. I have to close one eye to do this, and the efficiency of my shooting is impaired. I would never take a

The maximum range of motion to the right.

Demonstration of increased range of motion afforded the right-handed shooter who has developed the skill to shoot from his left shoulder.

difficult shot in this manner, but I have killed gobblers by shooting from my left shoulder. It is an important skill to develop.

OBSERVATION AND DATA COLLECTION BEFORE CALLING

Once you are situated, it is wise to engage in a period of intense observation—observation with the sense of hearing as well as sight. This is the time to collect information that will allow you to answer the following questions:

1. Is the gobbler where you thought he was?
2. Does he appear to be undisturbed?
3. What class of gobbler is it—mature, immature?

4. Are there hens with him?

5. Is there any evidence of other hunters?

6. How "hot" does the gobbler sound?

WORKING THE BIRD

If you are fortunate, the answers to the above questions will be that the gobbler is hot, mature, undisturbed, without hens, at an appropriate calling distance, and there are no other hunters in the vicinity. Assuming it is still too early for hens to have left their roosts, your first call should be the tree call of the hen. Make it very softly, and make only a few. From the time you finish your first call, you should be in a position of readiness for the arrival of the turkey by either air or ground. Some gobblers will acknowledge the tree calls by more active gobbling; others will not. The lack of an answer should not make you relax your vigil. If the bird increases his gobbling in response to your tree call, wait to call again until it is light enough for hens to leave the roost. Obviously, experience is a factor in calculating this timing, and some birds will fly down earlier than others, but a good general estimate would be about 40 minutes after first light. This is not 40 minutes after official sunup, which is well after prime gobbling time, but 40 minutes after the first hint of dawn. You needn't make a perfect estimate, because the gobbler does not expect all the hens to descend at precisely the same time; however, you don't want to make ground yelps at first light, and you certainly don't want to wait until bright daylight. When you decide the hens are on the ground, make your best series of snappy, quick-paced hen yelps. Some hunters make loud yelps; some make very soft, low-volume yelps. Some are coarse and raspy, and others are clear and bell-like. The tones and volume will vary tremendously, but the snappy, quick cadence or rhythm will remain similar.

It is reassuring, and incredibly exciting, if the gobbler cuts off your series of yelps with an aggressive gobble. If he does, you will need to determine whether the response is a direct communication or simply fortuitous timing. That is not difficult—even inexperienced hunters recognize that there is something directed and purposeful about the gobble that is made in response to your call.

As soon as I call, regardless of the response, I check my watch. It is very easy to exaggerate the amount of time that has passed after you call. If the turkey begins to gobble incessantly and if some of his gobbles are right on top of one another—creating what hunters refer to as the double or triple gobble—you have him right where you want him. Now is the time to allow him to grow impatient. Do *not* continue to call. If you make too many calls at this juncture, the bird will expect the eager hen to come to him. I have made this mistake, and the gobbler has stayed on the roost well into the morning, satisfied the dumb little hen is still eager and a few more gobbles will convince her to come.

If you refrain from calling, some gobblers will go crazy trying to decide what has happened to the hen. They will become frantic—and probably furious that their gracious invitation has apparently been ignored. If all goes well, they will decide to show the hen what a marvelous opportunity is available. I am not suggesting that you should never call more than once—that ancient advice is very poor. I normally wait approximately 10 minutes and then make a second call.

Timing the Response

When working a turkey that is gobbling frequently, I try to time my call so it is made just as the bird completes a gobble. I make my call as soon as I hear the first sound of the bird's gobble. In this way my call reaches the bird shortly after he finishes gobbling. In my experience, this "timed response" is advantageous. I will be particularly optimistic if, prior to my making this call, the gobbler is off the roost and closer to me. As soon as I conclude the timed call, I prepare myself for his approach. If his last gobble was within 100 yards, even if I cannot yet hear him walking, I will raise my gun and look just over the rib in the direction from which he last gobbled. If I have to adjust my body slightly to gain the correct angle, I will do that. By looking over the rib of the gun, I do not restrict my vision, and the only motion I have to make if he appears is to lower my head slightly. In most cases I will hear him walking toward me and will be able to get a better fix on the direction. When sighting him is imminent, I will lower my head to the comb of the stock so that I need to make no visible movement to shoot. Do not expect to be able to lift your gun from your knees after the gobbler is within sight. You will not be able to do that successfully on many gobblers.

In these "perfect case" situations there is no need to make another call. The bird may gobble and strut like crazy, but if he is making progress toward you it is foolish to do anything but wait patiently.

WORKING GOBBLERS
OF DIFFERENT AGES

I have just described the perfect situation. Most of the time gobblers will not be so accommodating. One factor which contributes to the challenge is that gobblers of different ages will respond differently when being called. To achieve consistent success it is imperative that you learn to determine the age of birds and alter your techniques accordingly.

The Young Gobbler

All of us enjoy taking mature gobblers with thick beards and long spurs. Many hunters claim that they will never harvest a young gobbler. A very few hunters will in fact maintain this policy. For most of us, the development of a specific strategy for young gobblers is a valuable way of increasing our enjoyment of the sport. Also, if you have limited time to hunt, a young gobbler can save the day.

Young gobblers will come to conventional calls and hunting techniques; however, the development of special tactics will prove much more effective. I always exercise the young-gobbler strategy after I have tried unsuccessfully for mature birds. The strategy is normally used after prime gobbling time. On a morning when I don't hear an old gobbler, I will typically try some blind calling for mature birds until I have approximately one hour left to hunt, or until a companion is too fatigued to hike into another area. Then I find a good place and commit myself to 45 minutes of calling — without changing position — for a young gobbler.

My calls, which I begin as soon as I am situated, consist exclusively of the lost call of the young gobbler. The lost call consists of a series of coarse yelps — often as many as 12 to 15 yelps in each series. I make the calls as loud as the type of caller allows. You can make these calls on any type of caller, but I have had my best results on boxes and slates with particularly deep

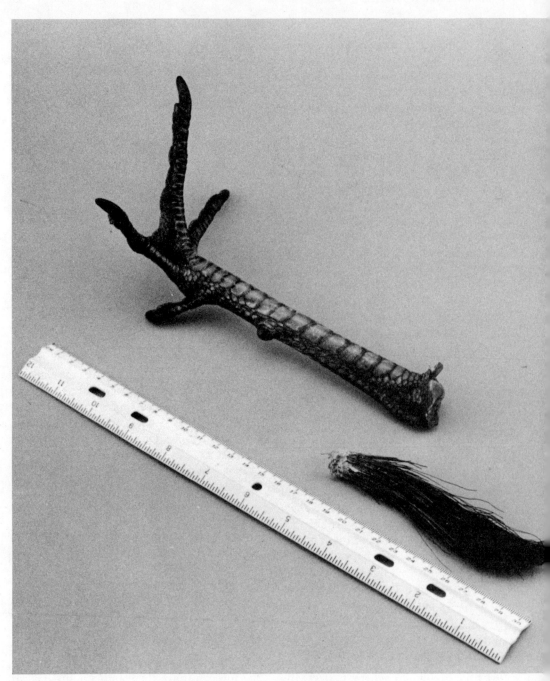

A spur and beard of a young gobbler.

and coarse tones. I have had several manufacturers design calls specifically for young gobblers.

The Silent Approach

Most of the time—I would say 85 percent—the young gobbler will come without making a call. Unlike a silent mature gobbler, the bird will usually come boldly and without hesitation. In fact, often you will detect his determined, direct approach by the surprising volume of noise created by his walking. His approach can be so loud that many hunters are sure they are listening to the gait of another hunter. There are times, however, when the approach is silent. Often this may be due not to a conscious effort to be quiet but to the fact that the bird is approaching on an open woods road or trail on which his walking simply does not generate much noise. So be prepared. Do not expect the young gobbler to answer your calls. Also, unlike the fall season, when young gobblers may run frantically to the lost call, they rarely do that in the spring. The approach is usually steady, direct, and determined.

Patience

Patience and persistence are important attributes for any gobbler hunter; however, the hunter of young spring birds must be particularly patient. Forty-five minutes is a long time to wait. Many young birds will come in less time, but some are very slow. I suspect these late arrivals are traveling extremely long distances in response to the call. I am confident many hunters spook birds by not waiting long enough. If you are going to

make this strategy work, you must be patient.

The Scattered Group of Young Gobblers

It is not unusual in the spring to encounter small groups of young gobblers. Three to six birds will typically stay together. If you by chance scatter such a group, either during actual hunting time or while trying to roost birds in the evening, your chances of calling one are excellent. In these situations you are in essence implementing a fall-season strategy. The birds will try to regroup at or near the spot from which they scattered. In the spring the young gobblers usually take longer to regroup than is the case in the fall, but the process is similar. The key is to give the birds time to come. I have such confidence in the vulnerability of young gobblers to the lost call that it is often difficult for me to decide to leave a blind even after an hour of calling.

Variations in Young Gobbler Behavior

Occasionally you will encounter young gobblers that behave like mature birds. That is, they have isolated themselves from other gobblers, they gobble to attract hens, and they engage in the sexual display. The question of their sexual maturity remains unanswered. I have never observed one mount a hen, but I have seen them display exactly like a mature bird. It is not uncommon for experienced hunters to call one of these birds in and kill it, only to be surprised that the bird that strutted boldly was immature. Some sections of the country seem to produce more of these "of-age" young gobblers than others. An experienced hunter from New

York told me most of the young gobblers in his area act exactly like mature birds. In areas to the south, this is much less common. The point is that you cannot be confident that every young gobbler will follow a specific pattern of behavior.

A Young Gobbler Hunt

I was worried. I had said to my friend, "Come for just one day if that is all your schedule will allow," but now the harsh reality of the odds against calling a gobbler on one day late in the season made me question the wisdom of my invitation. I stared out the window, my concern exaggerated by the fatigue the season had already imposed. "You know Mr. Schielke will understand that you can't guarantee a turkey," my wife said, trying to allay my concern. I smiled and said, "It's a long trip from New Jersey, and we just haven't been hearing that many birds." Nell added, "You and George will have a great time, turkey or no turkey." I knew she was right, but I was determined to show him a gobbler.

These were special guests, George Schielke and his wife Barbara. George is one of a handful of great American gunsmiths, a master craftsman who does *all* the work in building magnificent sporting rifles. The two he built for me on pre-1964 Model 70 Winchester actions are prized possessions. We had become friends in his elegant small shop near Trenton, New Jersey.

Hunting became an important part of my life at an early age. My father was not a hunter. George helped teach me about hunting and the tools of hunters. In addition to the practical information, he also stressed the need to develop a sense of etiquette that included courtesy for other hunters, respect for game, a deep interest in nature, and common decency in all activities associated with the hunt. He felt that the rigorous expectations that are made of the European hunter, in terms of learning about game and hunting techniques, should apply to all hunters. His normally soft-spoken and sensitive manner would turn to intense anger when he related stories of inconsiderate hunters that he had encountered. He had been hurt by the fact that many intelligent non-hunters in America viewed these coarse, stupid, and insensitive hunters as typical.

He also told me about wonderful hunting trips he had enjoyed in distant areas after exotic game. I enjoyed all the stories. In reflecting on them, I realized that there had never been one about the wild turkey. George Schielke had never killed a turkey.

George and his wife, Barbara, arrived on a cool April Sunday. A quick lunch was followed by a wildflower walk. The Schielkes' knowledge of the flowers was impressive. Halfway through the walk, we were drenched by a cloudburst. The cold rain was not a good omen for the following day's hunt. My anxiety increased.

George asked me where we would hunt in the morning. I admitted I was still not sure. I hunt a number of areas, and I was trying to decide which would be best.

After dinner he pulled the drilling, or three-barrel gun, from its handsome case. It was a beautiful gun of exquisite workmanship; built in Germany before the war, its 12 gauge barrels were an unusual 30 inches long and chambered for three-inch magnum shells. The rifle was a 30-30. George asked if I thought it would do the trick. I said it was perfect, realizing that there was a good chance it would not be fired at a turkey.

I was accustomed to the 3:30 a.m.

wakeup hour, but George seemed more rested than I as we ate a quick breakfast. I decided to go to a small farm that has been very good to me. I looked anxiously out the window. There were no stars, but there was no rain. I searched for signs of wind, the nemesis of the spring hunter; there were none.

As we drove out into the hills, I wondered about the climb. Could George, in his mid 60s, handle it? The nagging uncertainty distracted me. Several friends of mine, 30 years his junior, had not been able to make it up the hills. I know people kill turkeys at places you can reach with a Jeep, but when you check into the consistency of their success, you learn that it is a once-every-three-or-four-years affair. If you want to take Appalachian turkeys with consistency, you must be in condition to climb.

The first stage of the climb would be the toughest. The steep hill loomed in front of us as we dismounted from the vehicle. We talked in low voices as George assembled the gun. The strong smell of fine leather and Hoppe's No. 9 permeated the air. I took my camera, checked for my calls, and we headed toward the slope. Halfway up I stopped to assess my companion's situation. I asked if he was O.K. "Don't worry about me, Johnny; I'm doing fine." I turned to the hill reassured. It was a long, tough, 20-minute climb. George, a large man, was equal to the task.

We finally found the spot from which I'd heard a gobbler before the season opened. I motioned for George to sit down, and I crouched next to him. The rest was a great relief for me—even at 34, about one-half of George's age.

Dawn came slowly. I felt my heart begin to pound even faster in anticipation of the gobble. I was desperate for George to hear

one. It came, but it was far off and George did not hear it. Twice more the distant gobbler called, and still George could not hear it. The years of shooting before anyone worried about the effects of noise on one's hearing had taken their toll. I wondered, with growing concern, how close the bird would have to be before he heard it. Realizing the futility of continued worry, I directed my attention to the gobbler. I was sure the bird was still on the roost. I wondered about trying to get closer. The turkey was a good 400 yards away, but we were in a nice position, and if the bird were so disposed, he could come to us without encountering any difficult terrain features. I decided we would stay put. The bird was gobbling frequently, and I began to think there was hope. It sounded as if there were no hens with him.

When I saw the headlights at the base of the mountain, my hope was transformed to anxiety. I knew the course of the logging road and the spot where the hunters customarily parked. I was sure it would be close enough to hear the eager gobbler. My mind raced as I considered our alternatives. Finally, I turned to George and said, "Can you climb another tough ridge?" "Sure, don't worry about me, Johnny." I stashed the gear I had taken out of my pack, made a quick assessment of the best route, and started toward the bird and the approaching lights. The climb was tough. I slipped and heard George slip behind me, and I wondered about the stress my decision was imposing on a 64-year-old man. Every time I looked back at him he just nodded at me and motioned me on. Despite the tough terrain, it was not long before we were within 200 yards of the bird. His gobbles were still frequent. George grabbed my leg, and when I turned around I knew he could now hear the gobbler. Enjoying the fact he had heard the bird, I began to look for an appropriate place from which to call. I saw a large fallen log in a fairly open area and pointed at it, and we moved to it without another word. The old tree was pitched down the angle of the slope so that when we sat down I was somewhat uphill of George. We settled in, and I got my calls out and wondered about the location of the now-invisible vehicle.

Light came quickly, and the gobbler continued to call. The other hunters would be below him, and I wondered where they were. They had to be on the logging road. Suddenly, I registered a different tone in the gobble and strained to listen again. The last gobble had been discordant and shorter than the ringing calls that had attracted us. As I strained to hear, I was greeted again by the ringing, prolonged gobble characteristic of mature birds. That wasn't what I had just heard. George whispered something, but I did not acknowledge it as I again strained to hear. There it was again—a short, discordant gobble. And then the two gobbles almost together. Two birds, one a young gobbler, I thought.

I began to prepare myself to call when I heard the Jeep struggling up the road. I kept hoping it would stop, but the engine kept grinding. It grew louder, and I marveled at the way unnatural sounds penetrate the woods. Finally, after the level of noise began to make me wonder if a German Tiger Tank were below us, it stopped and an instant later there was the harsh sound of the doors. The lack of care with which the doors were closed convinced me we were dealing with either inexperienced or incompetent hunters, and I began to worry about our safety. Despite the intru-

sion on their domain, the birds continued to gobble. Next I clearly heard the sounds of guns being loaded. I decided against calling. We waited. When the turkeys stopped gobbling, I knew that the hunters were moving in. The sharp rifle shot made us both jump, and I looked over toward the spot from which the gobbles had come. I saw the huge bird pump his wings and then set them rigidly to glide out majestically over the valley. The rifle barked again, and it was followed by a barrage of the more hollow-sounding reports of shotguns. The bird glided with uninterrupted dignity. "Miss him, you . . . clowns," I said out loud as I watched him sail off the ridge. I began to curse softly but with feeling, and George simply said, "They must have shot at him on the roost, Johnny." I said, "No question they did." "Too bad, but at least I got to hear one!" replied George. As I smiled back, I began to wonder if we might still have a chance. I was confident a young gobbler had been with the old boy, and I doubted if he had been killed. I hadn't seen him fly, but if he had flown in the opposite direction I wouldn't have been able to see him. It was unlikely that the hunters below us would spend too much time in the area. If we waited an hour or so, we might have a chance to call the young bird back. I sat down and told George that I thought we might still have a chance despite the interference. George was keyed. I decided our best plan would be to just lie low and hope the intruders left.

I listened to the excited voices well below us as we rested by the log. Fifteen minutes passed, and I heard a man walking loudly through the brush. He appeared below us in an open glade, and I identified the rifle with its big scope. George and I ducked down low and watched him. He stopped once and made a few terrible yelps on a box, then turned it over and rattled it in a poor imitation of a gobble. He was answered by an invisible friend back by the car, and they called back and forth for a couple of minutes. I began to worry about the calling spooking the young gobbler. Soon they stopped, and the man walked back toward the car. Ten minutes later we heard laughter, a few calls, and then the sound of the vehicle's engine. I followed its progress down the mountain. Long after the sound was no longer audible, the Jeep emerged at the edge of the woods and pulled onto the hard-surfaced road. I wondered what stories would be told of their hunt.

Bright sun penetrated the woods, and it was hard to imagine that there was a realistic chance of calling a gobbler. I glanced at my watch—only 7:35 a.m. I whispered my new plan to George. We would try to get in position just above the spot where the birds had been roosting and wait another hour without making a sound. Then I would make a lost call for the young bird I suspected was still in the area and separated from his companion. We made the walk to the spot where the gobblers had been roosted and constructed a blind. Then we waited. I enjoyed the warmth of the sun and relaxed—my eyes heavy with three weeks of spring hunting. The woods were absolutely quiet. I checked my watch, and finally the long hour was up. The old box was chalked and ready, and I prepared myself for the rhythm of the call. George's body jerked at the loud gobbler yelps. I finished the long series, thinking it seemed louder than usual. I watched George strain to hear the answer I was confident would not come. I looked at my watch and waited. At the 15-minute mark I made the same series of calls. I was tense

now because I had confidence that somewhere out there a young gobbler had heard the calls and was coming. George was looking down the gradual slope; I was looking up it. The time passed. Numerous squirrels attracted my attention, the characteristic bouncing pace of their movement identifying them before they were seen. At the half-hour mark I called again and tried to inject a sense of urgency into the mechanical call. The call sounded good, but it was greeted by empty silence. After 40 minutes of calling with no response, most inexperienced hunters would grow restless. They would begin to move in the blind and clear their throats and cough. George sat still, never made a sound, and never looked at me for a comment. At the 45-minute mark I picked up the call and made the loud series for yet another time.

I placed the call gently on the ground, shifted my weight slightly—and immediately heard footsteps. It was no squirrel. The rhythm was regular, and the pace was steady. I glanced quickly at George, but he had not heard the sound. Frantically I searched in the direction of the sound. My eyes found the turkey at a range of 50 yards. He was angling down toward us, his head picking at the ground. I moved my head and eyes back slowly toward George, my heart pounding in my chest. George was just beyond my reach, staring downhill. How could I get his attention without spooking the turkey! I couldn't reach George, and the bird was too close for me to speak. I made a fist and tapped the log we were both leaning against with a sharp, light blow. There was no reaction. At the risk of warning the turkey, I tapped the log hard, and George's years of hunting paid us a dividend. He heard me; however, instead of jerking around to the strange signal, he moved his head slowly until our eyes met. I used my index finger to point behind me, hoping that George would find the bird. I saw his eyes move, searching for the turkey he knew was there. With frantic frustration, I realized he was looking well below where the bird was. He looked back to me, and his eyes told me he had not found the bird. I decided to turn slowly to the bird myself in the hope that his eyes could follow the position of my head more effectively than my pointing finger. I moved my head slowly backward to the bird, and picked him up quickly. He was at least five yards closer to us but partly hidden in some light cover. After looking at the bird, which continued to peck at the floor of the forest, I turned my head back slowly toward George. There was no need for an acknowledgment that he had seen the bird. George's eyes swept past me and were riveted on the spot behind me. I watched as he slowly moved the three-barrel gun up over the log and aimed it up the slope to my left. I turned to watch. My eyes found the bird, and I waited for the roar of the shotgun. There was no shot! Perhaps he thinks it is a hen! The beard of the young gobbler was not visible, but the large blue-red head and the size of the body were clear evidence of the sex. The gobbler was looking up from time to time now, and I knew he wouldn't stay long. I turned back to George to see why he had not shot. With a look of anguish on his face, he pointed and mouthed the sentence, "I can't see the sight." I had no answer. I turned back to the bird, and George brought the gun up again. As I watched, I suddenly realized he must be trying to use the rifle barrel! My mind raced with the question of why he wanted to use the rifle when the sharp crack of the 30-30 split the air. I watched in awe as the big bird was knocked backward with the energy of the 170-grain bullet. More feathers flew out of that turkey than any I have ever seen shot. The bird did not move after rolling from the initial impact.

I turned down to George, and the words ran together as we pieced together the intense 45-minute drama.

"Why the rifle?"

"When did you see him?"

"How did he get above us?"

"I couldn't see the sight."

"I thought he was a bit too far for the shotgun."

"I looked up when I heard a slight noise, and there he was!"

"How could he have gotten there without us seeing him sooner?"

"Why didn't he call?"

"I wasn't sure it was a gobbler for a while!"

"At first I couldn't find him."

"I knew he was there, but I couldn't see him!"

"I tried to point at him!"

The walk out of the woods was fun. The words continued to run together as we retold various stages of the experience. We also spent a number of rest stops admiring the beautiful bird. George said, "That is as fine a trophy as North America offers." I thought of the huge set of elk horns I've seen in the Schielke home, and I smiled and felt the relaxed warmth that comes from having done something difficult well.

We had a little celebration at home. We took the bird in back of the house and laughed as Nell and Barbara brought out two additional cameras to take more pictures. The four Brittanies in the pen added their excited barking to the event. We even took the four-month-old puppy out to inspect the immense bird. The older Brittanies screamed with jealousy, and we laughed as the little dog cautiously investigated his first wild turkey gobbler.

That evening we invited two young turkey-hunting friends over for a wild turkey dinner with the Schielkes. We ate a mature bird I had killed one week before. We packed him with a peanut stuffing, coated him in butter, and put two thicknesses of tinfoil around him. He roasted at about 350° for 3½ hours. A lot of people will tell you that a spring turkey is not fit to eat. It is not true. Every gobbler we have eaten has been delicious. The evening was a joy. We all sat down before dinner and took a long look at the beautiful German drilling that had just that day taken its first American wild turkey. My friends handled the gun with respect and admiration, and then Gary said to George, "Well, tell us the whole story." George began, "Well, last night Johnny said we'd have to get up at 3:30 . . ." We roared, knowing the story would be complete in every detail.

The Two-Year-Old Gobbler

All aspiring spring hunters should have the good fortune to encounter two-year-old gobblers. A normal two-year-old bird is a lot like a college freshman. He is oversexed and inexperienced. He tries to make up for his lack of knowledge and experience by being persistent and aggressive. A two-year gobbler will respond to a good call in a manner similar to that of a freshman responding to the smile of an attractive co-ed at his first fraternity party. There will be very little caution and not much grace in his approach. Two-year-old gobblers are the guys who come running. They are the ones who fly off the roost, land in your lap, and then gobble at you.

They have no manners. They are direct, aggressive, and foolish. The comparison with the fraternity initiate is probably unfair to the turkey because no wild turkey would survive a week if he acted as irresponsibly as most freshmen; however, the arrogance and lack of grace are similar.

Even a two-year-old bird will not tolerate a clumsy hunter. Instinctively the bird is ready to flee at the sign of a predator, and his sexual ardor does not alter his magnificently acute senses of vision and hearing. If you do your part and you are not interfered with by another hunter, the two-year-old bird can appear easy; however, he will not tolerate mistakes.

An undisturbed and not-previously-shot-at two-year-old bird will usually gobble like crazy on the roost. Often he will seem to become so intoxicated by his own display that it impedes his progress to your calls. It helps to call sparingly because too many calls will induce him to gobble and display in one place. In effect he becomes so hot he can't move. If you stop calling, you can often sense the increased urgency in his gobble; he will begin to get frantic as he begins to think the unthinkable about another gobbler. When he is about to tear himself apart gobbling and strutting, make one nice quick series of yelps right as he ends a gobble. The next thing you might see is a rapidly approaching young gobbler with purpose in his eyes.

Just like the freshman, the two-year-old bird is bold as long as the upperclassmen are not around. If you think you have a two-year-old, stick to traditional hen calls. This is not the guy who is going out to challenge the old gobbler for his girl. He will quickly gain caution if he hears the booming gobble of a three-year dominant gobbler. He does not relish competition with the old boy. My strategy for what I think is a mature but young bird is to make a modest number of traditional hen calls. I will increase my frequency of calling only if the bird does not seem to be responding. In most cases basic calls, and not too many of them, are the best bet.

Identification of the two-year-old mature gobbler is not easy. In general, if a bird gobbles frequently—at any time of the day—it is likely that you are hearing a two-year-old bird.

You should anticipate a rapid approach by such a bird and be prepared for it. When a friend tells a story about making one or two calls and then being all but run over by a gobbler, you can bet the bird was a two-year-old.

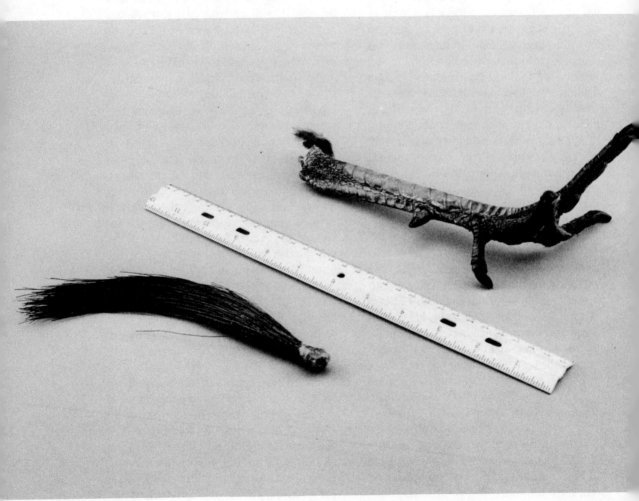

A spur and beard of a two-year-old gobbler.

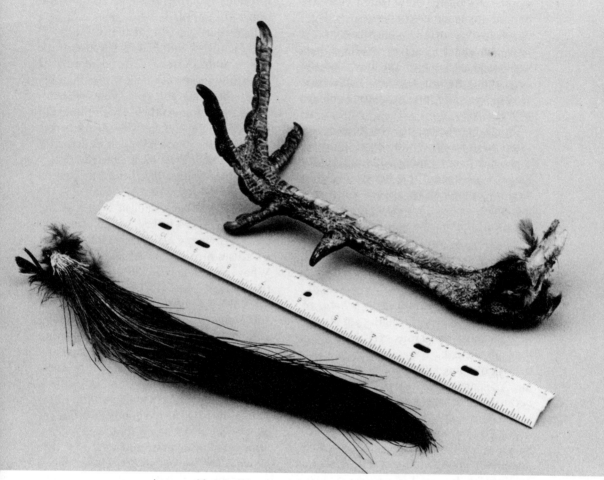

A spur and beard of the mature three-year or older gobbler.

The Dominant Old Gobbler

The dominant gobbler is without question one of the world's great hunting trophies. I have hunted elk in Idaho, and moose, goat, and grizzly bear in British Columbia and none of those great game animals is more challenging than an old gobbler. I have not hunted in Africa, but I have hunted with men who have, and the above statement stands. To the best of my knowledge, no man has yet been charged by a wounded gobbler, but despite some macho writing to the contrary, the quality of a trophy should not be assessed by the damage an animal can inflict. The trophy value should be based on the difficulty inherent in killing the animal in a sporting fashion. If this criterion is used, an old gobbler ranks with any trophy in the world. Obviously, other game creatures impose tremendous challenges, and attempts to make detailed comparisons are a counterproductive exercise. Suffice it to say that those hunters who have had the opportunity to hunt the great game creatures of the world rank the mature gobbler with the best.

The three-year-old or older gobbler is a formidable adversary for even the most experienced spring hunter. If you find any hunter who suggests that he has reached a level of expertise that makes three-year-old and older gobblers easy prey, I would question the accuracy of his self-appraisal.

Behavior of the Old Gobbler

Many old gobblers develop a habit of infrequent gobbling. Since the gobble is a turkey's most dangerous act, those birds that are silent have significantly reduced the risk of being killed by a human predator. A silent gobbler is particularly tough because in most cases you are not aware of his presence until you have alerted him.

Some old gobblers develop mating behavior that demands the hen come to their domain. A gobbler of any age may expect cooperation by the hen calling to him; however, the long-term survival of some old gobblers may be primarily due to their absolute refusal to accommodate the hen. Either she comes to him or mating does not take place. Obviously, a bird that refuses to alter this behavior will be impossible to call.

Some old gobblers have adopted unusual breeding areas. A bird may set up a strutting area in a huge, open field. This is unusual because of his vulnerability by sight detection; however, an immense, flat field with little vegetation can afford tremendous security. Another secure location is an unusually dense area such as a cutover. The old story is that turkeys will avoid cutovers and thickets because of the risk of ambush from hidden predators. If you study turkey behavior rather than believe everything you read, you will learn that turkeys frequently use such places. In the spring the hunter who encounters a gobbler calling hens into such an area may be facing an impossible challenge.

Another interesting behavior pattern characteristic of some old gobblers is the relationships they establish with a young gobbler. The two turkeys will tolerate each other's company and benefit from the extra senses provided by the additional bird. What stimulates the establishment of these unions and how long they persist is difficult to determine. It is not at all uncommon to be working an old gobbler and have him come in, reluctantly, with a young gobbler in front of him. Frequently the young bird gets so close that he spots the hunter and the old gobbler escapes. This is not to suggest some anthropomorphic scene with the old gobbler putting his wing around the young bird and saying, "Boy, you go in first, and we'll fool that clown." The key is that the relationship is not uncommon and it imposes an additional challenge.

If an old gobbler does decide to come to a call, his approach will often be slow and silent. It is rare that he will come sprinting like a two-year-old. The silence of the old gobbler is reflected not simply in his lack of calling but also in his stealthy movement. It is incredible how silently a gobbler can move through heavy cover. The hunter will occasionally have the tremendous thrill of suddenly being presented with a view of the entire body of a mature gobbler within easy range—without his ever having heard a sound. Often the hunter will not have time to react to the opportunity before the bird is gone.

Strategies and Techniques for the Mature Gobbler

Success with three-year-old and older gobblers must be measured in a realistic way. You simply cannot assume that you can go out and collect a set of 1¼-inch spurs whenever you put your mind to it. A good analogy exists with the exceedingly difficult challenge of being asked to bat against a Major League pitcher. An experienced hitter who can succeed four times out of ten at-bats during a season will be immortalized in his profession. In the last 43 years, only one man achieved this level of success. If you plan to duel with dominant gobblers under all conditions over an entire season, you too must develop a reasonable system for evaluating success. No one will succeed every time.

Accepting the magnitude of the challenge is the first important step in developing a strategy. The next is to locate a specific old gobbler and learn about his behavior. Often identification of a specific gobbler and the first phases in the collection of data about him will occur by chance. In one instance, I had a silent gobbler move within my range of vision with his entourage of hens. In the subsequent week I invested many hours trying to affix a pattern to his behavior. I learned that the only predictable elements were that he would not gobble and that he never repeated a specific route with his female friends. My calling would be met with interest but no gobbling. Often I was in a position to observe him from a range of 100 to 125 yards, and when I called, he

engaged in increased display but would never come. The one pattern that did emerge from observation was that he would typically move up the mountain as the day progressed. The hens would usually follow him, sometimes at distances that would take them out of his vision. This behavior stimulated me to try an unconventional tactic.

Unconventional Tactics

Often the only way a hunter will succeed with a difficult old gobbler is with an unconventional technique. To continue relating the above episode—which took place in the spring of 1981—I decided that I might be able to get a shot by pretending to be one of the hens trailing behind the gobbler as he went uphill. I knew the terrain and vegetational cover would have to be perfect for this to work, but I thought there was a chance of success. (*Author's Note:* In general it is dangerous to call and then move. In this situation, though, I was hunting on an isolated farm that two friends and I had leased. I was confident I could identify any poacher who might trespass. Also, I always checked with my two friends to make sure they would not be hunting the area at the same time I was.)

One morning I got particularly close to the gobbler and his several hens. As they angled by my position, they were invisible because of the land contour. I realized they were heading up a steep gully that terminated in a tangle of grapevines. I decided to try moving up behind them, calling as I moved. As soon as I perceived them to be in the thick cover, I began to move up the slope, trying to make my pace sound like that of a walking turkey. I scratched at the leaf cover and made a few very soft calls with my mouth diaphragm call. When I encountered the dense grapevines, it was very difficult to move without making a good bit of noise, and I expected to hear an alarm putt and the scurrying of spooked turkeys. To my surprise, I moved 20 yards into the rather dense cover and the woods remained silent. After stopping one time—I paused after every couple of steps—I heard the low, communicating calls of a hen that sounded 10 yards above me. I tried to imitate the call and then boldly walked toward the sound at what I hoped was a turkey pace. I am not sure how close I came to the birds before they flushed. It was very close. There was no alarm putt, just two hens catapulting into the air in front of me. Identifying them as hens was easy. Knowing the gobbler had to be near, I rushed forward to the spot from which the hens had flushed, and stopped, my shotgun at port arms and my heart beating wildly. An instant later he leaped into the air directly in front of me, and I fixed my eyes on his huge body and enormous head. The barrels of the shotgun entered the scene—sweeping from behind the bird, overtaking him, sweeping past him—and then the whole picture was blurred by the recoil of the gun. Several frames were lost to the brief interval of recoil. My next picture was of the large bird frozen in the air and then plummeting to the ground. The vegetation and contour made him invisible for an instant right before I heard the crash of his heavy body. I fixed the spot where he had fallen, and reloaded the shotgun. I was thrilled, and confident the bird was immobile on the ground. Whenever a bird freezes in the air, the chances of his recovering on the ground are not good. My confidence was well founded, and I was soon inspecting a 12-inch beard and 1⅜-inch spurs. I am

sure that a season of conventional tactics would not have harvested that gobbler.

The Competitive or Pugnacious Gobbler

Late in the season, some gobblers are best called by imitations of other gobblers. The birds that are susceptible to this type of calling will be of various ages, but in general the young and the old turkeys are most susceptible.

I rarely begin my calling with gobbler sounds. Two factors make this unwise: First, there is a measure of risk involved in making any gobbler call, particularly the gobble itself. In some areas and at some times during the season—such as the first day—I am simply afraid to make gobbler calls. In public areas that are relatively accessible, I will refrain from such calls at any time. The second reason I am reluctant to make gobbler sounds is that a lot of gobblers will not respond to them. Hence, in all cases I will consider making gobbler calls only if I feel I am in a safe area, and then I will use them only after other calls are unsuccessful. However, they have saved the day for me.

My best results have been with the imitation of the gobble itself. The gobble must be a realistic imitation. It is true that you can locate gobblers by using poor imitations of a gobble, but to actually bring birds in, the call must be realistic. Every time I have called a bird in with the gobble, it has been after I have tried unsuccessfully to interest him with conventional hen calls. There have also been many occasions when the gobble failed. When it has worked, the gobbler has usually made his way to me gobbling regularly. The gobble does not seem to stimulate a silent, stealthy approach; on the contrary, the gobblers usually come boldly.

When making the gobble, I make sure I am in a position that allows me to see well to my front and to the sides. I sit against a large tree or rock, and I try to maintain a constant vigilance for another hunter who may attempt to sneak in on the "gobbler" he is hearing. I have not been stalked yet, but I never let my guard down.

Don't let anyone tell you the gobble cannot be used to bring in—not just locate—gobblers. It is the most difficult call to master, but it can be the key to turning frustration into gratifying success.

It has been my experience that the other mature gobbler sounds, the deep, coarse yelps and the aggravated purr of fighting gobblers, are not as effective as the gobble.

What to Do When the Bird Does Not Come Running

In most instances the gobbler will not come running. The intelligent hunter will then adjust his tactics.

One of the most frustrating developments is when one or more hens intercept the gobbler. Often the hens will move quickly to the gobbler, yelping eagerly, as soon as it is light enough for them to leave their roosts.

The presence of hens creates a difficult problem for any hunter. The following tactics will increase your chances of success in that situation.

If it is early in the season, before the hens are staying with their nests, you should try to get close to the gobbler at first light. This increases the risk of being detected, but it often allows you to position yourself between the bird and his hens. If you are detected, the game is over, so you must be extremely careful. Once again, the correct distance is one you must

determine. In some areas it may be under 100 yards; in other areas it may be 200 yards. Regardless of the area, you should attempt to get as close as possible. This tactic, obviously, is effective only before the turkeys get together.

When the above tactic has failed and you hear the hens with the gobbler, you need a different strategy. The best is to attempt to call the entire group to you. To accomplish this, call to the hens. Usually when they are moving to the gobbler, and just after they arrive, they will be quite vocal. At this time, I try to sound like several other relaxed but noisy birds. I use a variety of calls to give the impression of birds of different ages. In addition to basic yelps, I make low-volume feeding and contentment sounds (all these calls will be described in detail later). I call frequently. My goal is to make one of the hens curious in the hope she and her cohorts will seek me out and the gobbler will follow them. Usually it is possible to get a response from one of the hens. In most cases the hen will not come immediately, so considerable patience and persistence are necessary. Another ploy to add to this strategy is for the caller to move while he is making these calls. Obviously, you must move with caution to avoid being detected. Changing your location makes your calling more realistic since a group of hens rarely calls from precisely the same spot for long. Moving just 15 or 20 yards in any direction will make the calls sound much more realistic.

If the basic hen calls elicit no favorable response after a reasonable time, I begin to throw in some excited mating calls. Fast-tempo calls such as the popular cackle are appropriate at this time. In some cases these calls will bring the entire group of birds. When I have employed this tactic successfully, the hens usually lead the gobbler to me. This has happened too frequently for it to be due to chance. I am now confident that the hens are also attracted by these excited calls. If you hear a bird moving to you when you're making these excited calls, do *not* assume it is a gobbler.

At times several hours of calling will not convince the birds to come. Often they will answer you but gradually move away. If you become too impatient, you may jeopardize an opportunity; however, it is foolish to sit in one place for five hours if you hear the birds moving progressively farther away from you. When I am convinced the birds are not coming — after at least one hour of patient hoping — I implement a strategy that is drastic and desperate. This tactic is to separate the gobbler from his hens. To intelligently exercise this tactic you must have several more hours of hunting time available to you.

If you do have the time, it is worth a try. Effectively scattering a mature gobbler and his harem is much more difficult than scattering young birds. Often when you try to get close to the old gobbler, the birds will simply disappear and avoid being scattered. Your chances of success will be increased if you can get below the flock and then move quickly up toward them while they are in heavy cover. The chances are poor of getting close enough to them in open, flatland hardwoods.

If you do surprise them and they flush in several directions, make a concerted effort to see where the gobbler flies. Usually he will be one of the last birds to flush, and often he will not go in the same direction as many of the hens. Unlike my strategy in the fall, in the spring I select a location for calling the gobbler that is not precisely where the birds scattered but rather in the direction in which the gobbler traveled. After I get in position, I wait at least one hour without making a call. If it is still relatively early in the morning and I have several hours available for calling, I wait even longer. Once I commence calling, I commit myself to waiting for the bird for whatever legal hunting time remains. (In the states in which I have done most of my hunting, there is an 11 a.m. or 12 noon daily closing.) One final, and important, point is that it may be worthwhile to return on the following morning to an area from which you scattered a flock. I have had a gobbler come boldly from what appeared to be the precise area to which he had flown the previous morning.

Changing Your Position on a Reluctant Gobbler

Occasionally you encounter a gobbler that does not have hens with him but refuses to come to your calling. One of the most effective strategies is to change position on such a bird. Any time you change position there are risks. First and most critical is the risk of being detected by the gobbler. After first light, it becomes extremely difficult to avoid being detected. The other risk is that the gobbler will decide to come to your original position. This has happened to every experienced hunter. There is no foolproof guide that will tell you whether or not to move. Some gobblers will seem totally uninterested in coming to you and then, just as you have given up and made a move, decide to go to the spot they ignored for the previous hour. In general, you should not move until the gobbler has had at least 45 minutes to make up his mind or until he is moving away and almost out of hearing range. The key again is not to be impatient. A balance between patience and decisiveness must be maintained. When in doubt, wait before moving to a new position; however, a new location can be the key to success. At times the same call from a slightly different spot will bring the gobbler immediately to you.

Poor planning of a move on a recalcitrant gobbler is one of the most common mistakes hunters make. You should consider the following before you move:

1. Is there a route that will allow relatively silent movement? An old logging road can be a great asset.

2. Are there land contours you can use to decrease the chances of noise reaching the gobbler? Map 3 shows two routes a hunter could take in achieving a new position from which to call. Clearly, route No. 2, which imposes a more difficult climb, should be selected because it will decrease the chances of being detected.

Be ready to move. Select equipment that will let you move quickly and quietly. I have taken people with me who sounded as if they were carrying their child's half-filled piggybank. Also, you should be able to secure your equipment quickly so that you do not waste time.

Coping with Interference

The worst sound a turkey hunter can hear is the report of a firearm between him and an approaching gobbler. The sound is not just depressing, it is also frightening. No one can be sure if another hunter is in the area. We should all try to locate other hunters, but sometimes that's just not possible.

If another hunter or a free-ranging dog has disturbed your hunt, you have to weigh your options carefully. Safety should be the primary consideration. It is depressing to give up, but I will not tolerate being close to hunters I do not know. If it is possible to move to another area, that is a good choice. Also, you may see a hunter or hunters leave an area you are planning to hunt. If they have not called a bird up and shot at it, there still may be a good chance to call a bird.

Turkeys are accustomed to disturbances. It is easy to attribute too great a significance to a dog disturbing a gobbler. Obviously, the gobbler will react to the dog and cease gobbling; however, he may be susceptible to being called much sooner thereafter than many hunters anticipate. Giving up just because a dog has run through your hunting area early in the morning is foolish. If a turkey went into hiding every time he encountered a dog or a cow, the bird would never have a chance to engage in the normal activities of life. He must cope with disturbances. The intelligent hunter accepts the fact that a disturbance does not mean the hunt is ruined.

The most impressive experience I have had indicating how quickly a gobbler will return to normal behavior after a disturbance, occurred during our 1984 season. On the first Friday, I selected a property that had never received heavy hunting pressure. From a nice listening post, I heard a gobbler at dawn. I had to move only 100 yards to get myself in perfect position. From my new perspective, I took out the Chisholm call and made a single tree call. The bird screamed back at me. I put the call down, checked my watch, and gave myself a pep talk about the need for patience. He continued to gobble, and I just knew he wanted to hear from the sleepy hen. It may have been my imagination, but his gobbles began to sound impatient.

The minutes passed slowly, and I strained to hear him come out of the tree. Finally, I heard him land just down the ridge. I shifted my body, more quickly than necessary, to adjust to the spot where he landed.

I picked the D. D. Adams slate up and prepared to offer him an invitation he would find irresistible. The call sounded good—and his hot response sounded better. I knew he was coming. I put the call down and eased the familiar gun into position. He gobbled again, 20 yards closer. The thrill of his approach began to work on my nervous system.

I had just told myself to stay calm when I heard the box call. It sounded as if the hunter was just below the gobbler. The call came again, and the gobbler did not respond. I waited, powerless, and my emotions ranged from anger to self-pity and back again.

Several minutes later I heard human voices, and soon not one or two, or three, but *four* young men walked up the ridge. I hate to encounter one other hunter, let alone four. I wanted to escape the imminent confrontation, but they were too close. I stood up and soon determined that at least one of them had permission to be on the property. After a strained conversation, I glanced at my watch and realized it was only 6:30 a.m. I made a quick excuse and turned to get as far away from the group as possible. As I started to walk away, I heard them decide to call it a morning.

I had to be back in town by 8:30 a.m., so I would not be able to go too far. Thirty minutes of hard walking took me over two small ridges and, I hoped, far enough away from the disturbance the four men

had caused. I sat down and rested. It was with less than effusive enthusiasm that I took out the call in the now bright and very quiet woods.

As I called, I reflected on the disappointment. I was angry and impatient, and after 15 minutes I began to think about going home. I stayed with it until 7:30, then retraced my morning route. Making better time going downhill, I arrived at the place where I had called at dawn and glanced at my watch. It was 7:45. I had 30 minutes before I had to be at the car, which was 10 minutes away. I thought there probably wasn't a chance in the world, but . . . why not call? You can anticipate the rest. He gobbled back as soon as I called. It took him five minutes to come. Less than 90 minutes before, five men had stood and talked on the same spot from which I called him.

How frequently will a bird be ready to respond after such a disturbance? I have no idea, but this experience indicates it is not wise to write off a morning even after a major disturbance.

The Influence of Weather

Spring weather is fickle. There will be glorious days, and some wet, cold, and windy ones.

An important lesson for the spring gobbler hunter to learn is that bad weather will not always make gobblers refuse to gobble. I have had success in rain and on unseasonably cold mornings. On one memorable morning, I was dressed in my down waterfowling jacket to face the below-freezing temperature. I called a very cold, but sexually hot, gobbler to me in 10 minutes. The key to hunting in adverse weather is to persevere.

High wind is the one condition that always seems to be highly disadvantageous. The wind makes it very difficult for you to hear gobblers and for them to hear your calling. In addition, under normal conditions the hunter's hearing allows him to identify a bird that is approaching. High wind makes it very difficult to hear the sounds of a bird walking. Also, turkeys, like many other game animals, seem particularly wary during windy conditions. It seems reasonable to assume that the birds sense their vulnerability in high winds. Several of the best hunters I know refuse to hunt in high wind.

It is very difficult to combat windy conditions. In some types of terrain you can escape the most violent winds by hunting in protected hollows. It is surprising how much protection such places afford. If you can predict the direction of winds, the use of a topographical map can allow you to gain some cover. If there is no area that affords protection, you still can adjust to windy conditions by taking the following steps:

1. Find a calling area that provides a maximum range of vision and the least chance the bird will sneak in from the rear.

2. Use loud calls to combat the effect of the wind.

3. Stay longer in a given position. The high wind will probably deprive you of a warning that the bird is coming.

4. You can take advantage of the wind by moving in areas where, under normal weather conditions, your progress would be obvious because of the noise you would make.

THE MOMENT OF TRUTH

The game is not over when the gobbler is within 35 yards. The last episode in the drama is in many ways the most challenging. Choosing the correct time to shoot culminates the affair, and an error in judgment at this stage obviates all that you may have accomplished previously. If you are impatient and shoot too soon, you may well cripple the bird; waiting too long greatly increases chances the gobbler will detect something amiss. Also, when you delay, even if the bird is not alerted, the shot becomes much tougher. At ranges of less than 20 yards, the width of the shot pattern is reduced dramatically. When you pattern your gun, try a shot or two at a distance of only 10 yards. You will see how little room there is for error at such extremely close range.

So you must be both patient and decisive. Quickness must be tempered by restraint. The key element is poise. I have watched men who seemed unable to restrain themselves from shooting when the bird was still out of range. Do not underestimate how difficult it is to resist the temptation to shoot too soon. Bringing a mature gobbler within range is an accomplishment. That accomplishment is rewarded only if the bird is killed cleanly.

Too Soon

More turkeys are crippled or missed because they are shot at too soon than for any other reason. One experienced hunter I know has the honesty to admit, "John, I just have to hold my shooting hand in a fist until he is within range. Used to be that whenever I would put my finger on the trigger, I'd shoot at him before I wanted to even though I kept telling myself not to shoot. It was like another part of my brain was operating my trigger finger."

A mature gobbler at 55 yards looks like

he is close enough; however, you must have the composure and willpower to wait for him to come—usually with agonizing slowness—another 20 yards closer. I have had inexperienced hunters whisper to me when the bird was a full 80 yards away, "Is he close enough?"

A mature, 20-pound gobbler in full strut at under 100 yards does something to the nervous system of *all* hunters. One good friend and excellent hunter still hears himself hyperventilate as the bird gets close. Another man said, without trying to be humorous: "John, there have been several times I thought I was having a heart attack—I mean, I almost got up to try to get back to the truck because my heart started beating irregularly."

I have tried to articulate, in another section, the captivating appeal of this sport. Certainly one of its powerful attractions is the thrill generated during the intense seconds when the gobbler comes those final yards. It seems contradictory, but while we relish that thrill, we are eager to terminate it. Our nervous system has evolved to respond to challenges that evoke thrills, but the quickened heartbeat, the sweating, and the hyperventilation can become incapacitating if maintained too long.

Any experienced hunter is aware of the fragile nature of the opportunity. It is not easy to achieve, and it can disappear with frightening quickness. All of these factors combine to provide the strong temptation to shoot too soon.

Too Late

Some hunters are so desperate to kill a bird—often because they have failed before—that they wait for the perfect opportunity. One man I guided failed to shoot when a gobbler projected his entire head

and neck above a downfall at a range of 20 paces. My guest was looking directly at the bird but refused to shoot. After the bird darted away, and before I could calm myself, I said, "Why didn't you shoot?" My friend's response was that he could not see the entire turkey. Do not wait until you see a turkey's spurs. If you have a decent shot at a vital area, strike decisively. In this game, those who hesitate will carry very few mature gobblers from the field.

Should You Risk a Shot at a Moving Gobbler?

The question is difficult because only you are in a position to define what constitutes a good shot. I am convinced that if you limit your shots to stationary gobblers, you will waste many opportunities. You must develop the skill and confidence to take a shot at a bird that is walking. I am not suggesting you shoot at all moving birds within range, but if the bird is clear of cover, you'd better have the confidence to take him on the move. If you wait for him to stop, there will be a number of occasions when you will never fire your gun.

The Clear Shot

If there is one subject that has not received adequate attention in the turkey-hunting literature, it is the effects of brush on shooting. Shotgun efficiency is dramatically reduced if vegetation interferes with the shot charge. It is very easy to overlook light brush, saplings, and low-hanging branches when your eyes and brain are focusing on a gobbler. Even a shot that appears to be open will often pass through a gauntlet of brush. I have had hunters who did not notice saplings three inches in diameter between them and the target. If you do not believe that such interference will affect the shot charge, try patterning your gun, as I have, through such brush. The lessons provided by one such exercise will be very sobering. A bird screened by dense brush is much less vulnerable than one in the open. If you do try to shoot through brush, you will sooner or later cripple a turkey. Make sure the shot you have is a *clear* shot.

Reducing the Loss of Crippled Gobblers

The loss of a wounded wild turkey gobbler is a traumatic experience for any responsible hunter. In many European countries the hunter must demonstrate his shooting skill before he is allowed to hunt, hence reducing the chances of his crippling game. We face no such tests before we are allowed to hunt these marvelous birds. The desire to kill cleanly, and the development of skills that will result in that goal, must come from within each hunter.

Any form of game can be crippled and lost; however, it is difficult to imagine a creature that imposes more of a possibility of crippling loss than a mature wild turkey gobbler. The turkey is both tenacious and tough, and his skeleton is heavy. Ringneck pheasants are extremely tough birds, but you can't compare the size of the largest cock bird that ever strutted through a cornfield with a mature gobbler. The gobbler will be four times the size of the pheasant.

Anyone who has hunted upland birds is aware of the varying ways in which gamebirds respond to injury. The ringneck pheasant will run even after sustaining serious injuries. In contrast, the elegant woodcock will rarely try to move after being wounded. Why natural selection has endowed some creatures with greater tenacity of life is difficult to understand. No bird, the pheasant included, makes a more determined effort to escape after being wounded than a wild turkey gobbler. I have seen turkeys that have sustained horrible injuries muster the strength and coordination to fly or run long distances. Every experienced hunter has such stories to tell, as well as tales of mortally wounded birds that used their last seconds of life to push themselves under a felled tree or into a hole.

A turkey has two escape routes; he can go by air or by ground. A quadruped creature like a whitetail deer may not be killed by a rifle bullet that smashes the pelvic bones and severs the spinal cord, but he will not move far on his front legs alone. A wild turkey can sustain a similar wound and still fly hundreds of yards. Conversely, a turkey with broken wings has the capacity to use his legs to elude the most athletic of hunters.

Another challenge to the hunter is that the areas inhabited by wild turkeys are conducive to easy hiding. Very few spring gobblers are shot in cut cornfields. The hunter is forced to find the wounded bird in dense swamps, briar thickets, hardwood forests, pine jungles, and virtually impenetrable cutovers. In some of these areas a blaze-orange bison would be tough to find.

To offset these formidable challenges, we must take a shot that immobilizes the bird. It is important to realize that this goal is not the same as that of responsible hunters of other game animals. For example, the efficient bowhunter who places his arrow through the chest cavity of a deer knows that penetration of the lungs will usually result in the coordinated and rapid departure of the deer. The deer will normally run 75 to 200 yards; however, the blood trail should allow the hunter to find the animal easily. With turkeys the situation is different. If we are determined to recover a turkey easily, we cannot afford to allow it any coordinated movement after the shot. So we must either disrupt the central nervous system, by penetrating the brain or severing the spinal cord near the brain, or smash the skeletal structure by fracturing the largest bones of the body.

The head and neck shot is the most effective and sure way of disrupting the central nervous system. The anatomy of this area is fragile. Many excellent hunters have established enviable records for clean kills by using shot sizes as small as No. 7½ and shooting only at the head or neck at ranges under 35 yards. If you decide to adopt this strategy, you must learn to determine what 35 yards looks like under varying conditions and *never* take a shot if there is not a clear path to the target.

If you adopt the strategy of breaking up the skeletal structure of the bird, you must use a gun capable of effectively patterning large shot. The challenge here is to determine what constitutes reasonable range and then develop the ability to define that range with accuracy and have the discipline not to attempt a longer shot. Again, it is important that the hunter shoot only if he has a clear path to the bird. Light brush can drastically reduce the effectiveness of even large shot.

Assuming that you have had the discipline to pattern your gun, to determine by time-consuming tests what is the best load, and to practice, you can use either strategy to establish a responsible record.

The major challenges to both strategies are similar. First, it is not easy to accurately estimate range under the varying situations encountered in the field. Second, it takes only a modest error in range estimation to cripple a bird. Records I have kept of my own hunting experiences and those of close friends indicate that approximately five yards of error in range estimation at the extreme maximum effective range of a given gun and load will result in the crippling of turkeys. It is enlightening to see how many turkeys have been crippled with good small-shot loads at ranges of 38, 41, 42, 43, and 44 yards — all of which were estimated to have been 35 yards. Obviously, many birds have been killed cleanly at similar ranges; the point is that chance becomes a factor at these ranges.

It's a disturbing fact that even experienced hunters will make five-yard miscalculations in range estimation. If you meet a person who says he never miscalculates by more than a yard, take him into the woods and test his accuracy on steep slopes and in thick areas. I am confident the tests will embarrass him. We all should recognize how easy it is to make errors of five yards or more in estimating range under hunting conditions; moreover, we have an obligation to understand that at the maximum effective range of a shotgun, these errors will result in lost birds.

I believe the best way to address these challenges is to use a gun that allows the instant choice of either large or small shot. This means a gun with two barrels and either double triggers or a barrel selector. With this gun and the appropriate loads, you can select the small shot if you are confident the bird is within 35 yards. At this maximum range, and if there is no brush between you and the bird's head and neck, an accurate shot will make the turkey incapable of coordinated movement. If you estimate the range to be a long 35 and if you are confident it is not over 50, the heavy shot load to the body will be effective. But at that range you must have a *clear* shot at the entire body of the bird. And you cannot afford to misjudge the maximum 50-yard range. It has been my experience that the use of this load for the 35-plus-yard shot will result in fewer crippled turkeys. Fifty yards is a long distance in normal spring gobbler cover, and it is much easier to resist the temptation of what you judge to be a plus-50-yard shot than it is to pass up a 40-yard shot. The problem with the small-shot philosophy is that few hunters can resist the temptation to shoot at "just over 35 yards." If we are going to be honest, we have to admit that most people will try it. That is the primary way birds are crippled. The large shot is devastating out to a full 50 yards. Also, the small-shot user must remember that he should take the shot only if the head and neck are clearly visible.

What does the hunter do if he has called the bird to within 20 yards in thick cover and suddenly it flushes, presenting a rapidly departing target at 25 to 30 yards? Under such circumstances small shot will often result in a lost bird. For the man who has the option of large shot, the departing turkey is vulnerable. The large shot will smash the structure of the bird regardless of the angle.

Recovering the Crippled Gobbler

It should be the primary goal of every hunter never to cripple a turkey. However, every experienced hunter, regardless of the discipline he exercises, will at some juncture experience the sickening emotion of watching a turkey run or fly off after the shot. Each hunter, hence, should prepare for the challenge of recovering the crippled bird. An intelligent strategy can be employed to increase your chances of recovering the bird. That strategy does not consist of running toward the gobbler. It is an error to immediately race to the turkey. The following steps constitute an intelligent approach.

As soon as the shot is made, use all your powers of observation to determine the reactions of the bird. Careful observation should indicate the nature of the wound. If the bird has been shot in the head or neck, the reaction will usually be one of two types. Most frequently, the bird will flap its wings violently and bounce spasmodically. If the bird is on a slope, gravity can carry it a substantial distance downhill. Though the powerful movements may be sustained for some time, they will be without coordination. There is no need to race frantically after a bird making this display. The second reaction to a head or neck shot is for the bird to be knocked over and either remain totally motionless or make only a few feeble movements. This is most common if the bird is at very close range and the shot charge has impacted a major part of the brain or central nervous system.

A bird hit in the body by large shot will normally be knocked over. In some cases the bird will be fatally injured and only have the ability to spasmodically move its extremities for several seconds before expiring. The more common reactions are of two types. The first is that the body shot will break up large bones and anchor the turkey on the spot. In many cases the immobile bird will have to be dispatched by hand. The bird will be immobile if any of the large bones of the upper legs are smashed. Often a bird's head will be up as the hunter approaches but he will not be able to move. A second common response to a lethal body shot is a feeble attempt to move despite multiple injuries to its skeleton. The careful hunter has little threat of losing such a turkey.

If you are confident the bird received a lethal shot such as those described above and is incapable of coordinated movement, you should:

1. Keep your eyes fixed on the bird.
2. Immediately stand up to deliver a follow-up shot.
3. Hold the gun on the bird until you are convinced he is incapable of coordinated movement.
4. Reload the magazine, or one barrel, of your gun while keeping your eyes fixed on the bird.
5. Walk at a steady but not frantic pace toward the bird with your gun at port arms.
6. Upon reaching the bird, wait until any spasmodic movement has stopped — the spurs of a flopping gobbler can inflict injury — and then reach down with your most powerful hand, grasp the bird by the neck, and, with one quick and powerful snapping motion, jerk his weight upward to sever his spinal column. The last action is not pleasant, and often it will result in somewhat disfiguring the bird; however, no turkey with a broken neck will either escape or suffer.

The Crippled Yet Coordinated Gobbler

Someday you will have the sickening view of a rapidly departing gobbler clearly capable of coordinated escape. In such cases you should try to be instantly ready to deliver another shot. The recoil of a heavy shotgun and the cramped confines of a blind will make this very difficult. Often the follow-up shot is made frantically, in desperation, and from an awkward position. Probably no opportunity is more frequently missed than that taken at a crippled gobbler.

If the bird is not within range, direct your entire attention to the bird's escape route. Use all your powers of observation, both visual and auditory, to increase the chances of finding the crippled bird. A key at this juncture is to try to remain calm so that you can collect valuable information. The sight of a rapidly departing turkey can shake even experienced hunters. Running frantically after the bird increases the chances it will be lost. As soon as the bird is no longer visible, ask yourself the following questions:

1. How did the bird react to the shot?
2. How did he make his escape?
3. What evidence of a wound did he display?
4. What was the precise direction of his escape?
5. Was there any indication, either by sight or by sound, of his escape being disrupted or interrupted?

As you try to collect this information you should be stationary. Your powers of observation decrease if you are moving.

After the bird has disappeared, you will feel a surge of anxiety, a pounding heart, a dry mouth, and trembling hands. It is no fun to cripple a gobbler. This is the time for cool, efficient behavior.

Make sure, first, that you mark the spot from which you shot. In most cases this will be easy because your pack, a call, or some other piece of equipment will be there. Next, move slowly to where the bird was standing at the shot. In most cases small feathers and disturbance of the ground cover will allow you to find the spot with relative ease. If you have trouble finding it, follow the path of the shot by observing the twigs it cut on its way to the target. In some types of cover it will be more difficult to find the spot than in others. When in doubt about the location, return to the place from which you shot and attempt to recreate the position in which you were sitting, the precise position of the bird, and the path the shot charge traveled. Always begin your search just in front of the area in which you believe the bird was located, since walking on the spot can obliterate evidence.

A large gobbler can cause surprising disturbances in many types of spring ground cover if he is knocked over, runs, or stumbles violently. Often his trail will be easy to follow, especially in a hardwood forest where a compost of decaying leaves covers the ground. In such areas leaves will be raked up by violent leg action or the dragging of a wing. As a test of the way a bird disturbs the ground cover, look carefully at the trail left by the next bird you kill cleanly as he bounces down a small grade. Such a trail can be easily followed by a composed and careful hunter.

Do not be surprised if you encounter significant blood. Once I trailed a turkey in excess of 400 yards, and there were bright drops of blood every three or four feet.

If the trail gives out, try to determine the general direction the bird took. Follow likely paths of escape. Have your eyes keyed for the tiny breast feathers or the feathery down that often falls off in small strands. After following likely paths of escape, begin to search in likely hiding areas. Explore downfalls, thickets, creek bottoms, and along old fences. Above all, you must persevere.

For the bird that takes to the wing, it is important to stay in one place and intently observe the flight. Also, use your ears! On one occasion I recovered a bird that I heard fall to the ground after its flight path had taken it from my sight. A 20-pound bird falling to the ground can be heard a long distance. Listen and watch carefully. As any experienced waterfowl hunter knows, a mortally wounded goose can fly several hundred yards before suddenly plummeting to the ground. In such cases it is probable that internal bleeding is steady and the effect is cumulative. Such birds usually are found dead at the spot at which they fall. It is imperative that you mark the spot carefully. In many types of terrain, this is not easy as the hunter's path to the bird will often take him off a line of sight. A compass is an invaluable tool. An azimuth reading can be shot to the point at which the bird fell, and then the hunter can descend off his vantage point and follow the direction of the compass even as he loses eye contact with the site. The precise distance to the site will remain an unknown, as the compass only gives direction, so the hunter should mark a clear feature near the site of the bird's fall—say a tall tree. When you reach the general area, begin a broad search. Marking a spot and searching out from it in ever-widening circles is an efficient method. Again, the key is to persist.

How Long Is Long Enough?
How much time should you invest in the

search for a wounded bird? To suggest that you search "as long as possible" provides no effective guide. The hunter who spends 15 minutes of aimless wandering and looking has not met the implicit responsibility we have to the wounded bird. At least 2½ hours should be invested immediately after the shot is taken. Obviously, the chances of finding the bird after that much diligent searching are significantly reduced; however, the responsible hunter should return the next day with friends and perhaps a dog. If you don't recover the bird that day, it is unlikely that you will. Two *diligent* searches are a reasonable investment.

It is critical not to give up. I found one crippled gobbler after two hours and fifteen minutes of searching. That experience provided an important lesson because I realized that I had begun to lose hope after only about 30 minutes. I am sure my searching after the half-hour mark was not as aggressive or effective as it was during the first 30 minutes. Candidly, I was lucky to find the bird. You must try to maintain the intensity of your search. It is not easy, but we have an obligation to the gobbler to search effectively and persistently.

7

The Tools

THE SHOTGUN

Spring gobblers should be hunted with shotguns. The challenge of the sport is to call gobblers to within shotgun range. There are responsible hunters who call turkeys close and shoot them with rifles. In my opinion their choice of the rifle is unwise. Even when used by the most responsible hunter, a rifle increases the possibility of accidents at long range. Also, no matter how accomplished the rifle user may be, a moving turkey presents a difficult target. A shotgun is simply a better choice for the bird that is called up. The rifle will allow you to kill more turkeys—at ranges of 50 to 125 yards—but such opportunities take unfair advantage of the bird.

Many hunters make the error of assuming that if they acquire the "perfect" gun the possibility of crippling turkeys is elim-inated. There is no gun, or load, that provides such a guarantee. It is important to select an efficient gun and load; however, the lessons of the previous chapter remain critical.

A Personal Choice

Your search for the most efficient spring gobbler gun is a personal exercise. No author, this one included, should mandate which gun is best for you. If you have an old Model 12 Winchester with 2¾-inch chambers and you shoot it well, it would be foolish to trade it in on a gun that you have not tried. The heavier shot loads of the three-inch 12 gauge magnum and 3½-inch 10 gauge magnum have significant ballistic advantages over the standard 12 gauge; however, these advantages are relevant only if the hunter can shoot the gun

A 12 gauge three-inch magnum Browning Superposed. An example of a superb spring gobbler gun.

efficiently. One of the common errors committed by turkey hunters is failing to determine if a particular gun is efficient in *their* hands. Many men have missed several spring birds before they realized that they really couldn't shoot a 10 gauge. Do not allow my pattern and velocity data to obscure this critical point. Increased efficiency is an advantage only if you can harness that efficiency.

I have been an outspoken advocate of the advantages of the 10 gauge (McDaniel 1980). My attitude toward the 10 gauge has not changed. As I said in 1980, in a well-balanced double such as the Beretta,

the 10 gauge is my choice. However, it may not be the best choice for you. The only way to determine whether it will be or not is to try it.

Every experienced gunsmith has horror stories of the great game shot who gave up a gun he used with consummate skill to gain access to "The Perfect Shotgun"— which was often of English origin. The new gun was unquestionably excellent in design, mechanical performance, and appearance, but the sad story ends with the man being unable to shoot the new gun as well as his old one. So be careful before you embark on the search for the perfect gun. If you are buying your first gun, make sure you try it and determine it is the best for you.

The Need to Pattern Shotguns

You need to test any shotgun. Don't assume a gun will shoot to the point of aim. My many tests have proven there are a lot that don't—even expensive ones. If the gun shoots high, it frequently is a function of the dimensions of the stock reacting to the contours of your face. In these cases a gunsmith can help you alter the stock to change the point of impact. Many shooters have never determined the point of impact of their shotguns. Most hunters using rifles recognize the need to "sight in" their guns. The reason for the infrequent testing of shotguns is that hunters assume a shotgun will hit the point of aim. We tend to visualize broad patterns of pellets flying toward a relatively large target. We accept the shotgun as being quick rather

A 10 gauge 3½-inch magnum Beretta double barrel, my choice as the ideal spring gobbler gun.

Patterning shotguns is time consuming but absolutely necessary.

An essential step in the testing of your gun is the preparation of a suitable target.

than precise. In the spring season, you must develop *precision* with a shotgun. When a gobbler sticks its head over a log 15 yards away, you had better be able to put that small wad of shot precisely where you want it.

Advantages of the Double-Barrel

My experimentation with various types of shotguns has convinced me that having two barrels is an advantage. A double or over-and-under with double triggers or a selective single trigger allows the hunter a quick choice of shot size and choke constriction. With the double, the hunter can develop two types of loads. One load can be efficient for short-range shots—by the use of smaller shot and less choke constriction. The other can be designed for the longer-range opportunity, using larger shot size and greater choke constriction. A double-barrel allows the immediate choice of either. The idea of stacking loads in a repeater for progressively longer shots — on the assumption the first opportunity will always be close — is flawed. Often the first chance is not close. One expert espoused the strategy of No. 6 shot followed by No. 4 shot followed by No. 2 shot. In response to my question about what he did when the bird was not at the correct distance at the appropriate time, he said he "just fired the 6 load to 'get rid of it' and then had the correct load for the long shot." That's ridiculous. The instant the No. 6 shot is fired, you no longer have a good shot at a turkey.

Another advantage of the double or over-and-under is that it is more compact than a repeater. Stand a double and an automatic next to each other, and if the barrel and stock lengths are the same, the double will be significantly more compact. While this compactness is irrelevant in most duck blinds, it is a distinct advantage in the confined positions spring gobbler hunters find themselves. Many who sing the praises of efficient repeating shotguns will obtain a short, 24 to 26-inch barrel to make their gun compact. The fallacy of this solution is that shorter barrels reduce ballistic efficiency. My tests confirm that shorter barrels reduce velocity, and a reduction in velocity converts to less energy and hence reduced killing efficiency. Also, my patterning tests, to be addressed in detail in a subsequent section, confirm that the tightest and hence most efficient long-range patterns are encountered in guns with barrels approximately 30 inches in length.

Another advantage of the double is that it can be loaded with very little noise. It is incredible how far the sound of a sliding bolt in an automatic or pump-action shotgun can be heard on a still spring morning.

Finally, the quality double or over-and-under is usually mechanically tough. Obviously, there is no possibility of shells jamming in a double. Neither mud nor dust will influence the functioning of a quality double.

I will grant that in a waterfowl blind the third shot of a repeater can be an advantage. In spring turkey hunting, 999 times out of 1,000 a third shot is used to call other hunters' attention to the fact you missed your two legitimate opportunities. Two shots are adequate.

Shotgun Weight

Regardless of the type of gun you determine is best for you, I would be very careful about choosing an exceedingly light gun. For many people a ten-pound gun is too heavy; however, fewer people realize that for them a six-pound gun may be too light. Shoot the six-pound gun at a skeet range before you buy it. One friend who was missing too many grouse with a five-pound gun finally took it to the skeet range. He proceeded to break only 4 of 25 targets. Confident the experience would convince him to go back to his old 8½-pound automatic, with which he had killed many grouse, I was appalled when he said, "Hey, this isn't a skeet gun; it is a grouse gun." Because an "expert" said the grouse gun should be light, he was convinced the gun he couldn't hit anything with was still perfect.

The American fascination with light guns is interesting. We all read about the light, quick guns that are perfect for upland birds. Take a look at the weight of

A heavy gun is much easier to hold on the target than a light gun.

the guns the great wingshots in your area shoot. I'll bet they weigh more than six pounds. I believe most men of average size and strength should shoot a gun that weighs somewhere around eight pounds. If heavy shot loads, let us say 1¼ or 1½ ounces of shot, are to be used, it is important for the gun to weigh about eight pounds. Excessive recoil is disadvanta-

geous. Great wingshots know that a six-pound gun will punish the shooter — any shooter. None of the big 10 gauge guns I have hunted with, or tested, generated as much punishing recoil as a six-pound German combination gun chambered for the three-inch 12 gauge shell. The weight of the gun is as relevant to the recoil produced as the size of the load. All my 10 gauge guns have weighed at least ten pounds.

Another reason for taking a critical look at the very light gun is provided by observing the weight of the guns used in the most demanding shotgun sport in the world—live pigeon shooting. Pigeon shooters need quick, responsive guns. The finest shotguns in the world are built for these shooters. These guns never weigh five or six pounds. Most pigeon shooters use guns of about eight pounds in weight. I suggest you experiment, but I urge you to be careful before you convince yourself the five- or six-pound gun will be best.

The Sighting Plane and Auxiliary Sights

Traditionally the sight on a shotgun has consisted of a small bead at the muzzle. This sight is occasionally supplemented by a raised rib on the barrel that allows the shooter to look down a flat plane. On guns designed for target shooting a second bead, smaller than the one at the muzzle, is often placed approximately halfway down the rib. If the stock fits the shooter and if the gun is mounted correctly, the relationship of the intermediate bead to the bead at the muzzle will be consistent.

Most good shooters will state that they are not aware of the bead or beads when they are shooting. In fact, one classic story about proper shotgun use describes an accomplished wingshot who enjoys a particularly successful day of shooting only to find the gun's front bead in his gun case at the end of the day.

As I have said, the use of a shotgun for spring gobblers demands a kind of precision not required in most field shooting. It

is true that a hunter with a perfectly fitting shotgun could kill turkeys by simply looking down the rib of his gun; however, most of us are aware of the front bead when we aim our guns at stationary spring gobblers. I have, in fact, altered the height of beads to provide a modest adjustment in the impact of the shot charge.

The use of a scope, or one of the optical sights that allows you to place a suspended dot of light on the target, is growing in popularity among turkey hunters. The idea is that the crosshairs or dot of light will always indicate where the shot charge will impact, regardless of the position of your face on the stock. It is very easy to miss a gobbler if you do not have your face down on the stock. I once called up three mature gobblers to within 20 yards of an experienced hunter who is a fine shot. The birds were below us on a relatively steep slope, and my friend failed to place his face down on the stock. He missed a 20-pound-plus stationary gobbler at 20 yards. I have seen the same man kill a limit of doves (12) with a box (25) of shells. If he'd had one of the sighting devices on his shotgun, it may have allowed him to hit the gobbler even with his elevated head position—or, more accurately articulated, it would have made him lower his face to superimpose the point of light on the bird's head.

I have tested these sights, and I do not have them on my shotguns. I do not feel comfortable with them. I have never seen a great game shot or the winner of a major pigeon shoot with one of the contraptions on his gun. My final argument against the sights is aesthetic. I don't think a beautiful shotgun should have an ugly hunk of metal screwed onto its receiver. I suggest you try the devices, but if your gun fits you well, you can fill a pickup truck with turkeys over the years without an optical sight.

Brush Deflection

Light vegetation—saplings, heavy weeds, small branches—can significantly reduce the effectiveness of shotgun loads. The hardwood forests, swamps, and scrubby plateaus that comprise good turkey habitat invariably contain cover that is capable of deflecting or stopping shot. Often the opportunity that appears to be open will be screened with light vegetation. If you appreciate how brush can deflect a rifle bullet, test what it does to shotgun pellets. A lack of understanding of this effect is a major factor contributing to the wounding of turkeys.

Table 2 presents data relevant to the performance of shotgun loads through brush. These data indicate not only the significant reduction in the effectiveness of all loads but also the implications of pellet size.

Gauge

The best turkey gun for you is the most potent shotgun you can shoot efficiently. For most hunters there is no reason to use a gauge smaller than 12. For many, the increased weight of the 12 with three-inch chambers does not decrease the ability to shoot the gun efficiently. On the other hand, some of the best game shots in the world have stayed with guns with 2¾-inch chambers.

For some hunters the three-inch gun or even the big 10 gauge offers no disadvan-

TABLE TWO
BRUSH DEFLECTION DATA
(40 yard range 2 screens light brush, 5 and 10 yards in front of target)

10 Gauge 3-1/2-in. magnum
Ithaca Automatic no. 0000 4229, 32'' full choke
2-1/8 oz. BB shot (116 pellets) buffered filler
Average velocity chronographed: 1299 feet per second

12 Gauge 3-in. magnum
Browning Superposed no. 9431758, 30-in. full choke
1-5/8 oz. no. 6 shot (366 pellets)
Velocity published as 1315 feet per second
Chronographed as 1227 feet per second

WITHOUT BRUSH 10 SHOTS	Mean number of pellets in 30'' circle at 40 yards = 105		Mean number of pellets in 30'' circle at 40 yards = 238		
		91% OF TOTAL LOAD ON TARGET			65% OF TOTAL LOAD ON TARGET
WITH BRUSH 7 SHOTS	Mean number of pellets in 30'' circle at 40 yards = 77		Mean number of pellets in 30'' circle at 40 yards = 106		
		66% OF TOTAL LOAD ON TARGET			29% OF TOTAL LOAD ON TARGET
BRUSH INFLUENCE	clear shot 105 pellets	brush shot 77 pellets	clear shot 238 pellets	brush shot 106 pellets	
		BRUSH INFLUENCE = 27% REDUCTION IN PELLETS ON TARGET			BRUSH INFLUENCE = 55% REDUCTION IN PELLETS ON TARGET

NOTE: This table and the nine which follow present data which were collected over a period of ten years (1975-1985). Unless otherwise stated, averages for performance have been calculated from at least five test shots to as many as twenty-five. The process of testing demonstrated that weather—particularly wind velocity and temperature—can significantly alter shotgun performance. Attempts to replicate these findings should be exercised with the knowledge that weather variation will have an impact on the results.

tages. The only way to prove if this is true for you is to try the gun at a skeet range. Obviously, you can't expect a 10 gauge gun with a full-choke barrel to perform with the efficiency of a 12 gauge gun with skeet choke. The meaningful comparison will be to stack the full-choke 10 against a 12 gauge gun also bored full-choke. Many hunters will not be able to shoot the 10 gauge efficiently. Try it, and be aware that a poor average on targets has implications for the field.

The 12 gauge gun chambered for three-inch shells provides significant ballistic advantages over the 12 gauge gun with 2¾-inch chambers. In most cases the maximum load of shot that is practical in the 2¾-inch shell is 1½ ounces. In the big three-inch shell, there recently (1983) has been the introduction of an efficient load that provides a full two ounces of shot. I have used these Federal Premium two-ounce loads and found them to be effective. Often the shooter overlooks the fact that the three-inch shell's advantages go beyond the increased amounts of shot. Some of the most efficient three-inch loads contain less than maximum amounts of shot but loads that produce high velocity. The best of them will propel 1½ ounces of shot at significantly greater velocity than will the 2¾-inch load that carries the same weight of shot. Many experienced waterfowl hunters make use of three-inch magnum guns with shot loads of 1⅜ ounces propelled at high velocities (often in the 1,350-feet-per-second range). I have used these loads, and they are extremely effective.

The contemporary three-inch magnum gun makes a wonderful spring gobbler gun because it can be built to weigh around eight pounds and yet not produce too much recoil. It is my belief that for the

great majority of hunters a quality three-inch 12 gauge gun is the best choice.

The 10 gauge magnum gun finally came of age in the seventh decade of the 20th century. Until 1977 there was no decent ammunition available for the 3½-inch-chambered 10 gauge. The pre-1977 two-ounce load was 15 years behind the fine three-inch magnum 12 gauge loads being produced at the same time. Table 3 indicates the way in which an improvement in ammunition has altered the performance of the 10 gauge gun. The table demonstrates that at 60 yards the best factory load available in 1976 provided half the energy of the best factory load available two years later.

Unfortunately, the reputation of the 10 gauge gun was damaged by the inferior quality of this pre-1978 factory ammunition. The handload listed in Table 3 demonstrates that spectacular performance was available to the 10 gauge aficionado before 1978; however, most of the literature concerning the 10 gauge did not address the capabilities of handloads. Now, as Table 3 demonstrates, even the best of the three-inch 12 gauge loads cannot match the currently available factory loads of the 10 gauge.

I am a firm believer in the efficiency of the 10 gauge if the shooter can handle the gun. My attraction is based not simply on the large quantity of shot it accommodates but also on the superior velocity, and hence greater pellet energy.

Recoil is high. In my opinion, no 10 gauge gun should weigh less than 10 pounds. However, if the gun weighs 10 to 12 pounds and has a well-designed stock, it will not be painful to shoot. I recently compared the recoil of an eight-pound 12 gauge gun shooting 1⅞-ounce, three-inch magnum loads with a 10½-pound 10

TABLE THREE

THE INFLUENCE OF AMMUNITION ON 10 GAUGE PERFORMANCE
(All shells fired in same 10 gauge gun used in Table Two)

	3 SHOTS AT 40 YARDS			3 SHOTS AT 60 YARDS		
	Mean number of pellets in 30 inch circle	Mean percentage of total load in 30 inch circle	Estimate of foot pounds of energy delivered to vital area of wild turkey	Mean number of pellets in 30 inch circle	Mean percentage of total load in 30 inch circle	Estimate of foot pounds of energy delivered to vital area of wild turkey
Best factory load available before 1977; 2 oz. no. 2 shot—no buffer, no copper plated shot, no BB size available	121	65%	82.5	47	25%	24
Best factory load available in 1979; Federal Premium 2-1/4 oz., buffered copper plated shot	107	86%	135*	63	49%	43
Handload: 2-1/8 oz. buffered, copper plated shot (This load was used in Tables One and Two.)	105	90%	135*	59	51%	53

*These numbers are the same because the greater velocity of the 2-1/8 oz. handload produces more individual pellet energy (15 foot pounds per pellet vs. 12).

gauge shooting 2¼-ounce, 3½-inch loads (both loads were Federal Premiums). The stock dimensions on the guns were identical. Two experienced shooters fired approximately 15 rounds with each gun. Both shooters offered the opinion that the eight-pound 12 gauge developed more painful recoil than the 10½-pound 10 gauge gun. The 3½-inch 10 gauge gun does kick, and one that weighed under 10 pounds would be dangerous for an inexperienced shooter; however, the idea that shooting a 10 gauge double is like being in an automobile accident is nonsense.

Obtaining Maximum Efficiency

Once you have selected the gun, you face the challenge of extracting its maximum potential. No shotgun is efficient if the load it shoots is a poor one. In a similar manner, the most expensive gun has to be choked for a specific task. If it were made with very open chokes, say for shooting woodcock over pointing dogs, it would perform poorly in situations where a dense pattern of shot was needed—such as for either long-range waterfowl shooting or for spring gobbler hunting. Once you have decided on the type of gun, gauge, weight, and stock dimensions, you need to consider the best barrel length, choke (or chokes), and load.

Barrel Length

A shotgun for turkey hunting is used with precision. The hunter must be able to deliver a dense pattern of shot to a relatively small target. A relatively long sighting plane makes this easier. Most experienced turkey hunters I know use 28-inch, 30-inch, or 32-inch barrels. As one who has patterned many shotguns in the interest of determining the most efficient loads, I can assure you that some guns are easier to hold on the target than others. Guns with longer — 30 or 32-inch — barrels tend to be easier to shoot with precision than those with shorter barrels. They may not be as "quick" in the grouse woods, but we are trying to find a gun that will shoot with precision. Do not go too far with barrel length. In my opinion, the "long Tom" guns with the 36-inch and 38-inch barrels are monstrocities. Don't forget, we also need to be able to take the occasional shot at a flying turkey, so pick the barrel length that feels best to you, but be advised that most accomplished gobbler hunters end up with moderately long (28 to 32-inch) barrels.

Choke

The term choke applies to the constriction applied to the muzzle of a shotgun barrel to concentrate the shot. Standard American descriptions of the degree of constriction are based on the percentage of shot that is placed within a 30-inch circle at a range of 40 yards. A constriction that places less than 40 percent of the shot in the circle has been called "skeet." A choke averaging 40 to 55 percent is called "improved cylinder." The barrel that shoots "modified" patterns will place approximately 55 to 65 percent in the 30-inch circle. A full-choke barrel is expected to place over 70 percent of the shot load in the circle. While these designations are standards, other descriptions provide a more precise definition. For example, the term "improved modified choke" is generally applied to a gun that places 65 to 70

percent of its pattern in the 30-inch circle. This term suggests that the "modified" title should be applied only to the gun that averages in the 55 to 60 percent range. Also an "extra full" designation is often applied to barrels that shoot patterns of 75 percent and above.

Choke performance depends on a variety of factors. The average hunter assumes, incorrectly, that what is stamped on the barrel defines the performance of his gun. In fact, the shotshell he selects — amount of shot, type of wadding, style of shot cup, velocity, and shot size — will have implications for performance. Another fact is that the degree of constriction necessary to produce a specific performance — in terms of the percentage of shot placed in the 30-inch circle — is not standardized. Contrary to popular opinion, not all full-choke barrels display the same amount of constriction. A popular myth is that if a dime will not enter the muzzle of a 12 gauge gun, the barrel will produce full-choke patterns. As my good friend and great gunsmith George Schielke said: "The only things a man proves when he tries to jam a dime in the muzzle of a 12 gauge gun is whether that particular dime will fit in the aperture and that he knows very little about choke." Tremendous variations in full-choke constriction exist because the bore diameters of guns of the same gauge vary significantly. The bore diameter quoted as "standard" in the literature for 12 gauge shotguns is .729-inch. As Table 4 indicates, a moderate-size sample of 12 gauge shotguns will show variations from that "standard." The guns selected for measurement included some of recent manufacture and some older ones. Also, an attempt was made to include guns made both in and outside the United States.

TABLE FOUR

BORE DIAMETER VARIATIONS
IN TWELVE GAUGE SHOTGUNS

	Measured Bore Diameter	Gun
EUROPEAN DRILLINGS AND COMBINATION GUNS	.720''; .721''	Welke Drilling
	.720''; .721''	Sauer Drilling
	.722''	Valmet Combination Gun
	.720''	Hyme Combination Gun
	.721''	AVERAGE FOR GROUP
EUROPEAN SHOTGUNS	.721''; .723''	Franchi-Italian
	.720''; .721''	Franchi
	.725''; .724''	Perazzi-Italian
	.725''; .726''	Perazzi
	.723''; .722''	Browning-Belgian
	.724''; .724''	Browning
	.727''; .729''	G.E. Lewis-English
	.724''	AVERAGE FOR GROUP
CURRENT AMERICAN SHOTGUNS	.732''	Remington 1100
	.733''	Remington 1100
	.732''	Remington 870
	.729	Remington 870
	.730''	Winchester 1200
	.727''	Winchester 1200
	.726''; .726''	Pugar Red Label
	.729''	AVERAGE FOR GROUP
OTHERS STAN BAKER ALTERED (overbored) 1100 REMINGTON	.735''	Baker Altered 1100 Remington

As the table demonstrates, only 11 percent of the bores measured were .729-inch or within .001-inch (.728 or .730) of the .729-inch standard.

Tight Bores

As the table demonstrates, the guns with the tightest bores are generally of European manufacture. Also, 86 percent of all the guns measured have bores tighter than the .729-inch standard. Obviously our sample is small, but it does suggest that tight bores are encountered frequently. The tightest bores, which average .721-inch, are found on European drillings and combination guns.

Since the 12 gauge gun with which I have done most of my turkey hunting was of tight, .726-inch bore diameter, I de-

cided to use it as a test gun to see how various degrees of choke constriction would influence its performance. I asked the Briley Manufacturing Company to provide choke tubes with increasing constriction, from .725 to .685-inch, with a tube for every .005-inch increase. Hence I had a set of nine tubes covering a .040-inch range at .005-inch intervals. The .685-inch tube provided the maximum reduction from "standard" bore diameter — of .041-inch. I tested those chokes with both large shot (size BB and 2) and small shot (size 6). The shells used in these tests were loaded with copper-plated shot and a buffering agent.

Since my goal was to obtain dense patterns, I have omitted the data from tests of the tubes that provided "skeet," "improved cylinder," and "modified" chokes. This

TABLE FIVE

THE EFFECT OF CHOKE CONSTRICTION
ON "LARGE" (SIZE BB) SHOT PERFORMANCE

Gun: Browning Superposed used in Table Two
Shells: Federal Premium 1-7/8 oz. # BB
Muzzel Velocity: Chronographed as 1150 feet per second.

Choke Constriction	40 YARDS		50 YARDS	
	Average # of pellets in 30 inch circle	Percentage of total shot load within 30 inch circle	Average # of pellets in 30 inch circle	Percentage of total shot load within 30 inch circle
.700"	80	83%	56	58%
.695"	81	84%	61	64%
.690"	84	88%	63	66%
.687"	88	92%	65	68%
.685"	79	82%	53	55%

A tremendous spring gobbler that weighed 21 pounds.

The hunter without camouflage.

Inadequate camouflage.

The beauty of the spring woods.

Wildflowers in the spring woods.

One step away from excellent camouflage.

Excellent camouflage. Notice the differences between this photograph and the three which precede it. The need to camouflage hands and face is clearly evident.

An area before turkey-management techniques were implemented.

Precisely the same area after it was cleared and planted to clover for wild turkeys.

The Virginia mountains and three great gobblers they provided.

Morel mushroom, a delicacy that can be collected by the spring turkey hunter.

Hen turkey decoy carved from pine and cork by the au

TABLE SIX

THE EFFECT OF CHOKE CONSTRICTION
ON "SMALL" (SIZE 6) SHOT PERFORMANCE

Gun: Browning Superposed
Shells: 1-7/8 oz. Federal Premium
Muzzle Velocity: Chronographed at 1155 feet per second

Choke Constriction	Average # of shot in 6'' circle at 30 yards	Size of pattern at 30 yards	Average # of shot in 30'' circle at 40 yards	Percentage of shot load in 30'' circle at 40 yards
.700''	59	22''	326	78%
.695''	58	21''	344	83%
.690''	83	20''	351	84%
.687''	77	19''	347	83%
.685''	57	18''	335	80%

selection process eliminated those choke tubes with a restriction from bore diameter of less than .026-inch. Data are provided for four of the original nine tubes tested. The first four tubes measured .700, .695, .690, and .685-inch. My first tests indicated the .690 tube afforded the tightest patterns. To determine if a slight increase in restriction would improve performance, I ordered a .687-inch tube. The data provided by that tube, the 10th tested, are included in the tables.

Table 5 shows the average percentages that the respective tubes provided for BB shot at 40 and 50 yards. Table 6 provides data on small shot at 30 and 40-yard ranges. As the tables indicate, there was an increasing density in the patterns as the degree of constriction was increased until the .685-inch, or tightest, tube was used.

With that degree of constriction, a less dense pattern was produced. The .685's patterns were not only lower in the calculated average but also were not as uniform in the general distribution of shot within the 30-inch circle. This degree of constriction — .041-inch less than bore diameter — in effect created *too much* choke.

As the tables demonstrate, my best large-shot performance was obtained with the .687 tube and the best small-shot work with the .690 tube. Fine "full"-choke performance in general was obtained when .036 to .039-inch constriction was achieved.

Open or "Over-Bored" Barrels

In the 1930s, Burt Becker of Philadelphia experimented with 12 gauge guns that were "over-bored" or had bore diameters in excess of the .729-inch standard. The fame of the performance of his guns was assured when their praises were sung by author Nash Buckingham. While I have never measured the bore of one of his guns, they were reported to be well above the .729-inch standard. The concept was that significantly greater bore diameter would allow more efficient performance.

To assess this theory I asked skillful gunsmith Stan Baker to over-bore a barrel of a standard 1100 Remington and provide me with a set of choke tubes for the gun. The bore of that Remington 1100 appears in Table 4 and measures .735-inch. I hence obtained a significantly over-bored gun.

The Stan Baker barrel is .009 larger than the bore of my Browning. Common sense would suggest that the choke constriction appropriate for this barrel should be different from that provided for the Browning barrel. My test of a range of tubes suggested by Mr. Baker supported

his belief that a tube providing .700-inch constriction would give the tightest patterns. Table 7 shows the results gleaned from tests made with the .690 tube in the Browning and the .700 tube in the Remington barrel. Both barrels and their chokes shoot 88 percent patterns with buffered copper-plated loads of BB shot. The shot distribution and general "evenness" of the patterns from both guns are excellent.

The critical point is that the size of the hole in the muzzle of the barrel—the choke—is not the factor which determines performance. It is rather the relationship of choke diameter to bore diameter, or the degree of constriction. Table 7 provides data from two guns with .010-inch variation in the aperture of the muzzle. Despite this difference, both guns provide the maximum pattern density currently available with modern shotshells. Most dimes will easily fit in the muzzle of the Baker gun with the .700-inch muzzle diameter.

TABLE SEVEN

ILLUSTRATION OF RELATIONSHIP OF BORE DIAMETER TO
CHOKE CONSTRICTION AND ITS INFLUENCE ON PATTERN DENSITY

	BORE DIAMETER	CHOKE MEASUREMENT PROVIDING OPTIMUM (88%) PATTERNS	VARIATIONS IN CHOKE CONSTRICTION BETWEEN GUNS	VARIATION IN CHOKE CONSTRICTION AS RELATED TO BORE DIAMETER
GUN #1 BROWNING SUPERPOSED	.726"	.690"	.690" vs .700" OR .010" difference	.726"-.690" = .36"- constriction from bore diameter
GUN #2 REMINGTON 1100 ALTERED "OVER BORED"	.735"	.700"		.735"-.700" = .35"- constriction from bore diameter OR .001" difference

Despite the larger muzzle size of the one gun, the actual decrease from bore diameter in both guns is very close (.036 and .035). It is this degree of constriction that is critical. So—any gun dealer who tells you a specific choke size will provide the tightest patterns in a gun of unknown bore diameter is guessing. The determination can be made only after bore diameter is calculated.

The advocates of over-bored guns suggest that you will enjoy denser patterns, more even distribution of shot, and even less recoil with an over-bored barrel. My test shows no significant differences. Excellence performance can be obtained with an over-bored gun—as demonstrated by my Baker Remington 1100—but excellent performance can also be obtained by a non-altered shotgun of rather tight bore constriction, as demonstrated by my Browning.

Choke Constriction and Shot Size

As Tables 5 and 6 demonstrate, the size of shot does not always significantly alter choke performance. This finding was of particular interest to me because I had encountered numerous comments in the literature indicating that with large shot the tightest patterns would be obtained with significantly less choke constriction than was the case with small shot. Tables 5 and 6 indicate this was not what I found. In fact, with the same load (1⅛ ounce of buffered copper-plated shot), I obtained my best patterns with essentially the same degree of choke with both the large (BB) and small (No. 6) shot. (The slight improvement of the .690-inch tube with the small shot was not, from a statistical perspective, significantly better than that with the .687 tube.)

Choke Constriction and the New "Heavy" 12 Gauge Loads

In 1983 the heavy (two-ounce) three-inch magnum 12 gauge loads from the Federal Company became available. My tests with these loads—and handloads I developed with a full two ounces of shot—indicate that significantly less choke constriction provides significantly better patterns. While the Federal loads were tested only with No. 2 shot—the only size available in these loads in my area in 1983—I tested handloads with both BBs and No. 3 shot, and the findings held up. Table 8 shows that in my Browning the best patterns were provided by the .700 choke tube—or with .013-inch less constriction than the .687 tube that gave the densest patterns with all other loads. I think it is the type of wadding/shot cup used with the heavy loads that results in their performing best with less choke constriction. A review of Table 8 should be made by anyone who expects to make extensive use of these heavy three-inch loads.

Shot Size

One of the most controversial subjects debated by turkey hunters is what size shot is most effective. For many years most experienced hunters relied on small shot. From a historical perspective, that policy had merit. Until the advent of buffered loads of copper-plated shot, the pattern densities that could be achieved were not high. The use of small shot increased pattern density because more small shot is available in a load of a given weight. Under optimum conditions, small shot is extremely effective. The head and neck of a turkey are vulnerable. Most experienced turkey hunters who grouse hunt in areas

TABLE EIGHT

THE EFFECT OF CHOKE CONSTRICTION ON THE "HEAVY"
TWO OUNCE THREE INCH MAGNUM 12 GAUGE SHOT SHELL PERFORMANCE

GUN: Browning Superposed used in previous tests
SHELL: Federal Premium "Heavy" 2 oz. # 2 shot

Choke Constriction	40 YARDS		50 YARDS	
	Average Number of Pellets in 30" circle	Percentage of Total Load	Average Number of Pellets in 30" circle	Percentage of Total Load
.705"	130	72%	88	49%
.700"	149	83%	110	61%
.695"	140	78%	105	58%
.600"	138	77%	102	57%
.687"	134	74%	100	56%
.685"	134	74%	100	56%

that the additional pellets obtained with No. 7½ shot are not needed. Also, the No. 6 pellets carry more energy because of their larger size.

The problem with small shot is that very few hunters will use it only under optimum conditions. As soon as you try to kill turkeys at 40 yards or shoot through "just a little" brush at 35 yards with small shot, you will cripple birds.

It is my belief that the hunter should either develop an all-purpose load with larger shot or have a large-shot load instantly available to him if the bird does one of the following: (1) stops at between 35 and 50 yards; (2) enters an area of brush at closer range; (3) comes very close to the caller and then leaps into the air to fly directly away. From my experiences in taking people hunting, I am confident

that contain turkeys have had the exciting experience of walking in behind a pointing dog with a 20 gauge and having a 20-pound turkey flush at their feet. I have cleanly killed turkeys with a ⅞-ounce load of No. 9 shot in a skeet-choked barrel of a 20 gauge gun. Anyone who doesn't think that is possible doesn't appreciate the efficiency of shotguns at close range. However, the fact that the small shot is lethal under optimum conditions does not make it the best choice for the spring hunter.

If the hunter has learned to calculate precisely what 35 yards is, and has the discipline never to shoot unless a perfectly clear shot is available, he can establish an enviable record with small shot. From my perspective, No. 6 shot is the smallest practical size. The high numbers of pellets available in the modern loadings are such very few hunters will pass up these opportunities. In these cases the use of small shot will cripple birds. Many of us have been lucky with small shot at 41 or 43 yards, but if a man has killed over 50 spring gobblers with small shot, he will have at least one story of a cripple. Table 9 demonstrates a comparison between the performance of large and small shot under controlled conditions. (The reason a non-buffered small-shot load was used is that at the time these tests were conducted, it was the only small-shot load available.)

I have no argument with the use of size 6 shot when the bird presents a perfect opportunity. A cool shot will put so many small pellets in the head and neck under such circumstances that it will be hard to count all the holes. More to the point, the kill will be quick and humane. Take that same turkey and have him stop 42 yards from you, and if you try it with No. 6 shot, it had better be your lucky day. There is a very good chance you will cripple him. Forty-two yards does not look very far in most turkey habitat. It looks even closer in poor light. A lot of turkeys have been lost right at that 42-yard range.

The specific small-shot size that will be best will depend on the gauge and chamber dimensions of your gun. For most 12 gauge guns, No. 6 shot is a good choice. For the 10 gauge you can go to larger shot and still maintain the requisite high pellet count. I have had excellent success with 2½-ounce handloads of No. 3 shot in the 10 gauge. These heavy loads provide ap-

TABLE NINE

LARGE SHOT EFFICIENCY

10 Gauge 3-1/2-in. magnum
Ithaca Automatic no. 000 4229,
  32-in. full choke
2-1/8 oz. BB shot (116 pellets)
  buffered filler
Average velocity chronographed:
  1299 feet per second

12 Gauge 3-in. magnum
Browning Superposed no. 9432758,
  30-in. full choke
1-5/8 oz. no. 6 shot
  (366 pellets)
Velocity published as 1315 feet
  per second-chronographed as 1227 feet per second.

	Mean # of pellets in 30-inch circle		Mean % of pellets in 30-inch circle		% loss from 40-yard performance		Energy per pellet in foot-pounds		Average # of 1/8-inch, 2-ply cardboard sheets penetrated	
RANGE	10 gauge	12 gauge	10 gauge	12 gauge	10 gauge	12 gauge	10 gauge	12 gauge	10 gauge	12 gauge
40 Yards 10 shots	105	238	91%	65%	—	—	15	2.5	25	6
50 Yards 5 shots	85	132	73%	36%	23%	45%	13	2.0	20	5
60 Yards 5 shots	60	85	52%	23%	43%	64%	11	1.5	18	4
70 Yards 5 shots	46	46	40%	13%	56%	81%	8	.75	14	3

proximately the same pellet count as the No. 6 shot load in the standard 1¼-ounce, 2¾-inch 12 gauge loadings. Obviously, if the pellet count is similar, the larger shot provides the dividend of greater energy. (Yes, No. 3 shot is available, from the Lawrence Company. I have found it to be efficient not only for head-shooting turkeys with the 10 gauge but also for geese in both 12 and 10 gauge guns.)

The Large-Shot Advantage

My argument is that with today's guns and loads you can be prepared for the 50-yard opportunity. Depending on the gauge and chamber length of your gun, an efficient load can be developed with either No. 2 or BB shot. In a well choked gun, these shot sizes will devastate the largest gobbler that ever lived. The myth that a turkey is not vulnerable to shot in the body is absurd. No. 2 and BB shot propelled from a 10 gauge or three-inch magnum 12 gauge will break the largest bones in a turkey's body at 50 yards. I have photographs of the awesome anatomical damage large shot inflicts. A single BB pellet that leaves the muzzle at 1,250 feet per second will penetrate the entire body of a gobbler at 40 yards. An efficient gun will provide numerous hits to the vital area of a turkey. In the great majority of cases the bird will be immobilized by the effect of the large shot on its skeletal structure. Frequently the largest bone of the leg, the tibiotarsus, will be shattered. Tremendous shock is transmitted by the fracturing of large bones. Tables 10 provides data on field use of small and large shot over a 10-

TABLE TEN
FIELD DATA: LARGE vs SMALL SHOT

Loads Used	Number of Turkeys Hit	Hit That Were Not Capable of Coordinated Movement	Number of Turkeys Hit and Recovered But Which Were Capable of Coordinated Effort to Escape	Turkeys Hit But Lost
10 Gauge Buffered BB Shot (2-1/8 oz.)	22	20	2	0
12 Gauge Buffered # 2 Shot (1-1/2 oz.)	15	12	3	1
12 Gauge Non Buffered # 6 Shot (1-1/2 and 1-5/8 oz.)	34	22	5	7
12 Gauge Buffered # 6 Shot (1-5/8 and 1-7/8 oz.)	20	18	0	2

Percentage of Turkeys hit with large shot (size two or BB loads) which escaped = .03%.
Percentage of Turkeys hit with small (size 6) shot which escaped = 16%.

The chronograph demonstrates the variations in velocity with shot load weight.

year period. The data demonstrate the efficiency of large shot.

In selecting a specific large-shot size, my experience indicates that No. 2 shot is best in most 12 gauge guns while BBs are the best choice in the 10 gauge. Again, you must determine what is best in your gun.

If your choice of a turkey gun is a repeater, I believe the best strategy is to use the large-shot load that patterns best. You can still make head shots with the large

shot at close range, and you have the ability to take the 45-yard chance when it is presented. One problem arises when you have a shot at the turkey's head at approximately 35 yards. At that range a good smaller-shot load will give you adequate density for the small target. The larger-shot load does not have great density at this range, and it is easier to miss the small target. As I have said, if you have a double-barrel this is no problem as you have the option of developing a load for body shots in one barrel and one for head shots in the other.

The Appropriate Load

Shot size is not the only consideration in attempting to select, or create, optimum efficiency for a specific gun. Two other variables are the amount of shot and the velocity of the load. When making a decision about these variables, you can't have it all. Obviously the higher the velocity and the heavier the shot load, the greater the energy generated. Greater energy converts to greater killing power and so is advantageous. Unfortunately, greater energy also converts to higher chamber pressures, and you must operate within safe limits. Since chamber-pressure danger deprives us of the opportunity to have both the heaviest load and highest velocity, we have

to decide which is most important. Table 11 indicates how shot weight influences velocity. An interesting aspect of this consideration is that what will be best for spring gobbler shooting will not necessarily be best for another field application. For duck shooting I think the most efficient load I have ever used in a magnum 12 gauge gun is one of very high velocity (1,365 feet per second) with a relatively light (1⅜-ounce) load of shot. I find the high velocity an advantage in helping me hit fast-flying ducks. In contrast, my turkey load in the same gun is the maximum shot loads (1⅞ or two ounces) at a necessarily much reduced (1,150 feet per second) velocity. Since most opportunities are at a stationary target, the advantages conferred by the fast load are to a degree obviated. The heavy load increases the density of the pattern and increases the chances of multiple wounds. A factor that

TABLE ELEVEN
THE EFFECT OF THE WEIGHT OF SHOT CHARGE ON VELOCITY IN THREE INCH MAGNUM TWELVE GAUGE SHOTGUNS

Gun: Browning Superposed
Ammunition: All Federal Premiums except for 1-3/8 oz.
       handload. All size BB shot.

Load	Muzzle velocity chronographed in feet per second	Average of 1/8 inch, 2-ply cardboard sheets penetrated at 40 yards
2 oz.	1148	21
1-7/8 oz.	1150	21
1-5/8 oz.	1227	22
1-3/8 oz.	1365	25

helps with this tradeoff to heavy loads is that the larger shot retain velocity more efficiently. Another disadvantage of the heavy loads in duck hunting is their brutal recoil. You don't have a problem with the cumulative effects of recoil in spring gobbler hunting.

CLOTHES

The subject of camouflage will be addressed in detail in the section that follows; however, camouflage is not the only consideration in the spring hunter's selection of clothes. It comes as something of a surprise to new spring hunters when they find that many of their hunting clothes are no longer appropriate. In North America, hunting has been associated with cold weather, and people assume that anything worn for hunting should be cold-adaptive. It will not take many warm spring mornings before even the most frugal hunter makes the decision to buy clothes that are light and cool.

In the spring, cotton should be the material for clothes—your socks, pants, and shirt or jacket. Cotton is light, cool, and quiet in the woods. Shirts and pants made of nylon or other synthetic materials are generally too warm and too noisy in the woods.

Intelligent hunters will be concerned about the weight of their clothes and equipment. Every extra pound imposes a handicap. Cotton is light, and, in shirts or pants appropriate for the spring, it doesn't have to be weighted down with heavy zippers, snaps, or other hardware.

When you purchase your spring clothes, make sure they fit well. This comment is not made in the interest of improving your appearance. When you are dressed for turkey hunting, there is little hope of looking fashionable. You may pull off the exotic look, but most of us look like clowns. A concern for good fit is important because you cannot afford to have clothes catching on brush or restraining your movement.

Footwear

Many experienced spring hunters will argue that no piece of equipment, gun included, is more important than footwear. The great majority of my hunting has been in the rough and rocky hills of Appalachia, and if you do not have appropriate footwear there, you simply will not hunt effectively.

I have had spring hunts ruined by hunters who used inappropriate boots. One man simply could not stand up. He hunted with a pair of army dress boots with flat, slick, leather soles.

Your boots should be as light as the terrain you hunt allows. In rocky areas, I believe a heavy Vibram sole is a must. The heavy Vibram adds weight, but it allows you to walk in rugged country.

When hunting in the low, flat, and wet country typical of many states in the Deep South, a heavy Vibram boot is a disadvantage. A light nylon boot that dries quickly and will not rot from repeated soakings is a good choice. You may argue that high, snakebite-proof, leather boots may be a better choice. I have a pair I wore for two years in the Peruvian jungle. These are comfortable, well-made boots, but they are heavy and warm. The careful person does not face much of a threat from snakebite. I suspect that a calculation of the ratio of snakebites received per hours that snakeproof boots have been worn would indicate the investment in such boots was unnecessary. If the boots give you a sense of security, fine; however, my bet is that after a few days you will get tired of both dragging the weight around and attempting to dry them out every evening.

In some types of terrain, very light running shoes have been used with success. These shoes—or the heavier versions designed for backpackers—will not provide much protection from rocks or water, but in some areas they may be adequate.

If you have had problems with your ankles, the decision to go to a light boot may not be a good idea. Do not sacrifice the support of a higher and heavier boot unless you have determined that you can accommodate it in the type of terrain in which you hunt.

The Vibram lug sole boot may be the most important piece of equipment used by the spring gobbler hunter in rocky, mountainous terrain.

I have allocated considerable space to boots, and the reader may wonder about my priorities. Whenever someone suggests that footwear does not demand careful attention, I think of an outfitter in British Columbia who responded to my questions about rifles for big-game hunting by saying: "Don't worry about the caliber of your rifle; just bring one you can shoot. I suggest you spend time considering your boots. Make sure they have a lug sole, are of good quality, and are broken in. In fact I'd sacrifice other equipment if necessary in order to bring two pairs of good boots. If you can't find them in your area, get a pair from the White Company in Spokane, Washington. Forget all your questions about the rifle—but bring good boots that fit."

Gloves

I like to wear a light pair of gloves in the spring. The reason is camouflage exclusively. Your hands are highly visible in the woods, and the gloves are less messy than camouflage paint or cream. I use a good pair of tight-fitting leather gloves of the type designed for target shooters. If you get caught in a rain, it is important to dry the gloves slowly and oil them, but with care they will provide long service. I don't see how some hunters tolerate ill-fitting cotton gloves. I have seen hunters who had to take them off to use various types of calls. It doesn't make much sense to wear gloves at all if you are going to take them off frequently.

Hats

Of all the things a turkey hunter wears, there is no greater range of variation than in hat style. A practical type is a compact baseball hat with a visor that is large enough to provide some eye shade. My wife improved upon the baseball hat by taking a fishing hat, with a baseball-type crown but a much larger brim, and sewing camouflage material over the light tan cotton. The extra shade for the face is an advantage, and yet the hat is still not large. Larger hats provide more protection, but they also tend to get knocked off. You don't need the aggravation of losing a hat while trying to get to a gobbler.

Stick with a Standard Outfit

One spring I experimented with several different styles of camouflage jackets. I never considered the possibility that my use of different garments could cost me a gobbler.

The morning it happened, I had been frustrated by mature gobblers, and with only a half hour left, I moved quickly to a high ridge to do some blind young-gobbler calling. After just 10 minutes of calling, three young birds came walking boldly and noisily toward me. It was late in the spring, and the ground cover had become very thick. I waited until the leading gobbler went behind a tree and then raised my gun. One of the gobbler's bachelor friends stopped instantly and putted. I could see the head of the lead gobbler through the dense vegetation, and since the range was only 20 yards I took the opportunity. At the shot, the bird's head disappeared and the two other gobblers flushed. I held the gun on the bird's location for an instant and heard nothing. Confident, I stood up, but the instant I broke the gun to reload, my gobbler flushed. Still watching the bird, I jammed my hands into my pocket for an extra shell. The jacket did not have a pocket. In my excitement I had forgotten that this new jacket had no pockets and, for the first time that spring, I had my shells in my pants pockets. I frantically jammed my hands into the jacket in a vain attempt to open the pocket that was not there. The gobbler's flight was not strong, but he was out of sight before I found the right pocket.

The story has a happy ending, though—the head-shot bird lost coordination shortly after disappearing behind the trees, and I distinctly heard the sound of his fall. I marked the spot and found him dead a short time later. I learned a lesson. Now I always wear the same style of jacket.

Being Prepared for Weather Changes

In some states the spring weather can fluctuate tremendously. Though my most frequent concern is for staying cool, I have suffered from the cold when I have not been prepared. If the temperature drops into the low 50's, you don't have to be very wet to get very cold.

I often find myself carrying a light down shirt in my pack early in the season. If the weather report indicates a particularly warm day, I will take the shirt out of my pack; however, when in doubt, I take it. I can remember two windy, damp mornings when the temperature dropped into the 40's. I know I would not have been able to endure the conditions without the shirt.

It is always a good idea to have a light rain jacket in your pack. I simply keep one there, and it allows me to be comfortable at least one day each spring. It is also welcome as a ground cover to sit on the day after a heavy rain.

The light down shirt and the rain jacket may add 1½ pounds to your pack, but someday they will allow you to hunt when you wouldn't otherwise have been able to.

OTHER TOOLS

The Decoy

One of the more controversial pieces of turkey-hunting equipment is the decoy. Many feel that the use of a decoy confers an unfair advantage on the hunter and is hence unethical. Several articles have suggested that the use of a decoy makes turkey hunting easy. The general thrust was that as soon as a gobbler saw the decoy he would unhesitatingly march directly to it. As is usually the case with reports on a new tool, the assessment of its advantages were exaggerated. In certain circumstances a decoy can be advantageous; however, to suggest that a decoy spells doom for any gobbler within a square mile is silly.

For a period of three years I experimented with decoys. In addition to testing two commercial decoys, I made the one of cork and pine shown in the accompanying photograph.

My experiences with the decoys confirmed my suspicions about their effectiveness. There is no question a gobbler will come to a decoy, but the critical point is that *you* must bring him close enough to see the decoy—that demands effective calling. The decoy does not replace efficient calling. How many of the birds that come to a decoy would have come anyway? The question is moot. All experienced hunters have had gobblers come directly to them as <u>if</u> they had their eyes fixed on a hen. When the decoy is out in front of you, it is natural to make the assumption that he came because of it.

The major problem I had with the use of a decoy was that in the terrain I usually hunt the decoy was often impossible for the gobbler to see. Even a modest contour change can hide the decoy. On several occasions when I had gobblers close, they seemed unaware of the decoy. When I subsequently put myself in the location of the gobbler and kneeled on the ground, the decoy was indeed invisible. It was easy to see from a standing man's perspective, but when my eyes were lowered to the height of a gobbler, the contour hid the decoy.

If you hunt near large, open fields and most of your terrain is flat, the decoy may be much more effective. If you hunt in areas with steep hills and considerable dense underbrush, I will predict that often the gobbler simply will not see the decoy.

Another problem with a decoy is that it

Hen decoy carved of cork and pine by the author.

Decoy the author carved from pine and cork is on the right. Commercial decoy is on the left.

is a burden to carry. Mobility is an important factor to the turkey hunter, and a decoy detracts from that mobility. It is true that some decoys are more portable than others; however, in most cases the more realistic the decoy, the harder it is to carry. It is not just the weight and size of the decoy that is disadvantageous but also the time needed to take it down, set it up, pack it away in your backpack, and unpack it.

My major concern about the decoy is that I think it is dangerous. If it is a good decoy, it looks like a turkey—a hen turkey, admittedly, but hens are killed in the spring by ethical hunters who simply get so excited they make a mistake. If we are quick to tell people not to wear blue, red, or white on their clothes because a small patch of these colors may cause some idiot to shoot at them, how can we justify placing a hen-turkey decoy close to our location? I used my decoy only in areas in which I was confident the chances of encountering other hunters were slight. As the hunting pressure has increased, the number of such isolated areas is rapidly declining.

In the context of ethics, I have no argument with attracting birds to a decoy. In my mind it is much more ethical than shooting one with a rifle.

So, if you want to try the decoy, I suggest you be aware of the fact that it is not the final solution, and, more importantly, you must be aware of the threat that some fool might shoot at it.

The Back or Belt Pack

I believe a compact pack can be one of the most functional additions to a spring hunter's collection of equipment. The small pack is a safe and efficient way to carry calls, rain jacket, lunch, survival pack, extra shells, a sling for your gun, and a variety of personal items. There are several advantages of the pack. First, if it is tied shut, nothing will fall out. If you had a dollar for every box call that has dropped from hunters' pockets, you could spend the rest of your life doing nothing but turkey hunting. Second, the pack becomes the place where you put everything the night before the hunt. If your pack is ready, all you have to do is get your gun and keys and go. The man who carries his equipment in a lot of different pockets is much more apt to forget something.

Small Accessories

Many superb turkey hunters have ventured into the woods with an inventory of accessory equipment that consisted of a pocket knife, period. However, there are other items that the well-equipped turkey hunter should carry. I believe the following are worth the extra weight they impose.

1. A survival kit. Mine consists of a light plastic tarp, a whistle, matches, a signal mirror, and three extra shotgun shells. I firmly believe no turkey hunter should venture out alone without such a kit. Its importance is not predicated on the isolation of the area in which you hunt. A broken leg just 500 yards from an interstate puts your life in jeopardy if you are without cover, fire, or a means of signaling for help.

2. A sling for my gun. I made a detachable sling of ⅛-inch nylon. I use it instead of a leather sling because it does not weigh as much and will never deteriorate. I carry it in one of the pockets of my pack.

3. Two diaphragm turkey calls. These are always carried in a small "Anacin" tin in my pack.

4. First-aid items. I have found commercial first-aid kits inadequate. I carry two tourniquets of adequate size and a half dozen bandaids. In packaged first-aid kits, the bandaids are rapidly used up while nothing else is ever used. The tourniquets are elastic and will allow you to address a serious hemorrhaging injury or construct a splint.

5. A silica Explorer's compass wrapped in a green army-surplus handkerchief. The compass, and the ability to use it, are valuable to the turkey hunter for obvious reasons. One comment: you should not assume that familiarity with a given hunting area eliminates the need for a compass. Until a dense fog has suddenly enveloped you on a familiar piece of hunting range, you can't appreciate a compass.

6. A compact and durable flashlight.

A pack is a valuable accessory.

The tiny flashlights that operate on two AA batteries are perfect for the turkey hunter.

7. An extra key for the ignition of my car. I carry it taped in my wallet.

8. A durable watch with a dial that is visible in the dark. You must keep track of time, and your timepiece must be durable.

UNNECESSARY EQUIPMENT

1. A big belt knife. The large knife indicates the individual carrying it has made the decision to carry weight that is not necessary.

2. A pistol of any caliber is worthless to the turkey hunter armed with a shotgun. Also, unless you have the discipline to wear hearing protection at all times, a handgun will damage the hearing that is so critical to your success as a turkey hunter.

3. A large flashlight. There is no need for a powerful flashlight. The use of one suggests the person is either not very smart or not above looking in the tops of trees for roosting birds.

4. A turkey sling. I've carried my share of birds from the field and felt no disadvantage in not having a turkey sling. If I kill a large gobbler, I sling my gun and carry the bird by its feet.

5. The "turkey vest." Several companies have brought out vests with multiple pockets specifically designed for turkey hunting. If you want to use one instead of a daypack, fine. I do not see any need for one if you use a pack.

6. A camera. As the photographs indicate, I take a lot of pictures of my turkey hunting. When guiding hunters, I frequently carry a camera; however, when I am hunting it is just too much extra weight. I know you can get a compact camera, but when my lungs scream as I try to go over one more tough ridge, I want to know that every ounce I carry is essential.

7. Binoculars. There might be one time in 20 days when binoculars would be advantageous. I do not want to carry the weight on the other 19 days, so I don't use them. In some types of terrain, however—for example, open western states—you may find that they are worth the weight.

8. The portable blind. Two experienced hunters and I were very amused by the cover of a catalogue put out by an outdoor supply store. The spring hunter depicted was surrounded by so much equipment that he would have needed a few bearers to move it. The largest item was a portable blind. Under ideal conditions such an item could be used; however, none of the experienced hunters of my acquaintance would consider trying to carry a portable blind into the field.

The same portable blind that is functional for the waterfowl hunter deprives you of the rapid and efficient mobility that is critical to the serious spring hunter.

8

Camouflage

The only time a hunter in full camouflage does not look like an absolute fool is when he or she is carrying an adult gobbler. Since most of us do not make a habit of carrying mature gobblers, we grow accustomed to looking foolish.

A good friend of mine had an experience which indicates how the use of camouflage may result in a hunter's being perceived as something more threatening than a fool. Gary was driving back to town after an unsuccessful spring morning. In a rush to make a nine o'clock meeting, he had not yet removed any of his camouflage gear, face paint, camouflage hat (complete with artificial leaves), or shooting glasses (which had camouflage tape over the bottom half of the lenses). He hoped no one from the University would see him before he made the refuge of his home.

Encountering our town's one major in-tersection, he stopped to allow the traffic to cross. The third car that passed was driven by a high-school sophomore on her way to school. The young girl's eyes found Gary's vehicle and, unfortunately, Gary. Horrified by the camouflaged figure, she lost control of the vehicle, and it bounced up on the curb. Thankfully, the car was moving at a modest speed, and it came to a rough but not injury-inducing stop. Gary jumped out of the Scout to see if he could help. As he stepped on the pavement, he realized that in anticipation of the quick change at home, he had kicked his boots off and was now in complete camouflage except for white athletic socks. Gary's stature contributed to his strange appearance. He is only five feet four inches tall, but as a former world-class wrestler, he has the upper body and arms of a large man. When Gary reached the girl's car he asked, "Are you all right?"

The girl slid across the front seat away from him and screamed, "Stay away from me!" Confused, Gary turned to greet several men who had come to help. They stopped in their tracks, and one said, "Are you an American?" Gary tried to explain: "I've been turkey hunting," he said as he attempted to rub the green, brown, and black paint off his face. Without the benefit of cold-cream, the colors merely smudged.

One man was staring at his shooting glasses, and Gary said, "I put the tape on the glasses so they can't see our eyes." The man said, "So *who* can't see your eyes?" Gary replied, "The turkeys." Two of the men stepped back and began whispering to each other. Gary desperately added, "This is camouflage I wear so the gobblers can't see me." One of the men was now staring at Gary's feet, and Gary glanced down, saw his white socks, and began to wonder if he could make it to the Scout before they decided to hold him as an alien or communist parachutist. Gary said, "I'll call the police from my house." Without looking behind him, he moved quickly to the Scout. Feeling very insecure, he waved at the men as he headed through the intersection. No one acknowledged his wave. The men simply stared at his vehicle. Finally, one said, "Homer, you call Chief Arbogast and tell him some kind of English-speaking dwarf in combat gear is driving south on Route 11. He's in a red and white 1982 Scout, and the little bastard is armed!"

THE NEED FOR
EFFECTIVE CAMOUFLAGE

There is no type of hunting in which camouflage is more important than in spring gobbler hunting. In many types of hunting the hunter knows where he will be when he tries to call the game. In most waterfowl hunting, for example, blinds are established before the season in locations that will be used often. The spring gobbler hunter faces the immense challenge of needing to hide well at short notice in a location that has not been prepared; hence, there is a demand for excellent personal camouflage.

THE KEYS TO
EFFECTIVE CAMOUFLAGE

You cannot buy perfect concealment. The best camouflage clothes on the market will not hide an individual who does not understand the need for appropriate behavior. Conversely, some hunters hide very effectively in solid-color clothes by being attentive to their behavior.

No type of clothing—and very few permanent blinds—will allow an individual to move and not be detected. Obviously, the goose hunter in a good pit blind can move without detection, but it is incredible how well game can detect movement within blinds. The spring gobbler hunter must learn to sit without moving. It is not easy. As I have said, in trying to determine the experience level of a hunter, I look for the way he sits when I am calling. Watch a novice on a stand, and his "sitting" is an exercise in motion. The two most difficult challenges in taking people spring gobbler hunting are that most cannot walk without becoming exhausted and others cannot sit still. In the context of remaining undetected, no skill is more important than simply learning to sit still.

Wild turkeys are made alert by any unnatural noise. Their incredible hearing acuity lets them detect noises that many hunters are confident the birds cannot

Not all camouflage material provides adequate concealment. Notice how the hunter on the left in the darker pattern blends in so much more effectively.

hear. Hunters make many unnatural noises. The following list is not exhaustive, but it gives an indication of the range of sounds that can send an immediate warning to a gobbler.

Mechanical Noises. The loud clang of the sliding bolt of an automatic shotgun has put many gobblers on the alert. I'm not sure how far this noise can travel, but it is a long distance. Many stories have been told about turkeys that gobbled back at the slamming of a car door. Those stories indicate the penetrating quality of that sound. Any gobbler so warned will be much harder to call. The sounds made when loading repeating shotguns or closing car doors are the two most frequently heard; others include the clanging of gates, and the sounds made by vehicles as they travel over rough roads.

Human Sounds. The sound of the human voice strikes fear in all game animals. Wild turkeys will not respond naturally after hearing human voices. It is always a shock to me when a nearby hunter uses his normal tone of voice in a hunting situation. Spring hunting demands soft, low-volume communications. Human conversation at normal volume carries incredible distances. Under optimum conditions, the conversation of two hunters at the base of a mountain will be carried hundreds of yards up the slope. In such situations, we can only speculate on the distance at which the wild turkey is capable of hearing the sounds.

Other sounds such as coughing, sneezing, and clearing your throat simply will not be tolerated by a gobbler. I have been able to track the progress of hunters by the hacking coughs they made. On one occasion, I listened to a man cough constantly for two hours, at least once every five minutes. I was a full 400 yards from him,

and I am sure a gobbler would have heard the sound 1,500 yards from the man.

Bold human walking has a characteristic pace and produces a pattern of sound that is identifiable not only by alert animals but also by other hunters. In general the sound produced by the inexperienced hunter is characterized by an uninterrupted and fast pace. In comparison to the walking sounds produced by most other animals, it is also loud. It is not just the weight of men, but also the fact that when walking at a normal pace they will break limbs and sticks. The range at which a walking human can be heard by wild turkeys would probably have all of us shaking our heads in disbelief.

A Strategy for Reducing Noise

The first step in developing a strategy for effective hiding is to recognize the primary threats to detection. As we have just discussed, unnatural noises are one.

In many situations, reducing those noises does not demand incredible skill but rather intelligent plans. For example, it is easy to walk silently on a clear logging road, so whenever possible, this type of route should be used. It does not take much intelligence to solve many noise problems. Simply be careful, and remember that one cough is too much.

Effective Concealment

Even if you learn to sit without movement, the challenge of having a gobbler come the final 100 yards remains formidable. There is an art to the concealment that will enhance, but never guarantee, your chances of not being detected once the gobbler is within 100 yards.

Location

I believe the most critical decision—after accepting the fact that you must sit still—is where you decide to sit. It is important that your body not be silhouetted. Sitting up against a tree trunk that is wider and higher than your body works well. The area in front and to the sides of the tree should be clear. Some hunters suggest placing a screen of branches stuck into the ground in front of the tree to help break up your outline. I do not do this—for two reasons. First, there is a chance that you will touch these branches with your gun barrel when you mount the gun. Such disturbances can alarm the gobbler. Second, the acts of cutting, collecting, and installing the branches are time-consuming. Finally, if you do your part you don't need such a screen.

Personal Camouflage

It is critical to provide no indication of unnatural color to the turkey. Every visible portion of your body and equipment must blend in with the surroundings. The worst error is failure to cover the face or hands. The face is perhaps the most likely giveaway of all. A shining face, I'm certain, has saved more turkeys than were harvested in Alabama in the last decade. Some experienced hunters suggest that hiding the hands is equally important because hunters tend to move their hands frequently. Both hands and face must be camouflaged.

Equipment

A shiny gun is an unnatural item in the spring woods. The problem involves not just the light-reflecting barrel but also the wooden stock. No tree shines like a polished stock. Also, the gun is a likely offender because you must move it. When you bring it to bear on the gobbler, it must be moved at least a few inches and in some cases a couple of feet. Camouflage tape will help to hide your gun. Do a good job, and cover all visible parts of the gun.

COMMON-SENSE CAMOUFLAGE

As is true of most aspects of spring gobbler hunting, common sense provides effective answers in the area of camouflage. In my opinion, no one pattern of camouflage material is vastly superior to any other. Many patterns provide a fine beginning for the development of effective concealment. The key is to make sure that you are totally hidden. Hiding the face and hands is much more important than selecting a given type of camouflage material. Obviously, the hardwood-forest turkey hunter will not want to wear a camouflage pattern designed for desert warfare. The choice of a leaf, tree trunk, or tiger stripe pattern is a matter of personal choice. Any pattern can provide superb personal camouflage.

To test your concealment, I suggest you dress in full camouflage, sit down as you would up against a tree in the woods, and look at yourself in a mirror. Try to determine if there are any weaknesses in your concealment. This simple test lets you see mistakes that you might miss otherwise—just pick a time when your wife or children will not surprise you and fear you may have taken up a new religion.

The color photos between pages 128 and 129 show various types of camouflage under field conditions. The material that looks best in these shots might not be best under other woods conditions. You must

An example of effective personal camouflage.

It is essential to *totally* camouflage your gun.

be the judge of what pattern is best. These pictures make the critical point that in order to hide well, you must hide your hands and face.

I think a camouflage pattern for boots is silly. Camouflage boots will not detract from your concealment, but they offer no practical advantage. As long as you wear drab leather boots and dull socks above the boots and keep your feet still, you will not be detected. I also look askance at the advice I have read to wear one pattern camouflage in a jacket and another in pants, the idea being that the contrasting patterns provide better concealment. I don't buy it.

The four camouflage photographs included in the full-color pages demonstrate how personal camouflage enhances concealment. Pay particular attention to the importance of camouflaging your hands, face, and gun. Also, notice how ineffective the concealment is in the picture of the hunter who is simply wearing a camouflage jacket.

9

Calling, Calls, and Callers

THE CALL MAKER

One of the fascinating aspects of wild turkey hunting is learning about the calling devices that have been invented. Any attempt to identify all the variations would be an exercise in futility. There have simply been too many; moreover, the process is ongoing. The range of variations pays clear tribute to the creativity of the makers.

This section is a tribute to one call maker. I selected the man for the following reasons. First, my research has convinced me that he alone is responsible for the call that bears his name. Second, the call is a classic. Third, his production techniques, documented in the accompanying photographs, are characteristic of many creative makers who worked in their homes. Fourth, his creativeness and hard work did not bring a fortune to himself or

his family. He did not design the product for a large market, and did not engage in aggressive advertising or marketing. Finally, Raymond Chisholm of Laurel, Mississippi, died in 1979. It gives me satisfaction to honor the memory of a great turkey hunter and creative craftsman.

The photographs showing Mr. Chisholm at work creating his calls deserve to be placed in the Smithsonian Institution. (I do not deserve credit for the photographs. They were provided by another of Mr. Chisholm's admirers, Jack Lancaster of Sunflower, Mississippi.)

If you find a Chisholm call, and a man or woman who can use it, you will appreciate Mr. Chisholm's creativity. I would not hazard a guess at the number of wild turkey gobblers that have fallen to calls that he produced. Turkeys have been deceived by calls that are not highly realistic

Mr. Raymond Chisholm, call maker, at work.

in tone. The Chisholm call captivated me because of both the ingenious nature of the design and the remarkable tone it produced.

The turkey-call business is booming. Your local sporting-goods store may stock more calls than Mr. Chisholm's total productions. Many mass-produced calls are of high quality and extremely effective. In some cases the type of call evolved from the company, or man, that markets the product. Generally, what occurred was that a hunter who happened to be a clever craftsman saw a call and used it as a model for one he made for himself. His attempt to improve the call seemed natural. The success of the modifications caused local hunters to ask if the maker would produce one for them. As the popularity of the call grew, men involved in

The first step in the call-making process.

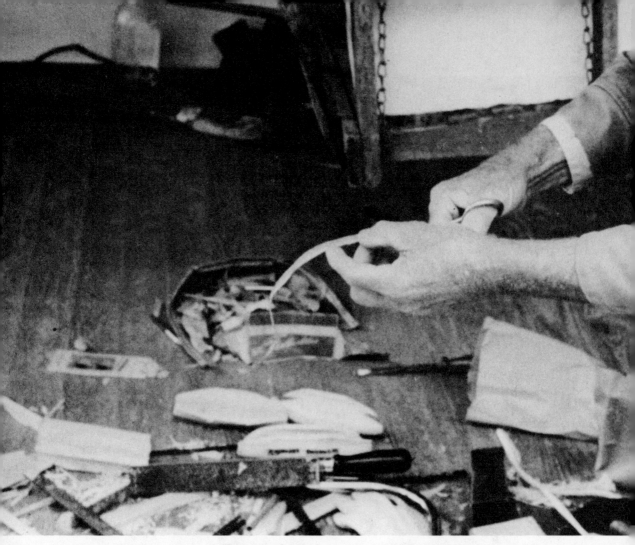

The great craftsman does not need sophisticated tools.

large-scale production of calls were attracted to the new product. In a few cases, the inventor would be given credit for his creativity and a mutually beneficial relationship would be established with the businessman. Frequently, the originator failed to protect his call with patents and suddenly a very similar call would appear on the national market and the inventor would receive neither credit nor financial reward.

A Raymond Chisholm call is like a Ward Brothers decoy. It is a work of art that is functional. It will remain a part of the American story. You don't stamp it out of plastic or make 4,000 of them in a morning. You don't have to try 20 to find one that works. If the man designed it, you can bet on the tone. And yet, no two will be precisely the same. That is part of the charm.

I trust the pictures convey to you the process. The wood he is working is wild magnolia, and Jack Lancaster says Mr.

The master with his product.

Chisholm would search diligently for the correct tree. You don't spend hours searching for the correct tree if you are interested primarily in the bottom line. Profit is not the motivation that produces a Raymond Chisholm call, any more than meat is the goal of a great turkey hunter. The call is folk art; the maker was an artist. How he ever came up with the idea of the shape, the size, and the components will remain a mystery. His call has been copied. So were the Ward Brothers decoys. In both cases, the originals are authentic; the copies are junk.

Study the man in the pictures. Look at the hands and the eyes. Here was an inventor/craftsman. I never had the pleasure of meeting the gentleman from Laurel, Mississippi, but I would be willing to bet that he was as authentic as his calls.

There are other Raymond Chisholms that invented, perfected, and produced wonderful calls. I doubt if any ever became rich. Each of us who enjoys all that is wild turkey hunting should give thanks for these great makers and the marvelous gifts they left us and our sport.

THE IMPORTANCE OF CALLING

Many experienced waterfowl hunters have said calling is not critical. An experienced duck hunter can select a great location, and if he hides effectively, he can enjoy tremendous success without using a call. It has become popular to suggest that calling is not as important as many turkey hunters perceive it to be. A common theme in some articles is that the importance of calling is exaggerated.

Spring gobbler hunting revolves around effective calling. The superb caller has a dramatic advantage over the average caller. There are *no* consistently successful spring hunters who do not develop considerable skill with their calls.

It has also become popular to suggest that successful spring hunting can be exercised with only one type of call. The theory is that developing skill with a variety of types of calls is a waste of time. I disagree. Developing multiple skills will provide dividends. It is true that the other skills necessary to successful spring hunting must also be exercised. For example, good calling will not overcome the disadvantages of poor location. However, no matter how proficient you become in the use of terrain, camouflage, and other skills, your success will suffer unless you become a proficient and versatile caller.

THE BASIC VOCAL SOUNDS OF THE WILD TURKEY

Before discussing the specific calls turkeys make to communicate messages, let me comment on the sounds that constitute the foundation of their communication.

There are four basic sounds: the cluck, the yelp, the whistle, and the gobble. Specific calls invoke variations or combinations of these basic sounds.

The Cluck. The cluck is a single note of short duration. It can be emitted sharply or softly, and the messages communicated by those differing sounds will vary drastically. The sharp, harsh cluck is an alarm putt. The soft, confident cluck communicates a sense that all is well.

The Yelp. The yelp is a fascinating sound. As is true of the cluck, it has many variations in tone and pitch. The basic "foundation" yelp is of two syllables, which starts on a high note and "falls" into a deeper concluding note. The variety of ways in which yelps can be joined together is tremendous.

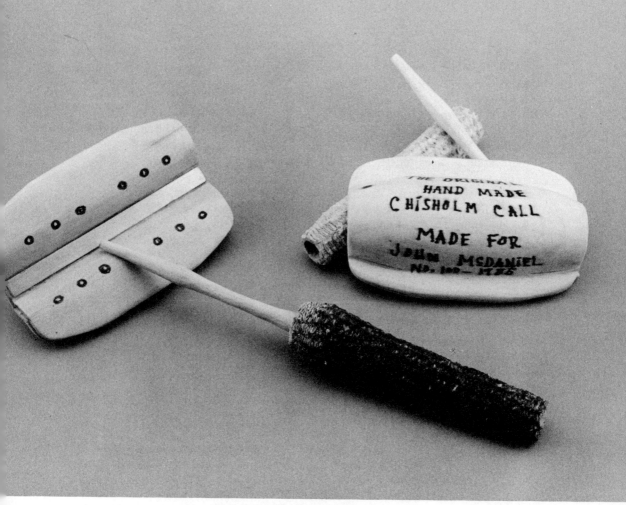

Two Raymond Chisholm calls.

The Whistle. The clear, sharp whistle is another distinctive sound that wild turkeys emit. It is always made in a series. Unlike the yelp or the cluck, you never hear a single whistle. Also unlike the yelp and the cluck, the whistle is exclusively associated with young turkeys.

The Gobble. The gobble is an unique call. In general, its variations are fewer than with the other calls. This is not to suggest that there is not significant varia-tion between gobbles but rather that the range is more restricted. Also, the combinations and variations in the messages communicated by the gobble are more limited than with the cluck and the yelp.

SPECIFIC CALLS

The Tree Call. The first call you will hear on a spring morning is the soft yelping of a bird on the roost. This call sounds as if the bird is not totally awake. It is muffled, soft, and made in a monotone or grunting sequence.

The yelp that is the base of this call lacks the sharp two tones characteristic of the yelping made after the bird leaves the roost. Its purpose is to establish communication between roosted turkeys.

The tree call is an excellent one to use at first light since birds that have been separated will often come to it as soon as there is light enough for them to see. Often the inexperienced caller will make an imitation of this call that is too loud.

The tree call can be effectively imitated with a variety of calls. Most of the best callers use the slate and peg, the diaphragm, or the wingbone types. Boxes and tubes are frequently difficult to tone down to the low volume necessary for realistic imitation.

As with many types of calls, do not use the tree call too frequently. Three series of soft, grunting yelps—separated by several minutes—is enough. Do *not* expect a response to the calls. At times a bird will gobble back, but more frequently there will be no acknowledgment.

Types of Yelps. To describe the yelp as a type of call is deceptive because it is used in a variety of ways to communicate different messages. The different types of yelps include the Old Hen Assembly Yelp, the Old Gobbler Yelp, the Mating Yelp, the Lost Call of the Young Gobbler, and Close-Range Yelps.

Two of these, the old hen assembly yelp and the old gobbler yelp, are essentially fall and winter season calls. The old hen assembly yelp consists of a persistent series of loud yelps, the purpose of which is to bring the hen's brood back to her. The old gobbler yelp is the communicat-

ing call of mature gobblers during those seasons of the year when they are in all-male groups. It is coarse in tone and characterized by a slow rhythm. Because of the maturation of the young birds and the dispersion of the old gobblers in the spring, neither of these calls is used regularly during the mating season.

All of these calls share the basic two-syllable sound that defines the yelp. Variations involve either tone—a function of the bird's age and sex—or the volume, sequence, and duration of the series of yelps.

Hen and Gobbler Yelps. The yelp of the gobbler is coarser and deeper than that of the hen of similar age. Experienced turkey hunters can *usually* use these variations as accurate indicators of the sex of turkeys. The clear, bell-like tone of the young hen contrasts with the coarse and raspy yelps of the young gobbler.

Another important sex difference is the rhythm of the yelps. The yelps in a series made by a hen will almost always be in a quicker rhythm than that of a gobbler. I think the cadence is best described by the words choppy or snappy. A gobbler series is more deliberate.

The challenge in determining sex is to differentiate between the old hen and the young gobbler. At times the old hen will develop a coarse tone that sounds like the young gobbler.

Lost Yelping. The wild turkey is a highly gregarious bird. As I have discussed, this gregariousness is influenced by mating behavior in the spring; however, there still is the bird's innate interest in being part of a group.

If a group of turkeys, of either sex and any age, are scattered, they will attempt to re-establish the group. In some instances this will take place only after a considerable period of time has passed; in other situations the effort to regroup will be very rapid.

When the birds are in their first year of life, the calls they make to establish contact with their peers reflect their age status. Typically these calls consist of whistles or whistles combined with yelps. At early stages in the year, this call consists of whistles exclusively; however, as the birds mature, the whistles terminate in a series of yelps to produce what is known as the "key-key run." As the birds approach the age of one year, they rely more on yelps.

The lost yelping is characterized by its high volume and the long duration of the yelps. A hunter can easily perceive the urgency in the call.

The lost call is associated primarily with the fall season because it is then that birds are flocked together and highly susceptible to being called after the flock is dispersed. The only exception to this is the rare occurrence of a mature gobbler who adopts a solitary existence. Most old gobblers will be members of small all-male flocks and will try to get back together after being scattered; however, they will not be as vocal in their efforts.

The number of yelps in a lost call can vary tremendously. I have counted over 20 yelps in some series. Often, a long series will be repeated after a short pause. The sex, age, and individual characteristics of the turkey will cause calls to vary in tone, pitch, and loudness; however, the basic rhythm and cadence will remain similar.

The volume and duration of the lost call often shock the beginner. The bold, loud calls seem to contradict what he has heard about the wariness of these great birds. You must remember that the lost call is designed to bring separated birds back together, and hence it must be loud.

The Lost Call of the Young Gobbler in the Spring. The lost call of the young gobbler is an effective one to use in the spring. I have used it to salvage a morning when I have been unable to stimulate an old gobbler (and despite the stories you will read about successes with old gobblers, there will be days when no one can find a cooperative mature gobbler). Also, I will use it early in the morning if, during a previous evening's scouting, I scattered a group of turkeys that I think is made up of young gobblers.

At first light, I will use the tree call in the hope that this low-volume call will be adequate to bring the birds back together. If it is not successful, and if there is no gobbling, I will make several series of lost calls. It has been my experience that young gobblers are more apt to be vocal in responding to lost calls made in the early morning than they are later in the day. My records indicate that approximately 85 percent of the young gobblers that respond to my lost calls *in the spring* come without making a call. Of the 15 percent that do call, most come during the first hour of the day. A second good time to use the lost call is when you scatter a group of gobblers during a hunt. This will usually be well into the day, and the response of the birds will be different than it is at first light. In most cases the birds will not expect a member of the group to start calling until at least 30 minutes, or more likely an hour, has passed. Don't forget that these birds have matured significantly since the fall, when they would begin whistling and key-keying a short time after being scattered.

When I scatter a flock of young gobblers, I make a blind and wait for at least 45 minutes. If it is early in the morning and I have the luxury of time, I wait a full hour. When I begin to call, I make three long and loud series of coarse lost yelps. Each series — consisting of eight to 15 yelps — is separated from the next by a few coarse clucks. The series is repeated at about 12-minute intervals. *No* calls are made between the series. At times, young gobblers may come shortly after you begin to call, but it is much more likely that they will not respond for a full half hour. That statement may be deceptive. They no doubt will have responded well before the half hour is up, but they will not reach you for a half hour or more. I never give up on my calling until I have waited an hour. Many birds have come to me at the 45-minute mark. As a matter of fact, I have learned to exercise particular attention at this time. The error most people make is not being patient.

The final situation in which I use the lost call is when I call blind from areas I think may well hold a young gobbler. My decision to use the blind calling is often stimulated by my failure with old gobblers. It is normally well into the morning and I have either not heard anything or been unsuccessful with a mature gobbler. In such cases I will often use my last 45 minutes to attempt to call up a young gobbler. In many of the areas I hunt, I have learned specific locations are excellent for blind calling. Usually these are on high ridges that give a command of a considerable area. You must be ready for an instant response. You are not calling birds you have just scattered so there is a chance your lost call may be heard by a young gobbler that is only 100 yards away and eager for company. They can come very quickly.

I have often heard the steady pace of a bird walking immediately after finishing my first series of yelps. Most such birds will come without calling. Listen intently for the sounds of birds walking because it is the one sound that is almost always present. They are usually determined in their approach, and the sound of their walking reflects this boldness.

The "Mating" Yelp. The most important call for the spring is the quick-cadenced yelp of the hen. Hunters who say that it's always a three-note yelp are simply wrong. The fact is that hens communicating with gobblers in anticipation of mating typically rely on a particular fast and choppy series of yelps; however, the numbers of yelps and their tone, volume, and duration will vary tremendously. The quick and snappy cadence, or rhythm, however, is characteristic. I believe the key to effective imitation of these yelps is to master this quick, choppy cadence.

The Cackle. Is the cackle derived from the yelp or the cluck? The natural cackling I have heard is made as soon as the birds leave their roosts and consists of a series of very fast clucks that terminate in yelps. This call is not heard frequently in the field. Most interactions between gobblers and hens consist of active gobbling and fast yelping. I define a call as a cackle if the yelps are so close together that they lose their two-tone cadence.

The cackle that consists of a series of yelps that suddenly explodes into very fast, short, harsh sounds and then tones down again to slower yelps is effective; however, I believe the more realistic imitation consists of a quick series of clucks that terminate in yelps.

Contentment Calls. The low-volume sounds that have come to be known as contentment calls are important for the spring hunter. Whines, purrs, soft clucks, and low yelps are examples of these calls, and they all can be effective. They are normally made when turkeys are resting. The term "contentment" is appropriate because the function of the call is to maintain rather than establish contact with other members of the group. At times the observer wonders if the sounds may not be analogous to the purring of a contented cat. They imply security and a sense of well-being. Birds look relaxed when making these barely audible sounds.

These low-volume contentment sounds are often very effective when used to convince a mature gobbler to come the last 50 yards to the caller. The ease with which birds hear these calls pays direct testimony to the acuity of their hearing. Often the softest call will elicit a response from a bird 100 yards away.

The Gobble. The gobble is one of the exciting wild calls of the world. The thrills it generates contribute directly to the appeal of spring gobbler hunting.

Many hunters who use the gobble to locate birds would not consider using it to call a gobbler during the day. This failure is unfortunate, as the gobble can be very effective under the correct circumstances.

The gobble arouses jealousy in gobblers. The response to the challenge will vary, but a dominant gobbler often responds by seeking out the "intruder." Also, it is common for a young gobbler to be attracted to the gobble. The young bird may come for reasons of curiosity rather than in the heat of anger; however, he will come.

An effective imitation of the gobble is not easy to produce. An indication of its inherent difficulty is provided by the number of times experienced hunters have heard effective imitations. We have all been impressed by good imitations of yelps, but most of us can easily detect the false notes of most gobble imitations.

Skilled callers make splendid imitations. The best I have heard were made with tube calls. A good man with one of these calls can fool an experienced hunter at close range. He also can call gobblers.

It is important to remember that the gobble is a dangerous call to imitate. It can be more dangerous in certain situations — such as in areas of heavy hunting pressure — but it is *always* dangerous. I use the call only where I am confident there are no other hunters. I have a few inaccessible properties on which the confidence is well founded; however, I am always extremely careful.

TYPES OF CALLING INSTRUMENTS

Many types of calls that were used by prehistoric and early historic populations have not survived. I suspect that these included animal membrane and vegetable material such as grass shoots. Obviously, such tools would be extremely fragile from the perspective of long-term preservation, and thus none have survived for us to inspect today.

Friction Calls

The Peg and Slate Call. Historical evidence from the beginning of European settlement suggests that the most popular early calls were probably of the wingbone and peg-and-slate types [McIlhenny 1914]. The peg and slate consists, in its simplest form, of a small, 3 x 3-inch flat piece of slate about one-eighth-inch thick. The "peg" is a pencil-sized stick striker fre-

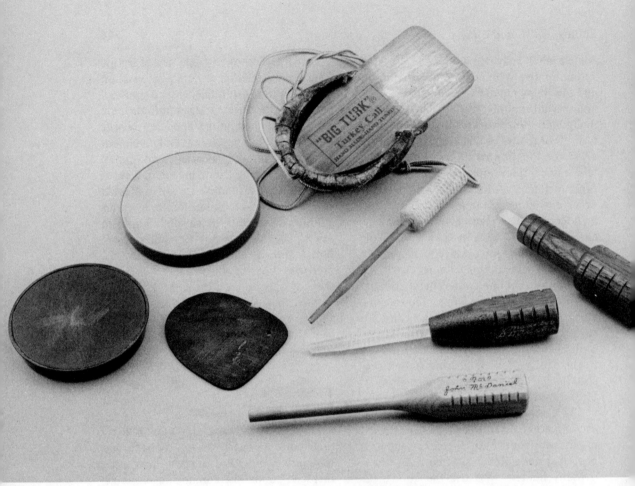

A collection of peg-and-slate calls.

quently made of cedar. The sound is produced when the end of the striker is pulled across the slate. Many variations of this call have been produced. In most, the surface of the slate is "prepared" by sanding. Critical to the tone of the sounds produced is the manner in which the piece of slate is held by the caller. The simple slates are cradled in the palm of the hand to create a sounding chamber. It takes skill and practice to hold a call so that it will produce the proper tone. To address this disadvantage, many makers have set the slate in a wooden frame, thereby incorporating a sounding chamber in the call.

The quality of sound produced by a good slate-and-peg call can be excellent. Many experienced hunters believe that certain calls—such as the cluck and soft whines—can be imitated more effectively on the peg and slate than with any other type of call.

I have used a variety of peg-and-slate calls successfully and always carry one with me while hunting. It is a fine call for the beginner. It is easier to master than the box call that most people use first. It has been my experience that the naturally high volume of boxes makes the slate and peg a better choice for most beginners. Also, it is hard for most novice callers to achieve a quick, choppy rhythm on a box. The long, stroking motion tends to draw notes out and make them slower than they should be. The short strokes used on a peg and slate help the user achieve the correct rhythm. The experienced caller can achieve a marvelous rhythm on a box, but it is much more difficult for the novice.

All slates are not created equal. I've tried every one I've seen advertised. The best I have found is the one developed by D. D. Adams of Thomastown, Pennsylvania. I own three D. D. Adams originals that I protect with a fervor that my wife finds humorous. The same call, essentially, is now being marketed—with credit provided to Mr. Adams—by Dick Kirby of Quaker Boy Company. It is a superb call. There are other good slates. The Stowe calls and those produced by Old Turk have fine tones, and you may find they fit your style of calling perfectly.

Different makers have experimented with various types of strikers and striking surfaces. Non-slate surfaces that have proven effective include wood, aluminum, and glass. The surfaces are set in a wide range of sounding chambers including coconut husks, turtle shells, and small boxes of plastic or wood. Some makers have set two pieces of slate or other surface material on top of one another in the sounding chamber.

Strikers have been made of virtually every conceivable type of wood. Recently plexiglass has become a very popular material as it affords the advantage of not slipping when wet. The non-contact end of the strikers are often stuck into corncobs or small wooden boxes to enhance the sound. Variations in the length and

size of the strikers have been tremendous.

The Gibson/Lynch Types of Lidded Boxes. These rather large box calls have a chamber with a floor, four walls, and an attached lid. Construction methods and the materials used vary. The Gibson type has a chamber made from a single piece of wood while the chamber of the Lynch type is constructed of five pieces of wood glued together. Many different woods have been used in these boxes. Among the most popular are: cedar, poplar, cherry, walnut, mahogany, and butternut. In many cases different woods will be used in different parts of the call.

One caution should be offered to the user of a box call: a wide variation in sounds will be produced by different boxes—even among those from the same maker. The reason is variations in the density of wood. One exercise that will aggravate even the most tolerant of sporting-goods dealers is to try every box in his inventory. One friend boasted, "I tried 75 Lynch boxes before I found this one. I got it back in '64, and I've never heard one as good since." Many experienced hunters claim that the older boxes made by certain manufacturers are superior to those produced more recently.

Excellent lidded boxes are being made today. Some, such as those made by Neal Cost, are not only fine calling instruments but also beautiful examples of American folk art that are destined to increase in value with age. At the risk of sounding biased, but in the interest of citing fine equipment, those boxes made by the Quaker Boy Company are the finest sounding I have encountered.

Few calls sound worse than a poor box. I have heard boxes so poor that it seemed incredible that the hunter could have convinced himself the sound could be

A collection of Gibson/Lynch-type lidded box calls.

effective.

A box can produce great sounds when used by an expert. Some hunters who have mastered mouth calls take the attitude that boxes are just for beginners. I would like to introduce anyone with such a prejudice to Jesse Suber of Quincy, Florida. He can make gobblers respond to his box when excellent callers fail with every other type of call known to the fraternity.

Many experienced hunters take advantage of the high volume that boxes produce and use them to prospect for, or try to locate, gobblers. A loud cackle or series of yelps produced by a good box can carry incredible distances. In one experiment I

made, a particularly high-pitched Neal Cost cedar box was clearly audible to a human at a distance of 3,600 feet. I can only wonder about the range at which this call could be heard by a gobbler under ideal conditions.

The key to using the lidded box is not to be mechanical. Obviously you must make strokes across the box with the lid; however, the strokes must have a quick and choppy rhythm that puts life into the call. If the strokes lack rhythm, they will not produce a realistic sound. My friend Mr. Suber "pops" the box with the lid, and the yelps are quick, harsh, and incredibly realistic. If you have purchased a quality call, you should work on the assumption that the sounds are there to be exploited. Any great instrument will yield impressive sounds only to one who has the skill to extract them. As one friend said after listening to a great pianist perform, "I never knew the University piano had those sounds in it. I mean, the guy made it sound like a different instrument." The same can be said of the manner in which a great caller can work a good box.

The Two-Piece Striker-Type Box. This type of call has been made in a variety of styles and sizes. It consists of a five-sided chamber which has a protruding lid. The chamber is small enough to be held comfortably in one hand. The unattached striker, usually a solid piece of chalked wood measuring about four inches by one-half inch, is held in the other hand, and sound is produced when it is struck on the lid of the small box.

Calls of this type are being produced by a variety of makers and can be extremely effective. I have had particularly good luck with the "Sweet Talker" and those made by the Old Turk Company.

Myths about Friction Calls

Find an inexperienced turkey hunter who thinks he has all the answers, and one

Four beautiful box calls made by Neal Cost.

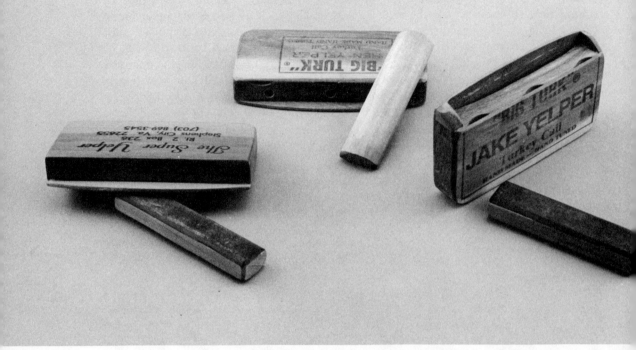

A collection of two-piece-striker-type box calls.

of the first things he will probably say is, "I use a mouth call exclusively because the gobbler will see your hands move when you operate a friction call."

Anyone who suggests friction calls put the hunter at an insurmountable disadvantage does not know much about turkey hunting. The experienced spring hunter has ample time to put the deadly friction call down and pick up his gun. The myth that you must continuously call to an approaching gobbler is just that—a myth.

At one local civic club meeting I was demonstrating some calls on my D. D. Adams and Raymond Chisholm calls. I was pleased with the acoustics of the room and was enjoying the remarkable tones of both calls when a young man in the audi-

ence stood up, interrupting me, and said, "I can see your hands moving from here—there's no way a gobbler will come to that." I said, "Well, I'll wager you $1,000 I can go out with you and call up and kill a gobbler with this call this spring. We have 50 witnesses. Do you take the bet?" The man sat down.

The point of the story is that some people who know very little pretend to know a lot. Don't let *anyone* convince you a friction call cannot be deadly.

Mouth-Operated Calls

Suction/Wingbone Types. The wingbone call, and others based on the same principle of operation, does not enjoy the

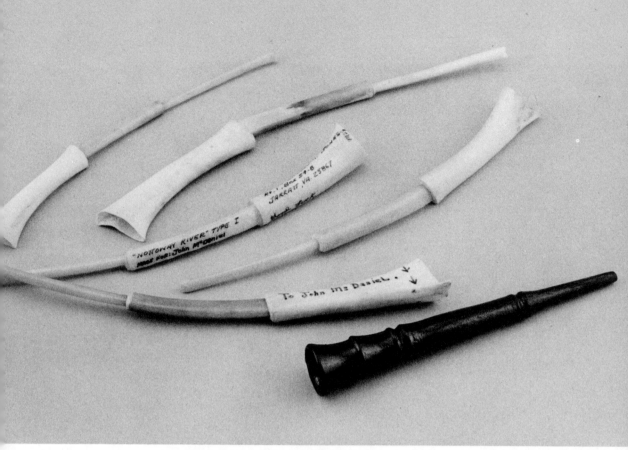

A collection of suction/wingbone-type calls.

popularity of the boxes or slates, but they can be very effective. They enjoyed greater popularity at the turn of the century than they do today. In McIlhenny's classic 1914 work, *The Wild Turkey and Its Hunting*, the wingbone call is described as "the most effective type of caller." The style described by McIlhenny was made by joining several sections of the wingbones of the adult hen wild turkey and inserting them into a small section of cane to provide a sounding chamber. Many variations have been developed. The basic type of wingbone call is a single section of bone that is worked on both ends to provide a convenient spot for sucking and a smooth exit. The call is used by holding the end of the bone in the mouth and sucking with a sharp and short breath. The call is difficult to master in comparison to many other types, which is no doubt the primary reason it has not maintained its popularity. At close range the tone does not sound nearly as realistic as it does at a distance. In the hands of an experienced hunter it can be very effective. The wingbone is particularly good for making two types of calls: the soft tree yelps of the hen and loud yelps designed to elicit a response from a distant gobbler. It does seem that gobblers respond particularly well to this type of call. I use the call for both situations, and I am convinced that there is some quality of tone to a good wingbone that will elicit responses when other calls will not.

A collection of tube-type calls.

The Tube Types. Many varieties of tube calls have been developed by turkey hunters. Often referred to as pillbox calls, many were made by stretching a latex membrane over the top of a small pill can. As with all types of calls, the variety of tube calls produced by individuals for their own use is incredible. A number of standardized types found their way onto the market and have enjoyed varying levels of popularity.

The tube call is another of the more difficult types to master. More people have expressed to me their frustration in trying to master the tube and the suction/wingbone type callers than any other types.

The tube call can produce superb sounds for the hunter who invests the effort and time necessary to master it. It is a particularly good type for imitating both the key-key run of the young turkey and the gobble. The most realistic *loud* gobble I have ever heard was produced by efficient callers using Ken Morgan's "Morgan Call" tube. Several types of tubes produce effective calls. Most of the good ones are larger—in both diameter and length—

than the pillbox styles from which they evolved. One of the key challenges is to determine the appropriate tension for the diaphragm stretched over the call. Most people try to use the call with the diaphragm too tight.

While the proficient caller can make a variety of calls on the tube, I think it is particularly well suited to loud yelps and cackles. Good tube calls can carry long distances. I have found them to be particularly effective in locating gobblers.

It is a tremendous advantage to receive instruction from an expert when trying to master a tube call. Learning to use a tube is never easy, but the process is made much simpler if someone can demonstrate how to position your mouth on the call.

The Mouth Diaphragm. In the last decade the mouth diaphragm has become very popular. Its primary advantages are that it is compact and produces highly realistic sounds.

The diaphragm consists of a light frame, usually shaped like a horseshoe, to which is affixed a rubber membrane or membranes. The diaphragms, referred to as reeds, come in a variety of types. In addition, some reeds are altered—small incisions are made into the edges—to change the tone. It would be interesting to know how many diaphragm calls have been produced over the last decade. There is no question that the figure would be impressive. Experienced hunters will carry several with them.

Perhaps your most important consideration in buying a diaphragm call is to make sure that it fits your upper palate. Your dentist can inform you about the variations in the shape of the human mouth. You must obtain a call that fits your mouth. Thanks to the number of calls on the market today, the chances are

good that you will find one that fits properly.

Even with a good fit, you don't learn to use a diaphragm call overnight. It takes practice, and even with help, there will be an initial period during which clean notes will be hard to obtain. Every hunter I have helped, including a few who are now excellent callers, went through a stage when the only sounds they made were of a huffing variety. My wife refers to this as "the chimpanzee call stage." As is true of all calls, you must persevere to become proficient.

The Diaphragm Danger. Diaphragm calls are not edible. The small size of the diaphragm makes it the type of object on which you can easily choke. Friends have had them lodge in their throats, and each has been terrified by the experience.

Every hunter should recognize the danger and not engage in acts that increase the chances of swallowing the call. *Never* run or even walk with the call in your mouth. A bad fall could easily make you swallow the diaphragm. If the call is not being used, and hence tight against the roof of your mouth, keep it between your teeth and cheek. In this position it cannot slip into your throat.

A STRATEGY FOR BECOMING AN EFFICIENT CALLER

It is not easy to become a proficient caller. You may be able to make a few rough yelps on a mechanical caller after short practice, but to achieve proficiency requires an investment of considerable time and effort.

Tapes can be instructive, and I urge you to acquire them for purposes of refreshing your memory about the tone and rhythm of good calling. The best first step, how-

A collection of mouth-diaphragm-type calls.

ever, is to enlist the help of an experienced caller. A tape cannot listen to you and comment on your efforts—a good caller can teach.

After you begin to practice on your own, a good tape recording system will allow you to assess how your calls sound. It is important to recognize that the acoustics of a room will alter the tone of the sounds you make. I have maintained tapes from my earliest attempts at calling, and it is instructive—and at times humorous—to go back and play those recordings from

years earlier. I also keep tapes of the great callers that I have visited.

Rhythm

The most important quality of good calling is realistic rhythm. The tone, pitch, and volume produced by superb callers will vary tremendously, but all of them have a rhythm that is "alive." You can listen to this tempo or rhythm on tapes or, better yet, listen to live birds in the woods. Nothing is so clearly unnatural as yelps that have no cadence. The inexperienced caller who strikes a box in a series of slow, even strokes produces a totally unrealistic sound. You must learn to impart natural rhythm to your calls.

Tone

After just having said that rhythm is the key, it is not a contradiction to stress the importance of tone. It is true that the cadence of calls is most critical; however, effective tone imitation is also important to producing a good call. Obviously, there are wide variations in the tones made by turkeys. This range allows hunters some leeway in their imitations. But you can deviate too far from the tonal range. Errors in tone imitation are frequently at the high end of the scale. It is true that some younger hens make high-pitched yelps; however, the inexperienced caller, particularly with a mouth diaphragm, will often make calls that are much too high in tone.

In my opinion, the call that has a measure of raspiness will be more effective than high-pitched calls. If you listen to hen wild turkeys in the spring, you will be impressed with the raspiness of most of their calls.

Volume

One of the most frequently repeated axioms of turkey hunting is that you should not call too loudly. In general, that is sound advice; however, if you have heard hens calling as they moved toward a gobbler, you know just how loud they can be.

I believe that certain types of calls are more prone to being too loud than others. One of the inherent advantages of the slate and peg is that it is difficult to make a too-loud call on one. The device simply tends to produce sounds of moderate volume. The box can make extremely loud calls, but the frequency made on a good box is such that even when loud they retain their realistic tone and pitch. It is with the mouth-operated calls—such as the wingbones, tubes, and mouth diaphragms—that extremely loud calls can create poor imitations. If you have ever heard an inexperienced diaphragm caller making very loud yelps, you can often detect a forced, high-pitched tone that I believe can repel turkeys. Please don't misunderstand me. An experienced hunter can make loud, raspy diaphragm yelps that are highly realistic. It is the inexperienced hunter who often loses the realistic tone when the volume becomes too high on mouth-operated calls.

WHAT MAKES FOR POOR CALLS?

The common denominator of most poor calling is unnatural rhythm or cadence. The experienced hunter can quickly detect the mechanical rhythm of the inexperienced hunter. The rhythm must imitate the choppy, alive sound of the hen turkey. It is interesting to see how hard it seems to be for some callers to acquire and maintain the proper cadence. One friend seems to hold it for only a few days before it eludes him. This may be a function of the variations in the "ear" of hunters. Some hunters seem able to acquire and then maintain the rhythm more effectively than others.

JACK OF ALL CALLS OR MASTER OF ONE

Most of us enjoy experimenting with a variety of calls. In fact, it's hard to imagine how many calls a dedicated turkey hunter can accumulate. Is this experimentation a foolish exercise that pulls us away from the one type of call we should be emphasizing? There is a temptation to suggest that the most proficient caller will be the man who works with only one call. However, the best callers I know have worked to master a variety of calls. The following reasons justify that practice:

1. Some types of calls are better suited to imitating certain tones than others. In my opinion, every serious hunter should have a good slate-and-peg call. The tree yelps, clucks, and soft contentment calls can be imitated with great realism on a slate and peg. In a similar manner, a good loud box is a fine call to have for the specific, and perhaps exclusive, purpose of making prospecting calls for distant gobblers. I know several hunters who use a loud wingbone in the same way. These wingbones are never used when the bird is close. So it becomes a special-purpose, long-distance call. Many hunters have a call with which they only gobble. I believe this strategy of adopting a specific call for a particular situation makes good sense.

2. At times a new type of call will come on the market that a caller may find is perfect for him. I know one hunter who has an old box that is his turkey call. He refuses to experiment. Because he is a good woodsman and knows the rhythm of the turkey, he calls up gobblers; however, I am sure that a call with a better tone would make him a more effective hunter. In this case, I would argue that his unwillingness to try other calls has limited his effectiveness.

3. Ability with a variety of calls can allow you to more effectively imitate the great variations in tones made by a group of turkeys. It is true that a skilled caller can produce a variety of tones from a single call; however, the same hunter can increase the diversity of tones manyfold by using several types of calls.

4. Having more than one call prepares you for the possibility that a specific call may be rendered ineffective by weather or — perish the thought — by being broken or lost.

CALL SELECTION

If you accept the concept that mastering a variety of calls is worthwhile, you will face the challenge of selecting the correct one for the appropriate times. It makes sense to determine a strategy before you go into the field. I suggest that you select the best call with which to make the following calls:

1. The tree call
2. The basic hen yelp
3. The cackle
4. The cluck
5. Contentment sounds
6. The gobble
7. The aggravated purr of the mature gobbler
8. The young gobbler's lost call
9. Long-range locating/prospecting/ stimulating calls

In addition, you should be prepared to make these calls in the rain (which will eliminate the use of several types of friction calls).

The Locating, Prospecting, and Stimulating Calls

As stated in Chapter 6, the owl call and gobbling calls can be very effective when used to locate gobblers the evening before a hunt. It is also important for the hunter to develop a series of hen calls that are designed to stimulate a response at long range during a hunt. Among the most effective of these calls are lost yelps, cackles, and "cutting." "Cutting" consists of a series of very fast clucks. When done at high volume, it often elicits a response when other calls will not.

An important factor influencing the efficiency of a prospecting call is the volume. Those types of calling devices that inherently provide high volume will be particularly effective. As I have said, the lidded box is a great example of an instrument that has the capacity to produce particularly loud calls. Many hunters claim a loud wingbone call also has the capacity to stimulate a response at long range. My personal preference is for a somewhat raspy lidded box. When I use the call for locating, I produce the maximum volume I can generate. On several occasions I have had birds respond at distances at which their gobbles were barely audible.

Wait for the Response

One error many hunters make when prospecting for birds is that they expect every response to be instantaneous. In some instances a quick answer will be forthcoming; however, in many cases a period of 10 or more minutes will pass before you get a response. If you have confidence you are in a good area, give your locater call time to work.

Call Selection in a
Typical Hunt Situation

Many intelligent and experienced hunters will be quick to argue that there is no such thing as a typical hunt. It is true that no two hunts are ever the same; however, it is worthwhile to reflect on what constitutes a reasonable selection of calls in a typical spring situation.

Let us say that you are in good position and it is 45 minutes before sunrise. At this juncture, you should listen as intently as you can for any sounds indicating wild turkeys. The light tree call or soft clucks can easily go undetected unless you are vigilant.

As soon as you are able to see the outline of trees clearly, make a few soft tree calls. It is hard to say precisely at what time this should occur in relation to official sunrise, as the cloud cover, topography, and vegetation of the area will have an influence. On an average, I make these calls about 45 minutes before official sunrise. This is still before flying-down time, and it is not fully light. Don't make these calls too loud or too long in duration. A few short, grunting yelps is what you want. I make about three series over a period of perhaps 10 minutes.

The difficulty in providing instructions about calling frequency is that it is impossible to predict the reactions of the gobbler. In some instances the gobbler may respond actively to the soft tree call. Then you may alter your anticipated sequence of calls to adjust to the specific response.

The Importance of Timing

Do not begin to make other calls—such as the basic yelp—at first light because it is too early for hens to make these calls. Many hunters make the mistake of relying on their basic yelps when it is still too early. Bold yelps and aggressive cackles should be made at flying-down time, not before.

After the Tree Call

In most circumstances a gobbler will not provide any audible indication that he has heard your tree calls. Be ready! Gobblers will often sail soundlessly into the spot from which a tree call is coming. As soon as you begin to call, you should be in a position to bring your gun to bear on a bird that suddenly appears. This may seem like common sense; however, I once guided an inexperienced hunter who wanted to try to call himself. Before making the tree call, he leaned his gun up against a tree and sat down more than an arm's length from the shotgun. When I asked him why he had placed the gun so far away, he replied, "Oh, I'll get it after he comes to the ground." At first I thought he was joking. You must be prepared from the moment you make your first call. If your tree calls do not get a response, don't relax your vigilance. Listen intently for the sounds of a bird coming off the roost.

When flying-down time arrives, you enter the next phase of the calling sequence. Even if the bird has been gobbling actively since first light, the key is to wait until flying-down time to make your first bold bid for him to come to you. When I believe hens should be on the ground, I make a quick, short series of choppy yelps, normally at good volume.

Your first yelps should elicit some type of response from the bird. The problem is that the response can be varied. The bird may fly or run directly to you or, at the other end of the broad spectrum of responses, may cease gobbling and never make another sound. Perhaps the most frequent response will be a bold gobble that salutes your call.

When the Gobbler Answers Your Call

Many hunters call too much at this juncture. Now is the time to take a look at your watch and discipline yourself not to call too frequently. Don't forget, he wants you to come to him. The more you call, the more likely he is to believe that you are excited and will soon accept his invitation. The key is to let him know you are interested but make him think you are not too eager. Make him consider coming to you. A lot of things can happen at this time that might make you doubt this basic strategy of a modest amount of calling. For example, the bird may move away from you while gobbling actively, or you may encounter competition from a hen that begins calling to the gobbler.

If such an interruption takes place, you need to make a quick decision. Before making the bold decision to change position, most of us will do more calling to try convincing the bird of our increased interest. In addition to more frequent calls, this is an appropriate time to try an excited cackle or some fast clucking to try to strike a particular chord that may convince the bird to come.

If there is no additional competition and if the bird remains at his original location, don't become impatient. Often the bird will be slow in coming. If there seems to be no immediate response to your calls, patiently continue to call at intervals of about 10 to 15 minutes. When the bird is gobbling well, you will be eager to call more than once every 10 minutes—in fact, 10 minutes will seem very long. However, remember that you are trying to make him grow impatient.

If the bird suddenly becomes silent, be prepared as he may have made the decision to come. If his gobble indicates he is coming progressively closer, don't allow the thrill of his approach to make you suddenly alter your strategy. On the other hand, don't do anything that will change his mind. For example, if you can tell that he is moving progressively closer to you, it makes sense to refrain from calling until he stops. Prepare yourself as much as possible for his coming into view. This is the time to make any modest shift in your position in anticipation of his approach route. You can't be ready too soon. All experienced hunters have had birds arrive more rapidly than they anticipated. Most of the time, the sounds of the bird walking will warn you of his imminent arrival; however, that is not always the case.

Inexperienced hunters often make many calls as the bird approaches. This causes several problems. First, the chance of your making a poor call is increased when you are under tension. Second, the most realistic of calls may stop the bird. A really "hot" gobbler may go into strut when he hears an excited hen yelp. So, if he is on his way, let him come.

Dealing with the Bird That Hangs Up

One of the most common phrases in the lexicon of spring gobbler hunting is "hanging up." A bird that hangs up is one that interrupts its progress to the caller. The challenge that this situation introduces is to convince the bird to continue his progress. This feat can be excruciatingly difficult. The reasons for the bird's decision to stop are almost always hard to ascertain. I believe it frequently relates to terrain features. Terrain features can interrupt a bird for both negative and positive

reasons. From a positive perspective, the gobbler may encounter an area in which he wants to engage in his display. His refusal to move from the spot doesn't mean he suddenly decides the hen calls are unrealistic, but rather that he has found the proper place for mating. From a negative perspective, a gobbler may hang up short of the caller because something about the caller's location (not his call) convinces the bird that it is not an appropriate place for breeding.

The frustrations that such a situation can impose on the caller are profound. There is no easy solution. The experienced hunter will typically try to encourage the bird to come the remaining distance by additional calling. Every conceivable calling tactic may be used. Most experienced callers will save their best excitement call, which is often a cackle, for such circumstances. If this does not succeed, calls with different tones may be used. The threat the hunter faces is making too many calls too quickly. You should not become desperate—desperation can be communicated in your calling. A balance between trying some different calls and the desire to avoid sounding like a desperate hunter trying all his calls should be maintained.

A strategy which is occasionally successful is to attempt to sound like a hen that is leaving the area. By gradually toning down your calls, you can create the impression the hen is walking away from the gobbler.

This is also the time when some people try to stimulate the emotion of jealousy by using gobbler calls. These would include the gobble and the aggravated purr call gobblers make when fighting. Most of us use these sounds as a last resort, however.

Moving

Often just changing location will do the trick, as the gobbler's reluctance to come may be a result of the caller's location. If the bird does not come to the new location, another move can be combined with the selection of a call with a slightly different tone.

The Error of Making Desperation Calls

Sometimes hunters become so frustrated by a reluctant gobbler that they begin to make what I consider "I've given up hope" calls, which normally consist of loud, incessant cackles and gobbles. It is used as a last resort, but it is almost never effective, because the calls communicate your frustration.

The caller must have the patience to stay with a reasonable sequence of calls and not succumb to this desperation calling.

A Special Strategy— Calling Without Yelping

A great tactic to employ on "difficult" gobblers, or in an area that has been subjected to heavy hunting pressure, is to avoid yelping and rely on low-volume calls.

On several occasions I have had birds come to me when the only calls I made were a few soft clucks and purrs. After the first hour of light, it is natural for hens to use these soft contentment calls; hence they are particularly effective later in the morning. Also, there are so many hunters making yelps that I am confident some

gobblers develop a reluctance to respond to yelping at any time.

The next time you encounter a bird that will not respond, or you are invited to try one that has humiliated a friend, try just a few soft tree calls right at dawn, and a couple of clucks and a few purrs after he hits the ground.

ATTRACTING GOBBLERS WITH SOUNDS OTHER THAN CALLS

The clever hunter can occasionally attract gobblers by imitating non-vocal sounds. One of those most frequently imitated is that made by the birds when they scratch for food in the leaf cover of the forest floor. It is surprising how far this can be heard. Obviously, a turkey that is scratching is not alarmed, so the sound suggests all is well. Scratching sounds can be used in conjunction with calling, but they are also effective—particularly on call-shy birds—on their own. The hunter trying to imitate the sound must learn the rhythm used by the birds in scratching. There is a distinct cadence to the motion. It has been my experience that birds tend to make three "strokes" followed by a pause.

Another sound, less frequently used, is that of a turkey walking. As I have said, in most turkey range this sound will be quite loud. Obviously, a gobbler hears the sounds made by a hen walking to him—he expects to hear them. You can imitate the sounds. The disadvantage of this tactic is that your movement increases the chances of your being detected by the gobbler; however, if you have a contour or very thick cover between you and the bird, you may be able to use the ploy. I have one friend who has used the technique alone to fool particularly wary gobblers. A most impressive story involving this technique was provided to me by Bill Rector of Stony Creek, Virginia, who told of one bird that would gobble at the sound of Bill's imitation of a hen walking. Dense cover allowed Bill to use the walking sound to "call" the bird to him. The final step in this tactic is to remain stationary and hence encourage the gobbler to come to the spot from which he last heard the "hen" walking.

10

The Physical Demands

SPRING FATIGUE AND
THE STORY OF NUMB

Most spring hunters have a story about how the physical demands of the spring season got the best of them. My story concerns a good friend who worked the 3 p.m. to 11 p.m. shift at a chemical plant. Every night he would make a tough one-hour drive home and rush to bed just after 12 p.m. When you retire at midnight, 3:30 a.m. comes very quickly. My friend found the courage—and I chose that word with care—to get out of bed at 3:30 a.m. *every day* of the season. Put in a week of 3:30 a.m. mornings, even when you are getting to bed at 9 p.m. rather than midnight, and you'll appreciate the toughness of that schedule.

My friend was okay for the first two weeks of the season. Oh, he had his moments. The drive home at 11 p.m. was tor-

ture, and he got tired of his co-workers sneaking up behind him to gobble in his ear as he drifted to sleep. By the third week he was in pain, but still giving the gobblers hell.

It happened the next to last Saturday. He awoke, and both his feet felt as if they were "asleep." He told me that he thought he had just "laid down the wrong way or something." As he drove out to hunt, though, the numbness in his feet remained. Suddenly he realized his hands were kind of numb too. "My God," he thought, "I'm going numb."

His co-workers were sure he was over the edge when he began to stomp his feet and shake his hands on the job. He told me, "It was terrible, John. At times the feeling would come back, but most of the time my hands and feet were totally numb."

Numb's wife, Louise Virginia, even called my wife Nell to ask her if I would prevail upon him to get some rest. She told Nell that their daughter kept asking, "Why does Daddy keep stomping his feet?" Once, Louise Virginia went to the kitchen for a moment during dinner and suddenly heard her daughter say, "That's not nice, Daddy." When she returned to the dining room, Numb was asleep with his face in the mashed potatoes.

The worst incident occurred the last week of the season. He had located a huge gobbler and had gotten close two mornings in a row. Numb or not, there was no thought of rest. "You know how it is, John—he had one of those super thick beards!" By this stage, the numbness and his general fatigue had become progressively worse.

In his words:

> I'd sit up against a tree and couldn't keep my eyes open. The only thing that would keep me awake was his gobble. It got so bad the last Friday, I was fighting sleep as he came toward me. I'd make a call, he'd double gobble back, and an instant later I'd feel my eyes start to drop. I kept calling so that his gobble would keep me awake. When he got about 75 yards away, I tried to lift the gun and I couldn't feel it. I jammed my hands into the ground a few times and got a little feeling back in my fingers. I didn't dare move my legs because I couldn't feel my feet. That bird came on toward me, and for the first time I didn't shake. God, it was nice not to be trembling and panting! Well, I finally got my gun up, and at the shot he just flopped on the ground. Instead of jumping up, I just sat there sort of stunned. I mean, I was so numb I couldn't move. It took me several minutes to get up. When I was finally up, I realized I hadn't picked up my slate call, and when I leaned down for it, I fell over! It was terrible. I must have looked like an old turtle rolling around. Finally, I got up and staggered over to the bird, and I started stomping to try to get the circulation back. It must have been a sight, John. There I am, standing over this great gobbler, stamping my feet and shaking my hands. I mean, most of me was numb!

Ever since that year, my friend has carried the nickname Numb. I wish I had taken Numb to a physician to get a clinical assessment of his physical condition. I'm sure the fatigue had reached such a point that a definite diagnosis could have been made about what physiologically was taking place.

PHYSICAL FITNESS

Spring gobbler hunting is never easy. The physical stress it imposes will vary from one part of the nation to the next, but there is no area in which it is not an advantage to be physically fit. Where the ridges are steep and the vegetation dense, a hunter's success will be directly correlated with his physical strength and endurance.

For most of us there are periods of the year when our occupations deprive us of exercise comparable to what we experience when spring gobbler hunting. If you, too, have periods of little exercise, try to develop a program for year-round physical conditioning.

One of the best exercises is simply walking. This activity is generally not too stressful for an individual who is not grossly overweight. The value of walking can be increased by carrying weight comparable to or heavier than your hunting gear. This weight handicap can be increased gradually as you begin to gain strength in your legs and enjoy more efficient cardiovascular function. A fringe benefit can be obtained if you walk in

It is important to engage in physical exercise in the off season.

areas in which you will be hunting since you can scout areas and become familiar with terrain features. Many hunters do not live close to areas they hunt and hence must develop more time-efficient ways to maintain physical condition.

Running

Running is superb for both attaining and maintaining excellent physical condition. An hour will allow most of us the time we need to dress, get to a place where we can run, run, return home, and shower. An intelligent running program, developed with the input of a physician, will

pay tremendous benefits to your general health and make you a much more efficient hunter. Such a program requires no greater expense than a good pair of running shoes. Also, if well planned, a running program is compatible with even intense occupational schedules.

Special Programs

There are some people for whom running is too stressful. If you have back, knee, or foot problems, the pounding of running, particularly on hard pavement, may aggravate the condition. There are a number of less stressful exercises that can provide benefits equal to running. Included among these would be:

Swimming—Many in the field of physical education have stressed the therapeutic and conditioning value of swimming. Certainly, it is a fine exercise.

Bicycling—Anyone's conditioning can benefit from the exercise obtained by either riding a bicycle or working on a stationary bicycling machine.

Cross-Country Skiing—Physiologists who study sports generally agree that the most beneficial of exercises is cross-country skiing. Unlike running, cross-country skiing places stress on the upper body, since propelling oneself with the poles involves significant use of the muscles of the back, chest, shoulders, and upper arms. Though swimming also involves most muscles of the body, it generally is agreed that the cardiovascular benefits of the cross-country exercise are superior. Cross-country skiing might pose a problem for a hunter in Florida or Alabama; however, there are exercise machines that simulate the skiing motion. An excellent cross-country simulator is available for a price comparable to that of a good exercise bike. It is available from the Nordic Track Company.

DEVELOPING A REALISTIC FITNESS PROGRAM

Most of us have limited time for exercise; hence, the program's time consumption is an important consideration. One of the benefits of a realistic program is that we are more likely to persist with the regimen. It makes much more sense to exercise for 20 minutes five times a week than for three hours once a week. Another consideration is that the program should not demand that you travel a significant dis-

tance to the place where you will exercise. Swimming demands not only a pool but frequently the accommodation of a limited schedule of access.

A very real measure of personal choice has to be exercised when developing a program. Exercises that are enthusiastically supported by some may not be what you prefer. For example, swimming is a hardship for many. It does not make sense for an individual to engage in a type of exercise he finds intolerable.

The keys to a successful program are:

1. Develop one that you will adhere to—the fact you can do it for a week is no measure of how worthwhile it will be to you over a longer period of time.

2. Provide some variation in the activities so that you reduce tedium and so that all parts of your body receive exercise.

3. Record your performance levels and physiological response to the program—weight loss, pulse rate, and speed with which you perform specific tasks.

4. Strive to improve performance—increase, say, the speed at which you complete specific tasks or maintain a constant level of exertion over a longer period of time.

5. Avoid injury-inducing exercise, especially as you enter the ages during which muscles pull more easily. One of the reasons I have not undertaken, nor will I suggest, weightlifting programs is that I have seen too many pulled muscles and back injuries among my 40-year-old age mates who lift weights.

How Much Is Enough?

You have to develop a program that is compatible with your physical abilities. If your occupation provides no cardiovascular stress, or if you are overweight, you must exercise with care. A physician is the best source of advice about what level of exertion is reasonable for you.

One point to remember is that your exercise program could become consuming. I had one friend who became so involved with running that he began to enter long-distance races. After a couple of years, the "training program" had become his consuming interest. He would rather race than hunt. That choice seems deranged to most of us addicted to hunting. At the other extreme of involvement is the person who exercises once a week. To hunt effectively, you certainly need to get more exercise than that. I believe most serious spring hunters need to exercise six days a week. During each period of exercise you should be taxing your body for at least 20 minutes.

A Reasonable Level of Exertion

Pain and suffering are not the only sensations that allow you to determine whether you are imposing too much physi-

cal stress. The best means of assessing the stress of exercise is to monitor your pulse. Take your pulse at rest and then after exercise. Your pulse rate will vary with your fitness and age; however, a standard rule is that in heavy exercise you should achieve a per-minute pulse rate that amounts to subtracting your age from 200. If you are in good shape and want to maintain a high level of fitness, try to bring your pulse to this level during your exercise. Again, each program should be developed with the input of a physician. If you are initiating intensive exercise for the first time, or for the first time since your youth, be careful.

As I have said, the stress imposed by wild turkey hunting will vary significantly from one area to the next. A level of conditioning that would be adequate in one type of terrain will not suffice in another. I have seen spring hunters with vast experience in relatively flat country come into our hills and be traumatized by the stress imposed upon them. Even in flat terrain, though, the individual who enjoys superb conditioning will hunt more effectively than the person who does not.

11

Safety

Spring gobbler hunting is dangerous. The hard, cold fact is that some hunters jeopardize the safety of others. The prudent hunter recognizes the threat. No precise data are available on the comparative dangers in different forms of hunting; however, most experienced hunters agree that our sport does impose particularly high risks. The reasons include the following:

1. Many hunters can realistically imitate the sounds of a turkey, and hence other hunters will assume their calls are being made by a turkey.

2. Because of the visual acuity of the wild turkey, hunters have perfected the art of camouflage and are inconspicuous to other hunters.

3. A wild turkey gobbler does things to a hunter's mind. Tremendous excitement is generated in a hunter who *thinks* he has a gobbler coming to him. This excitement can affect your normal powers of analysis. Officials who investigated shooting accidents have concluded that excitement can cause a hunter to imagine that a nongame object is game. The phrase "early blur" has been used to describe this situation in which the hunter's anticipation of seeing game allows him to "see" what is not there. It is suggested that the reason the blaze-orange color is helpful in reducing accidents is that it shocks the hunter from this "blurred" perspective.

4. Fatigue: One subject that has not received adequate attention in the literature on hunting safety is the effect of fatigue. A superb example is provided by a review of attempts to control industrial accidents. One of the primary factors contributing to these accidents is fatigue. Anyone who has invested a full spring to wild tur-

key hunting will usually have a humorous story or two to tell about how intense fatigue made him do something foolish. In most of these stories no danger was involved; however, they indicate what could occur. Here's one example:

My friend drove his car to work during the third week of the spring season. After what he admits "was not the most productive morning on the job," he walked out to the spot in the company lot where he normally parked his car. Fatigue had robbed him of the ability to remember that, because his place was taken, he had parked elsewhere. He had to enlist the help of several secretaries to find the car 45 minutes later. He stresses the fact he had no recollection of parking it there.

It is important to recognize that the fatigue which produces humorous stories can create tragedy. You must convince yourself that fatigue is a threat and that when you are tired you should exercise extra care. For example, when I return to my vehicle after a hunt, I break my gun and look through both barrels. The procedure ensures that there is no shell in either chamber. Upon arriving at my home, regardless of any pressing schedule, I recheck the chambers before taking the shotgun into the house. I know how easy it is to be careless when you are tired.

Fatigue in the field can cause many types of accidents. You may lose coordination and fall or trip more frequently. Any fall is potentially disastrous when you are carrying a loaded gun. Every fence, deadfall, or other obstacle should be deemed capable of causing a fall.

5. Hunting in groups: When you hunt alone, you reduce your risks significantly. Most accidents involve injury inflicted at close range by people accompanying the injured hunter.

6. Pick your hunting partners with care. I have often taken a new friend hunting and had the frightening experience of hearing a shell being chambered in his gun in the pre-dawn darkness. There is no reason to load a gun before you are sitting in the blind. To walk several hundred yards through the dark with a chambered shell is an exercise in stupidity. When a guest chambers a shell before light, I make it clear that the only way I will proceed is with his gun unloaded. If you hunt with people you do not know, I suggest you are imposing a very real threat on yourself.

REDUCING THE DANGER TO YOURSELF AND OTHERS

The assumption that acting in a responsible manner will eliminate threats to yourself and others is flawed. Unfortunately, it is not that simple. I believe the following steps will provide you with a measure of protection.

1. Hunt by yourself. No matter how responsible a companion is, the very introduction of another gun increases the possibility of accidents.
2. Try to hunt places where you know the numbers of hunters in the area. Private land on which access is controlled provides some security. You can't control access to public land, but you can go to the most inaccessible area. Most people will not make the effort to walk to secluded areas. There are public areas in which I hunt where I have never seen another hunter.

The growing popularity of spring gobbler hunting has made it impossible for some hunters to escape heavy pressure. If you hunt in such areas, you must recognize the threat. If there seems to be a hunter every 100 yards, I suggest you define the risk as too great. Maybe you can't avoid heavy pressure, but I think if you work hard at finding more isolated areas, you will succeed.

3. Hunt with the conviction that every call you hear could have been made by a hunter. This practice will not jeopardize your success as a hunter, and it will provide a check that could prevent a tragic error. The following points will help you predict whether a call was made by a hunter:

a. Most callers tend to rely on a consistent style of calling. One friend, a good caller, has developed such confidence in a series of four yelps that he rarely varies their number or rhythm. The wild turkey will display greater variations in calling than will most callers.

b. Most wild turkeys move while calling. In contrast, most hunters remain stationary. Obviously, a bird will occasionally call from one location; however, you should be suspicious about the authenticity of any call, no matter how realistic its tone or rhythm, if it comes from precisely the same location for an extended period of time.

c. Hunters, even those who have developed effective calling techniques, tend to call in response to all calls they hear. To clarify, an inexperienced hunter will want to answer each call a turkey makes. Turkeys will, of course, respond to other calls, but it is rare for them to respond to every call.

d. Be suspicious of calls that are consistently of one type. If all you hear are yelps, or clucks, or whines, or whistles, there is a good chance you are listening to a hunter who has confidence in a particular call. He may be clever enough to vary the tone, volume, or number of calls in the sequence, but if there is no variation in the type of call, it is probably being made by a hunter.

e. Listen for the odd call that even the excellent hunter may use as a last resort. On one occasion, I was not sure if the hen yelping I heard was being made by a bird or a hunter. However, there was so much calling at a relatively late stage in the morning that I was suspicious. My suspicions were confirmed when the hunter made an imitation of the gobble. Gobble imitations are often a giveaway. Hunters who have mastered excellent yelps will often, in desperation, shake a box to produce a very poor imitation of the gobble.

f. Calls that are extremely loud under circumstances when turkeys will normally not be calling with high volume should stimulate suspicion. In the spring, the loudest calling is usually heard when the birds get together after flying down from the roost in the morning. As the day progresses, there are fewer loud calls. During these later stages, the caller who continues to call with high volume gives himself away.

g. The inexperienced hunter occasionally makes a highly realistic call at an inappropriate time. The error most frequently heard is a mating yelp too early in the morning. The only call a gobbler expects to hear at first light is the tree call. Hearing an excellent mating yelp too early in the morning has helped me determine that another hunter was in the area. In a similar manner, even the best tree yelp will be unrealistic if it is made after tree-yelping time.

4. Assume the sounds of walking are made by another hunter. This point could have been included in the last discussion, but it deserves separate attention. The hunter must assume that the sounds he believes are being made by a turkey walk-

ing toward his calling could be another hunter. The gait of a turkey is very similar to that of a hunter. Once, I was hunting in a particularly inaccessible area, on private property, and was blind calling with confidence that I was the only hunter within 1,000 yards. After 15 minutes I heard the sound of footsteps coming up a very steep slope toward my position. The gait sounded exactly like that made by a turkey. I positioned myself for the bird and was looking down the rib of the shotgun as I waited. My heart was beating fast because I had previously called up a silent gobbler from precisely the same place. I was horrified when a man's head appeared at the end of my gun barrel. I knew the man, and I honestly believe there may be only two other men in Rockbridge County who could have climbed the steep slope at the consistent pace he maintained. Do not assume that what you hear walking toward you is a gobbler!

5. You must exercise common sense about fatigue. You can hunt when you are tired, but when you reach the point of acting irresponsibly, you have the obligation to rest.

6. Wear highly visible clothes whenever you feel you are in a high risk area or when camouflage is not of value. One of the most intelligent things you can do as soon as you kill a gobbler is to make sure you are visible for your trip out of the woods. I carry a blaze-orange pack that I sit on while calling birds. After killing a bird, I make sure the bright orange is visible as I walk from the woods.

7. *Never* wear or carry anything that is red, blue, or white. One friend still is traumatized by the fact he almost shot a man sneaking toward him on his hands and knees who wore a camouflage hat with a light-blue patch on it. My friend, an experienced hunter, was sure the blue patch was the head of a mature gobbler.

SHOULD WE WEAR BLAZE ORANGE ALL THE TIME?

One of the most controversial subjects discussed by spring gobbler hunters is the question of wearing blaze orange while calling the birds. Several studies — one of which I participated in — have been conducted to determine whether it is feasible to call up birds while enjoying the safety benefits conferred by blaze-orange clothing. The studies indicate that it is indeed possible. However, I believe most of us who engaged in the studies would agree that the blaze orange certainly imposes some disadvantage in the context of hunting efficiency. Also, I disliked using the orange vest. As I said in my report, I did not enjoy the way I felt in the woods while wearing it. One of the aspects of spring gobbler hunting that I enjoy is being able to achieve effective camouflage. I knew I could call a gobbler up while wearing the blaze orange, but I felt that the vest detracted from the hunting experience. The sad fact is that if hunters acted with responsibility and care, there would be no need for blaze orange. The data from Germany, and other countries where rigorous training is demanded before candidates earn the right to hunt, indicates that accidents can be avoided without bright clothing. For many of us, spring gobbler hunting provides an escape from the blaze-orange masses of the fall deer season. We enjoy developing effective camouflage rather than being dressed like fire fighters.

The bright clothes will provide protection, but the superb hunters I know hope they never will be required to wear them.

LET SOMEONE KNOW
WHERE YOU GO

You can die of exposure within 500 yards of an interstate. If you break your ankle and do not return to your home or camp, someone had better have an idea of where you went. I always leave a note for my wife telling her where I plan to hunt. The hunter who does not take this precaution is gambling with his life. No hunter is so smart, strong, or clever as to be able to avoid accidents. If you suffer a bad fall, you may need help, and the only way you will receive it is if you can be found in a reasonable period of time.

EYE PROTECTION

In 1974 I took one of my students spring gobbler hunting. Rushing to get to a gobbler before dawn, we were moving with the speed that youth allows. I was in front of the young man when he suddenly screamed in pain. He had jammed a branch into his right eye. He did not lose the eye, but when I inspected the damage I thought the eye was gone. Since that incident I *never* walk in the woods without shooting glasses. Protect your eyes.

HEARING PROTECTION

Spring gobbler hunting quickly indicates how many contemporary Americans have impaired hearing. High levels of noise can permanently damage hearing. Most of you probably have already suffered damage; however, it is never too late to protect your precious hearing. If you shoot a gun, run a chainsaw, or work around high levels of noise of any kind, wear earmuffs or other sound-insulating devices.

12

Ethics and the Spring Hunter

Turkeys can be killed in unethical ways. Many of these tactics are also unlawful, such as hunting out of season; however, other essentially unethical techniques are legal. In Virginia there is no law against shooting a strutting gobbler at 300 yards with a rifle. Any hunter who kills a bird in such a manner has acted unethically. By shooting a gobbler at long range you have not only deprived yourself of the sport's basic thrill but also—and more importantly—you have taken unfair advantage of the turkey. There is nothing wrong with long-range rifle hunting, but it is not an appropriate technique for a gobbler that can be called to the hunter. Killing a fine spring gobbler is a feat of which you can be proud only if it is done under a set of conditions, or ethical guidelines, that the hunter imposes. A man can kill ducks sitting on the water or upland birds before

they flush, but such acts are unethical. The kill is ethical, and should generate pride, only if some sporting standard is met.

If you have had a gobbler display in a small glade 125 yards from you on three successive mornings, you should be motivated to develop a plan that will convince the bird to come to you. If you decide that the answer to the challenge is your 222 Remington with its 6-power scope, I submit that you have thereby reduced that kill—though it is absolutely legal in my state and others—to an unethical act.

Some hunters exceed bag limits and make no bones about it. There is a narrow line between positive pride and damaging competitiveness. If you allow the spring season to become a vehicle for creating a reputation, the wild turkey becomes the victim. Some hunters are driven to prove they can kill more than anyone else. I have had individuals come to me with outrageous reports of the numbers of gobblers that a specific man is alleged to have killed. If the reports are true, they confirm an absolute lack of respect for the wild turkey. The interesting aspect of these multiple-kill reports is that sooner or later you hear that the braggart is using a rifle, hunting during illegal times, or shooting over bait. So what do the many kills mean? If you wanted to establish an even more impressive record, you could use poison. The point is that as soon as the number of birds killed becomes a statistic for public consumption, the hunter has fallen into the trap of trying to elevate himself at the expense of the wild turkey.

It is easy to make the error of allocating prestige on the basis of how many birds an individual has killed. From my perspective, a better approach is to assess a hunter's merit in the context of the contributions he makes to the welfare of the wild turkey.

A different kind of ethical consideration involves the belief many of us have that the wild turkey deserves to be sought by individuals who are hunting exclusively wild turkeys. I am frustrated by the fact many wild turkeys are legally killed by men hunting other game during fall seasons. An individual goes squirrel hunting, and a flock of turkeys walks past him. A quick shot, and the man has had a successful "turkey hunt." That is not turkey hunting. A wild turkey is such a valuable resource that it should be harvested only by those who have invested time in turkey hunting. The chance killing of turkeys frequently takes place during our fall deer season. From my perspective, it is unethical to kill a turkey just because it has by chance wandered into the field of fire you can cover with a high-powered rifle. What is achieved by the deer hunter who has an unsuspecting gobbler walk past his tree stand? Every time I see a young turkey that has been blown apart by a bullet designed to kill a deer, it makes me sick. As I said in my first book:

> In the context of rules and regulations concerning hunting, it is unfortunate that many states allow turkeys to be killed at the same time as small game. Turkeys should be harvested by hunters who are hunting turkeys. The rabbit or squirrel hunter who blunders into a flock of turkeys is not turkey hunting. The concept that wild sheep are not legal game for a rabbit hunter who happens to encounter one seems axiomatic, but we allow rabbit hunters to kill turkeys. I sincerely believe a mature gobbler with 1½ inch spurs and a 12-inch beard is as fine a North American trophy as a Stone Sheep with 40-inch horns. Both the sheep and the turkey should only be harvested by men who are purposefully hunting them [McDaniel 1980].

ETHICS AND THE OTHER HUNTER

The overriding ethical consideration of all hunters should be the safety of their fellow hunters. As I have said, the sport is inherently dangerous. It is hard to keep the concept of others' safety at the highest priority when the intensity of the hunt weighs upon you, but we all have the moral responsibility to do so.

If Another Hunter Is Working a Bird

It is not only rude but, more importantly, dangerous to move in on a bird that another hunter is attempting to call. We should all be able to recognize when someone else is closer to a gobbler than we are. However, under field conditions, it is frequently not as simple as the last com- ment would suggest. At times it is difficult to know that someone else is working a bird. Also, if another hunter simply makes a few calls at a bird from a distance of 400 yards, it is not unethical for you to wait to determine if he will continue his effort. At times you can be fairly confident that the other hunter has given up and left the woods. Often a few desperate calls will be followed by the sounds of a vehicle leaving the area from which the man was calling. Such proof is rare, so you must exercise care before you enter the area. If a sub- stantial time period passes and there are no calls, chances are good the hunter has left. You *never* should proceed to the other caller's spot, but if you can follow a route that takes you around the birds and puts you in a significantly different posi- tion, it is ethical to travel to that spot and—after a reasonable wait to make sure no one else is close—begin to work the bird. Under *no* circumstances should you assume the other hunter is no longer in the area.

Trying to call a bird away from another hunter is clearly unethical. It is unfortu- nate that such an "accomplishment" is often celebrated.

CAN WE AFFORD TO BE UNSELFISH?

It is ethical to be selfish? Early in my hunting career I was generous with infor- mation about areas in which I had found turkeys or other game. I learned my lesson with woodcock. I found a great cover and told a man about it. I suggested we hunt it later in the week and made the tactical error of divulging the location. Two after- noons later I called his office to see if he could get away to hunt. I was sorry to hear

he was out. Thirty minutes later I saw his car parked at my cover. I watched him and another man I know well walk out of the cover. To this day, I don't think they know I witnessed their exploitation of my gener- osity. I issued no other invitations.

Share your data with care. If you find a friend who will share information, you are both lucky. I've been blessed with more than one such friend. When you find one, you have a rare commodity.

I enjoy taking young people with me if they are responsible and respect the pri- vacy of my areas. After the woodcock ex- perience, I feel compelled to make it clear to anyone other than the two or three guys I know I can trust that the ground rule is that you return to one of "my" areas only with me. You also have a responsibility to the landowner to make sure that aggres- sive companions don't come back on their own.

ETHICS AND THE BIRD ITSELF

It is true that most questions of ethics relate to our behavior with other hunters. If we are too aggressive, too competitive, or too selfish, our behavior impacts other humans. We should also reflect on how our behavior interacts with wild turkeys.

As I said in Chapter 6, we each have a responsibility to work hard to develop the skill and tactics that will reduce the loss of wounded gobblers. It is unethical and cruel to shoot at birds that are out of range. Anyone can make an error in range estimation, but some hunters are guilty of shooting at birds so far off that they sim- ply don't expect to kill them. That wanton act is unethical.

The hunter who does not test his gun or load before attempting to kill a gobbler with it is also guilty of a careless act. You must be prepared to kill in a clean and humane manner. Taking the life of any creature imposes a responsibility that should not be taken lightly. There are no laws demanding that a hunter demonstrate competence. It is a sad fact that some hunters are poorly prepared to meet the challenge of killing efficiently. The sense of responsibility and the development of skills must come from within. We have an ethical responsibility to be efficient and we should insist that those with whom we hunt meet the same responsibility.

Each of us can spread that word. We should teach inexperienced hunters that they should be traumatized by the loss of a bird they have wounded. I know one man who thought the fact he had lost eight consecutive gobblers should elicit sympathy! Such stories confirm the worst suspicions of anti-hunters. Only an incompetent and irresponsible fool allows eight gobblers in a row to be lost.

13

Working for the Wild Turkey's Future

Every avid spring gobbler hunter should make a commitment to the present and future welfare of wild turkeys. Contributions can be made in a variety of ways.

ON THE LOCAL LEVEL

Each of us can improve habitat in the areas we hunt. This can be done with a modest dollar investment if you will seek out inexpensive sources of trees and shrubs and then plant them yourself. This is much easier to do if you own a tract of property or if you are a member of a club that controls property. If plants are not available from local, state, or federal sources, or if the costs are too high, a program of clearing small areas by a planned system of taking firewood can be helpful. Improvements are limited only by the industriousness of the hunter. It is easy

to procrastinate or find excuses for not working. I know of hunting clubs in prime wild turkey range that have done nothing of substance to improve habitat for a period of 20 years. Members acknowledge that the purpose of the club is hunting, and yet many members are unwilling to make even a modest commitment of either time or money.

A casual observer could argue that the effort to improve habitat is selfish—that hunters plant crops just to have more game to kill. But most dedicated hunters want to help wild turkey populations succeed in a biological sense. I have friends who have made significant investments of both time and money to improving turkey habitat in areas where they did not hunt.

At the local level another important contribution can be made by controlling free-running dogs and cats. In many areas

Planting shrubs such as autumn olive can provide multiple benefits for the wild turkey.

free-running dogs are by far the most vicious predatory threat to turkeys during both the nesting period and in the summer when the young poults are vulnerable. If you are interested in protecting your turkey population, don't tolerate free-running dogs. All such dogs are a threat. Those "pets" with collars can be as vicious as feral dogs. In most areas the fear of killing someone's pet keeps hunters from being as aggressive as we should in controlling dogs. There are no excuses for allowing dogs to run free—not even the fact that the dogs belong to fox-hunting clubs. I have seen this occur with two clubs in widely separated parts of the nation. If you are a member of a hunt club, you can publicize the fact that free-running dogs will not be tolerated on your property.

It is often helpful to join forces with other concerned hunters to implement programs that will benefit the wild turkey. Hunting clubs are perfect vehicles for pooling resources and talents which can be focused on the challenges. Local conservation groups have often been very effective in helping improve habitat. Often groups that are not directly oriented to the wild turkey can implement programs that will pay direct dividends to our bird. We should join the efforts of the many groups that are fighting to prevent habitat destruction.

Each person, on his or her own, can make a contribution. It is extremely gratifying to watch shrubs and trees grow over the years. The accompanying photographs provide illustrations of the improvements that can be implemented in a relatively short time at a relatively low cost.

Obviously, it makes good sense to develop a special program for a specific area. In the oak and hickory forests of western Virginia, we have had great success with two types of habitat improvement. The first is the simple clearing of openings in the forest. For turkeys it appears that the most attractive thing that can be done with these openings is to plant them in clover and then place autumn olive plants around the edges. There are costs involved here. The autumn olive can often be obtained from the state foresters at very reasonable costs; however, the clover seed and the labor and equipment needed to sow it are expensive. A tactic that can be used to reduce costs is to allow a neighbor with farming equipment to take hay from your fields and in return provide the labor and equipment to plant and fertilize the game plots. You may need to make a financial sacrifice by this tradeoff; however, it does allow you to help the wild turkey at a modest cost. Turkeys are not the only creatures to benefit from such a program. Other game and nongame species derive tremendous benefits. In fact, if your property had only modest open areas before the improvements, you may see larger increases in some other game animals—such as deer—than you will in turkeys.

Many crops in addition to clover are attractive to turkeys. But be cautious about making a commitment to some crops that are attractive for a relatively short time. Corn is a good example. Once corn has matured, it will attract many animals and birds. Unfortunately, it also makes some game highly vulnerable to hunters who use the corn as bait, legally or otherwise. Turkeys in cornfields are visible and very vulnerable. Also, such food crops have the disadvantage of having to be replanted every year, and the harvesting usually is scheduled during fall hunting seasons—an inconvenient time for many of us. Finally, such agricultural crops demand, from the

An example of an opening cut in a hardwood forest for the benefit of wildlife.

An example of an area seeded in clover for turkeys.

An area to be managed for wild turkeys.

farmer's perspective, a large and relatively flat field to provide a reasonable yield. In contrast, clover can be hand sown in any small opening in the woods. In the context of small openings, wood roads can be planted and can provide many square feet of food for turkeys and other creatures. As is true of all openings in the woods, it is not just what is planted in the area that is important but also the insects that are attracted. The grasshopper is one of the turkey's most valued food sources, and they thrive in most open areas.

The one type of management practice that is highly profitable to deer but not as helpful to wild turkeys is the woods clearing that is allowed to reseed in hardwood saplings. Deer benefit from both the dense cover and the food provided by the shoots and leaves. To benefit the turkey, sow the clearcut in a low type of cover such as clover and keep the area open. The modest cost of simply allowing a cleared area to grow back is attractive—and in some circumstances there can be positive dollar flow if there is marketable timber on the property. In fact, I met the costs of my clover plantings by the income created by the marketing of relatively small tracts of timber.

If there are no openings in a wooded area, the clearcut that is allowed to reseed and grow back in dense cover will be an improvement. Such areas are often used

The same area after it was cleared and planted to clover.

for nesting, and it can be surprising how frequently turkeys will use them at other times. They do not use such areas as actively as they will a nice secluded clover field, but if costs or lack of access to an area makes the clover planting impractical, you should consider the small clearcut.

In most of the areas I hunt, access to water is not a problem. But there are sections of the country where the creation of a small pond or other watering site could create tremendous benefits for the turkey population.

ON THE NATIONAL LEVEL

The greatest threat that the wild turkey, or any other species of game, faces in the future is habitat deterioration. In many cases actual destruction of the habitat takes place. A program in the wind that would allow clearcutting of all the public land in the western part of my state of Virginia would assure the elimination of the wild turkey. We should be grateful that such large-scale action would not be tolerated by the public. What remains a very real threat is the gradual chipping away of prime habitat. Each of us who hunts in prime turkey terrain has seen the effects of this gradual erosion of habitat. A prime farm is subdivided, and what was a productive 200 acres is eliminated. The cumulative effect becomes serious.

We should feel a commitment to the welfare of these great birds.

The problem is that the wild turkey demands relatively large range. Many stable and increasing populations of whitetail deer exist in areas that are densely populated with humans. Deer only need small blocks of security cover from which they can roam at night to exploit the rich food resources associated with small farms. Turkeys need hundreds of acres for their range. Ideal turkey range contains blocks of thousands of acres of prime habitat.

While the range necessities of the wild turkey are significant, they are not incompatible with twentieth century "progress." Unfortunately, the same may not be true of other great North American game species that appear doomed. The grizzly bear is a good example. It is unrealistic to expect the western states to provide the requisite 20 square miles of wilderness each bear needs. We may be able to protect a small, isolated population of the creatures in Yellowstone Park, but even that is currently being debated.

History has taught that the threat to wildlife is not imposed by those who hunt but rather by those who destroy habitat. Market hunters are portrayed as the ultimate villains because their purpose was to kill. However, when examined in an unbiased and disciplined fashion, the extinction of a species or the elimination of a species from a given area will be seen to be a result of habitat destruction. In most cases that habitat destruction was done in the interest of economic progress and profit. The culprits are not only the captains of industry who decided to build a plant on the shores of the Chesapeake Bay, but also the hard-working farmers in Minnesota who loved pheasant and duck hunting and fishing but never considered the implications of draining all their sloughs and eliminating all their fence rows and woodlots. More acres in crops provided a higher cash income, and there were few debates over the decisions. The ducks and pheasants declined precipitously, and their decline was lamented; however, it was rare indeed for a man to argue that perhaps acres that could provide a cash income should be left as habitat for gamebirds. The great numbers of waterfowl and upland birds suggested that there would always be enough. We have learned the grim lessons of our expectations of plenty.

Those interested in the declining populations of gamebirds, animals, and fish and the destruction of free-flowing rivers and mature forests have formed organizations which have addressed the need to maintain habitat. The success of Ducks Unlimited with waterfowl, and the various groups directed to maintenance of cold-water fisheries—among them Trout Unlimited and the Federation of Fly Fishermen—are examples of what can be accomplished by sportsmen who are generous with their money and time.

Sportsmen's groups have been complemented by conservation organizations of a variety of types that have helped protect public land. Anyone who suggests that all the work has been done by sportsmen and sportswomen is simply wrong. We all should acknowledge our debts to those organizations that are not oriented to hunting and fishing but rather have worked hard to protect free-flowing streams and large blocks of public property for multiple uses. We owe debts of thanks to the Sierra Club, the Wilderness Society, the Izaak Walton League, the Nature Conservancy, and many other groups that have worked hard and made significant investments in protecting the environment. Many of their efforts have benefitted the wild turkey. Obviously, habitat protection will help all those creatures native to the area being protected.

In the recent past, a group of hunters formed the Wild Turkey Federation, an organization that has the potential to provide tremendous benefits for these great birds. The group has funded valuable research and succeeded in focusing much attention on the wild turkey. To date, the dollars and time allocated to habitat protection and improvement have been modest when compared to the achievements of Ducks Unlimited, Trout Unlimited, and the Federation of Fly Fishermen. Those of us who enjoy being called turkey hunters must try to make our contributions compare to those made by these other groups.

Let us not forget the debt we have to the wild turkey.

Our concern should not be for how many new turkey hunters we have convinced to join the ranks of our organization but rather how many dollars those member-ships bring to bear *directly* on the improvement of habitat or biological research oriented to the long-term welfare of the turkey. The efforts to add members involve high administrative costs, but the bottom line is the influence we exert that directly improves the status of the turkey.

We should ask what individual turkey hunters or groups have done for habitat improvement in our home areas. As a case in point, in western Virginia the groups that have led the way in fighting for the preservation of public land, for the creation of wilderness areas, and for the protection of habitat have been trout fishermen and non-sporting conservation groups. We have had turkey-calling contests and turkey-hunting seminars in the major towns in the region, but to date no significant accomplishment in habitat protection has been realized by a turkey-hunting organization or those of us who are turkey hunters. The Trout Unlimited chapter in my area has implemented many work days devoted to improving stream habitat. I have seen no parallels from turkey hunters. We must not be satisfied with the entertaining seminars. The other conservation groups have shown us what can be done—now we must do it.

THE STATUS OF THE WILD TURKEY

One great step forward has been achieved by drawing public attention to the wild turkey. The Wild Turkey Federation has played an important role in that success. Experienced hunters have been ready to share knowledge and techniques to help people hunt more efficiently and, more importantly, to increase the numbers of people who care about the welfare of the wild turkey.

Our care can find expression by making public the grand qualities of this great American bird. We should be aggressive and determined to improve the status of the American wild turkey. Efforts to improve his image can be made in many ways. Educating young children can be a start. Most schools will be receptive to a program on the biology of the wild turkey. Adult education can be promoted to civic groups, most of which are usually desperate for evening programs. My experience has been that civic groups respond very well to slide lectures and a demonstration of calls. These sessions can be entertaining and informative, and a powerful case can be articulated for the wild turkey and the need to protect his habitat.

OUR DEBT

We should never forget that the wild turkey is responsible for all the enjoyment and satisfaction we derive from seeking him. We should periodically ask ourselves what dollar value should be attributed to those benefits. When we have made an honest and generous appraisal, we should make a financial commitment to improving or protecting habitat or supporting research. It is easy to procrastinate and avoid the responsibility.

The true measure of a serious spring hunter is not the efficiency with which he kills gobblers but the effectiveness of his contributions to assuring a bright future for the bird he loves.

Selected Bibliography

Barber, Michael B.
1978 "The Vertebrate Faunal Analysis of JC27 (James City County, Virginia): An Exercise in Plow Zone Archaeology," in *The Quarterly Bulletin of the Archaeological Society of Virginia*, Vol. 32, No. 3.

Barber, Michael B. and John Baroody.
1977 "Analysis of Vertebrate Faunal Remains from The Shannon Site, Montgomery County, Virginia," in *The Quarterly Bulletin of the Archaeological Society of Virginia*, Vol. 31, No. 3.

Brady, James F.
1973 *Modern Turkey Hunting*. New York: Crown Publishers.

Brister, Bob.
1976 *Shotgunning—The Art and Science*. New York: Winchester Press.

Burrard, Major Gerald.
1931 *The Modern Shotgun*. New York: Scribners (3 volumes).

Coggin, Joseph and C. Peery.
1975 *The Wild Turkey in Virginia*. Richmond, Virginia: Commission of Game and Inland Fisheries.

Davis, Henry E.
1949 *The American Wild Turkey*. Georgetown, South Carolina: Small Arms Technical Publishing Company.
1950 "Hunting Wild Turkeys with a Rifle." In *Hunting with the Twenty-Two*, Charles S. Landis, editor. Georgetown, South Carolina: Small Arms Technical Publishing Company.

Edminster, Frank G.
1954 *American Game Birds*. New York: Charles Scribner's Sons.

Elliott, Charles.
1979 *Turkey Hunting with Charlie Elliott*. New York: David McKay Company.

Evans, George Bird.
1973 *The Best of Nash Buckingham*. New York: Winchester Press.

Everitt, Simon W.
1928 *Tales of Wild Turkey Hunting*. Chicago: William C. Hazelton Publisher.

Fears, J. Wayne.
1981 *The Wild Turkey Book*. Clinton, New Jersey: The Amwell Press.

Gooch, Bob.
1978 *In Search of Wild Turkey*. Waukegan, Illinois: Greatlakes Living Press, Ltd.

Griffin, James B.
1952 *Archaeology of Eastern United States*. Chicago: University of Chicago Press.

Hanenkrat, William Frank.
1975 *The Education of a Turkey Hunter*. New York: Winchester Press.

Harbour, Dave.
1975 *Hunting the American Wild Turkey*. Harrisburg, Pennsylvania: Stackpole Books.

Johenning, Leon.
no date *The Turkey Hunting Guide*. Waynesboro, Virginia: The Humphries Press.

Kelly, Tom.
1973 *Tenth Legion*. Monroe, Louisiana: Spur Enterprises.

Latham, Roger M.
1956 *Complete Book of the Wild Turkey*. Harrisburg, Pennsylvania: Stackpole Books.

McDaniel, John M.
1980 *The Turkey Hunter's Book*. Clinton, New Jersey: The Amwell Press.

McIlhenny, E. A.
1914 *The Wild Turkey and Its Hunting*. New York: Doubleday & Co.

Mosby, H., and C. Handley.
1943 *The Wild Turkey in Virginia*. Richmond, Virginia: Commission of Game and Inland Fisheries.

Nash, Roderick.
1967 *Wilderness and the American Mind*. New Haven, Connecticut: Yale University Press.

Schorger, A. W.
1966 *The Wild Turkey*. Norman, Oklahoma: University of Oklahoma Press.

Trueblood, Ted.
1978 *The Ted Trueblood Hunting Treasury*. New York: David McKay.

Turpin, Tom.
1966 *Hunting the Wild Turkey*. Delmont, Pennsylvania: Penns Woods (Reprint of original).

Wheeler, Robert J.
1948 *The Wild Turkey in Alabama*. Montgomery, Alabama: Alabama Department of Conservation.

Williams, Lovette E.
1981 *The Book of the Wild Turkey*. Tulsa, Oklahoma: Winchester Press.

Index

Afternoon scouting, 72–74
Age of a turkey
    how to determine the, 38, 56–60
    spur length and, 60
    tail feathers and, 59–60
    tone of the gobble and, 38, 58–59
Aggravated purr calls, 179
Archaeology of Eastern United States, 22
Arrogance of turkeys, 50–51

Bag limits, 195–96
Bailey, W. W., 26
Baker, Stan, 130
Barrel length of shotguns, 125–26
Beard, age of a turkey and the size of a,
    57–58
Becker, Burt, 129
Bicycling, importance of, 186
Binoculars, use of, 145
Bird points, 22
Blaze orange, use of, 192
Blind calling, 164
Blinds, portable, 145

Bone tube, 22
Boots, camouflage for, 153
Bores of shotguns
    over-bored barrels, 129–31
    tight, 128–29
Box calls, 167–69
Breeding areas of old gobblers, 100
Briley Manufacturing Company, 128
Brush deflection and loads of shotguns, 123
Buckingham, Nash, 130

Cackle call, 164
Caller, how to become an efficient, 173–75
Calling
    bones used in, 22
    effects of excessive, 47
    effects of pre-season, 74
    frequency of, 89, 177
    how to start, 88
    imitating non-vocal sounds, 180–81
    importance of, 160
    information to have before, 87–88
    intense hunting pressure and, 75

of old gobblers, 100
rhythm in, 174–75
sitting strategy and, 83–87
timing of, 89, 177–78
tone in, 175
of two-year-old gobblers, 97–98
volume of, 175
what to do when there is a response to, 178–79
what to do when there is no response to, 103–5, 179–80
when hens are around, 103
of young gobblers, 89, 91
See also Gobble, the
Calling instruments
box, 167–69
friction calls, 165–70, 176
Gibson/Lynch lidded box, 167–69
mouth diaphragm, 143, 173
mouth-operated, 170–73
peg and slate, 165–67
pillbox calls, 172
raspy slate, 64
suction/wingbone types, 170–72
tube, 65, 172–73
two-piece striker-type box, 169
Calling site(s)
appropriate distance from birds and location of, 79–81
importance of topographic features, 78
locations for, 81, 83
when to change your, 104–5
Calls, selection of, 175
for locating gobblers, 177
Calls, types of
aggravated purr, 179
cackle, 164
Chisholm, 155–56, 158, 160
contentment, 164–65
development of, 156, 158
flying-down time, 178
ground yelps, 88
hen, 76, 98
lost call of young gobblers, 89, 91, 163–64
mating yelps, 104, 164
owl, 76
tree call of the hen, 88, 161–62
yelps, 162–65
See also Gobble, the
Calls made by other hunters, how to determine, 191

Cameras, use of, 145
Camouflage
for boots, 153
for face and hands, 151
importance of, 148
jackets, 139–40
patterns of, 151
sound and, 148, 150
tape for equipment, 151
Chisholm, Raymond, 155, 155–56, 158, 160
Choke constriction and shot size, 131
Choke of shotguns, 126, 128
Clearcuts for turkeys, 204–5
Clothes
camouflage jackets, 139–40
fabric for, 137
footwear, 137–39
gloves, 139
hats, 139
made from turkeys, 21
vests, 145
for weather changes, 140
Clover, planting of, 201
Cluck, description of the, 160
Colors of gobblers' heads, significance of, 54, 56
Commission of Game and Inland Fisheries, 25
Compasses, 145
Concealment, effective, 150–51
Conservation groups, importance of, 207
Contentment calls, 164–65
Corn, planting of, 201
Cost, Neal, 167
Crippled gobblers
how to reduce the loss of, 109–11
recovery of, 111–14
shot size and, 132
Cross-country skiing, importance of, 186
Cutting, 177

D. D. Adams, 167
Decoys
effectiveness of, 140–41
problems with, 141–43
Diaphragm call, mouth, 143, 173
Display, the
age of a turkey and, 59
description of, 39–41
predators and, 39, 54

pulmonary puff and, 40–41
Display areas, types of, 54
Disturbances, how to deal with, 105–6
Dogs and gobblers, 105, 199, 201
Ducks Unlimited, 207

Early blur, how to combat, 189
Entering the woods, techniques for, 76–77
Ethics
    and other hunters, 196–97
    and selfishness, 197
    of shooting, 195–96
    and turkeys, 197–98
European views on turkeys, 22
Eyes, protection for the, 193

Face, camouflage for the, 151
Fatigue, effects of, 189–90
Federal Premium loads, 124, 125
Federation of Fly Fishermen, 207
Fighting among gobblers, 41, 43
First-aid items, 143, 145
Flashlights, use of, 76–77, 145
Flying-down time and calls, 178
Food for turkeys, 204
Footwear, 137–39
    camouflage for boots, 153
Friction calls
    Gibson/Lynch lidded box, 167–69
    myths about, 169–70
    peg and slate, 165–67
    rain and, 176
    two-piece striker-type box, 169

Game-farm turkeys, 25
Gauge of shotgun, 123–25
Gibson lidded box calls, 167–69
Gloves, 139
Gobble, the
    age of a turkey determined by tone of,
        38, 58–59
    description of, 161
    distances and carrying of, 39, 77–78
    double or triple, 88
    imitation of, 102–3, 165
    mating and, 37, 38–39
    reason for, 38–39
    reasons for not using, 48–49, 102
Gobbler(s)
    arrogance of, 50–51
    colors of the heads of, 54, 56
    determining the age of a, 38, 56–60
    displaying areas of, 54
    display of, 39–41
    fighting among, 41, 43
    hearing of, 43–44, 148, 150
    relationship between immature and
        mature birds, 52, 54, 100
    and role of hens, 51–52
    roosting locations for, 54
    smelling sense of, 49–50
    that do not gobble, 48–49, 100
    vision of, 43–44
    wariness of, 43, 44, 46–47
    yelps of, 162
Gobblers, dominant old
    behavior of, 100–101
    breeding areas of, 100
    calling of, 100
    how to hunt, 101–2
    relationships with young gobblers, 52, 54,
        100
    scattering hens from, 104
    yelps of, 162
Gobblers, two-year-old
    calling of, 97–98
    identification of, 98–99
Gobblers, young
    behavior variations of, 91–92
    calling of, 89, 91
    description of a hunt for, 92–97
    lost call of, 89, 91, 163–64
    patience needed for, 91
    relationships with old gobblers, 52, 54,
        100
    scattering a group of, 91
    silent approach of, 91
Griffin, James B., 22
Ground yelps, 88

Habitats
    how to improve, 199, 201, 204–9
    importance of conservation groups, 207
    importance of preserving, 9–11, 15–16
    size of, 206
    sportsmen's groups and improvement of,
        207

turkey populations affected by the loss
    of, 23
Handguns, 145
Hands, camouflage for, 151
Hats, 139
Hearing
    of turkeys, 43–44, 148, 150
    protection, 193
Hen calls, 76, 98
Hens
    calling and, 103
    the display and, 39, 41
    gobbler behavior affected by, 51–52
    nesting locations for, 54
    scattering a mature gobbler from, 104
    tree call of, 88, 161–62
    wariness of, 39
    yelps of, 162
Hunting
    methods used during prehistoric times,
        21–22
    of turkeys by early Americans, 22–24

Improved cylinder, definition of, 126
Improved modified choke, definition of, 126
Insects for turkeys, 204
Izaak Walton League, 207

Jackets, camouflage, 139–40

Key-key run, 163
Keys, importance of spare, 145
Kirby, Dick, 167
Knives, large, 145

Lancaster, Jack, 155, 158
Lawrence Company, 134
Listening posts, 77–78
Loads for shotguns, 124
    brush deflection and, 123
    choosing, 136–37
    Federal Premium, 124, 125
    heavy 12 gauge, 131
Locating gobblers. *See* Scouting

Logging roads and calling sites, 78
Long-range rifle hunting, 195
Lost yelping, 162–64
Lumbering and effects on turkeys, 23
Lynch lidded box calls, 167–69

McIlhenny, Edward A., 24, 171
Mating
    display/strut and, 39–41
    role of the gobble and, 37, 38–39
    yelps, 104, 164
Morgan, Ken, 173
Morning scouting, disadvantages of, 72
Mosby, H. S., 26
Mouth diaphragm calls, 143, 173
Mouth-operated calls, 170–73
    mouth diaphragm, 143, 173
    suction/wingbone types, 170–72
    tube, 65, 172–73

Nash, Robert, 23
Nature Conservancy, 207
Nesting locations for hens, 54
Nordic Track Company, 186

Old gobbler yelp, 162
Old hen assembly yelp, 162
Old Turk Company, 167, 169
Optical sights, 122–23
Over-bored barrels of shotguns, 129–31
Owl call, use of the, 76

Packs, back or belt, 143
Pattern shotguns, need to, 117, 119
Peg and slate calls, 165–67
Physical fitness programs
    bicycling, 186
    cross-country skiing, 186
    how to develop, 186–87
    importance of, 184
    running, 185
    swimming, 186
    walking, 184–85
Pillbox calls, 172

Predators
    dogs as, 199, 201
    during the display, 39, 54
    how turkeys avoid, 44, 46-47
    types of, 46
Prehistoric period
    hunting methods used during, 21–22
    records of turkeys during, 19–20
    turkeys as a source of tools during, 20–21
Pulmonary puff, 40–41

Quaker Boy Company, 167

Ranges
    primary ranges and spring territory, 52, 54
    relationship between immature and mature birds and, 52, 54
    spring alterations on, 52
Raspy slate call, 64
Raymond Chisholm calls, 155–56, 158, 160
Recovery of shot gobblers, 110
    of crippled and coordinated gobblers, 112–14
    of crippled gobblers, 111–12
Reeds, 173
Re-nesting, 47
Restocking of turkeys
    game-farm turkeys, 25
    pure wildstock turkeys, 26
Ridge tops and calling sites, 78
Rifles, advantages of shotguns over, 115
Roosting areas
    how to attain access to, 76–77
    how to get a response from gobblers in, 76
    listening posts and, 77
    location of, 54, 75–76
    using hen calls in, 76
    using owl calls in, 76
Running, importance of, 185

Safety
    eye protection, 193
    fatigue and, 189–90
    hearing protection, 193
    how to combat early blur, 189
    how to protect yourself, 190–93
    use of blaze orange, 192
Scattering
    a group of young gobblers, 91
    a mature gobbler from the hens, 104
Schielke, George and Barbara, 92
Scouting, techniques of
    afternoon scouting, 72–74
    effects of pre-season calling, 74
    keeping detailed records, 71
    listening posts, 77–78
    long-range, 195
    morning scouting, 72
    scouting of the home area, 71–72
    sharing of information, 73–74
    use of scartch marks, 72–73
Scratching sounds, imitation of, 180
Scratch marks, scouting and, 72–73
Sex of a turkey determined by yelps, 162
Shooting
    angles and sitting techniques, 85–87
    how to reduce the loss of crippled gobblers, 109–11
    importance of a clear shot, 108–9
    at a moving gobbler, 108
    too late, 108
    too soon, 107–8
    See also Recovery of shot gobblers
Shooting glasses, 193
Shotgun(s)
    advantages of double-barrel, 119–20
    advantages over rifles, 115
    barrel length of, 125–26
    brush deflection and loads of, 123
    camouflage tape for, 151
    choice of, 115–17
    choke constriction and shot size, 131
    choke of, 126, 128
    gauge of, 123–25
    importance of determining the point of impact of, 117, 119
    loads and, 136–37
    over-bored barrels of, 129–31
    shot size and, 131–36
    sights of, 122–23
    slings for, 143
    tight bores of, 128–29
    weights of, 120–22
Shot size
    advantages of large, 134–36
    choke constriction and, 131

small, 132–33
type to use, 131–36
Shot weight and velocity, 136–37
Sierra Club, 207
Silica Explorer compass, 145
Sites
    effects of weather on, 75
    hunting pressure and, 74
    importance of resting, 75
    location of calling, 78–81, 83
    productivity and, 74–75
    See also Calling sites
Sitting techniques
    importance of, 83–84
    location and, 151
    shooting angles and, 85–87
Skeet, definition of, 126
Slate and peg calls, 165–67
Slings
    for guns, 143
    for turkeys, 145
Smelling sense of turkeys, 49–50
Sounds
    heard by turkeys, 43–44, 148, 150
    how to reduce, 150
    made by turkeys, 160–61
Sportsmen's groups, 207
Spring hunter, description of a, 68–70
Spring hunting
    adjusting to, 29–30
    appeal of, 34–35
    challenges presented by, 30–34
    description of, 61–68
    hardships with, 183–84
    importance of physical fitness for, 184–86
    risks of, 189
Spur length and age of turkey, 60
Stowe calls, 167
Strut, definition of, 39
    See also Display
Suction/wingbone types of calls, 170–72
Survival kit, 143
Swimming, importance of, 186

Tail feathers and age of turkey, 59–60
Timing of calls, 89, 177–78
Tools made from turkeys, 20–21
Topographic features and calling sites, 78
Tree call of the hen, 88, 161–62
Trout Unlimited, 207, 209

Trueblood, Ted, 83–84
Tube calls, 65, 172–73
Turkey populations
    effects of loss of habitats on, 23
    from 1960 on, 26, 28
    in the South, 24
    spring alterations on, 52
    in Virginia, 24–26
Turkeys
    adaptability of, 47–48
    beauty of, 14
    endurance and courage of, 12
    flight of, 14
    intelligence of, 47
    as a source of tools, 20–21
    See also Gobblers
Turkey sling, 145
Turkey vest, 145
Two-piece striker-type box calls, 169

Unethical techniques of killing turkeys, 195–96

Velocity and shot weight, 136–37
Vests, 145
Virginia, turkeys in, 24–26
Virginia Game Department, 24
Virginia Polytechnic Institute, Cooperative Wildlife Research Unit of, 25–26
Vision of turkeys, 43–44

Walking
    imitating the sound of turkeys, 180–81, 191–92
    importance of, 184–85
Wariness
    of gobblers, 43
    of hens, 39
    of turkeys, 44, 46–47
Watches, importance of, 145
Watering sites for turkeys, 205
Weather
    clothes for changes in the, 140
    site location and, 75
    windy, 106, 107

Whistle, description of the, 161
White Company, 139
Wingbone calls, 170–72
Wilderness and the American Mind, 23
Wilderness Society, 207
Wild Turkey and Its Hunting, The, 24, 171

Wild Turkey Federation, 207, 209

Yelps
    description of, 160
    types of, 162-65
    used to determine the sex of a turkey, 162